THE LAW OF
THE COMMON MARKET

THE LAW OF
THE COMMON MARKET

EDITED BY

B. A. WORTLEY

O.B.E., Q.C., LL.D.

HON. DR DE L'UNIV. (RENNES AND STRASBOURG),
MEMBER OF THE ROYAL NETHERLANDS ACADEMY, MEMBER OF
THE GOVERNING COUNCIL OF THE INTERNATIONAL INSTITUTE FOR
THE UNIFICATION OF PRIVATE LAW, MEMBRE DE L'INSTITUT
DE DROIT INTERNATIONAL, PROFESSOR OF JURISPRUDENCE
AND INTERNATIONAL LAW IN THE UNIVERSITY OF
MANCHESTER

MANCHESTER UNIVERSITY PRESS
U.S.A.: OCEANA PUBLICATIONS INC

© 1974 MANCHESTER UNIVERSITY PRESS

Published by the University of Manchester at
THE UNIVERSITY PRESS
Oxford Road, Manchester M13 9PL
UK ISBN 0 7190 0559 0

U.S.A.
OCEANA PUBLICATIONS INC
75 Main Street, Dobbs Ferry, N.Y. 10522
US ISBN 0 379 11914 5
Library of Congress catalog card No. 74–6695

Distributed in India by
N. M. TRIPATHI (PRIVATE) LTD
164 Samaldas Gandhi Marg, Bombay 400 002

Printed Great Britain by Butler & Tanner Ltd. Frome and London

CONTENTS

v

FOREWORD

In 1971 five Schill lectures were delivered in the University and early in January 1972 were published by the University Press as *An Introduction to the Law of the European Economic Community*. This was before the U.K. had acceded to the Community; the terms of the treaty of accession and of the enabling Act of Parliament were not known. The first fourteen chapters of the present work, by some of my colleagues and by myself, have arisen out of a series of lectures to the legal profession and to students given in the Easter term of 1973: the chapter by Dr Cukwurah is based on a lecture given by him on a visit to his old faculty in this university in 1972. In the main they attempt to bring up to date what was said in 1971 and 1972 and to extend our studies into fresh fields of the utmost importance to lawyers.

The views expressed are the individual, not the collective views of the authors. I should like to express my cordial thanks to all for their co-operation.

Special thanks are due to my old friend, Reginald Pilkington, O.B.E., LL.D., solicitor, for his work on the proofs, on the index and on the table of cases, and to my son, Richard J. A. Wortley, LL.B., solicitor, for preparing the list of the cited articles of the E.E.C. treaty, and last, but not least, to Mr T. L. Jones, M.A., Secretary of the Press, to whom every good wish is offered on the occasion of his well earned retirement.

Spring 1973

B. A. WORTLEY
Faculty of Law
University of Manchester

Since the above was written we deeply regret to record the death of Mr T. L. Jones shortly after his retirement.

Printing and other delays have meant that proofs became available only in March 1974. So far as possible within our budget, note has been taken of legal changes of importance affecting the text, but the editor cannot of course anticipate future political and economic developments in relation to the Market and its member States: *tempora mutantur . . .*

B.A.W.

Chapter I

GENERAL INTRODUCTION: BACKGROUND AND AIMS

B. A. Wortley

I. THE THREE COMMUNITY TREATIES

In his excellent background survey in *An Introduction to the Law of the European Economic Community*,[1] chapter II, p. 7, Mr Geoffrey North of Manchester University described the geographical and economic importance of industrial agglomeration around the Rhine and the Paris basin, and its impact on the surrounding countries. The complementary economies of Denmark (including Greenland), Ireland and the United Kingdom, will now strengthen this agglomeration, and we may look forward to the creation of an economic force comparable to that of the United States, with an equally large free market. The important 'summit' meeting of October 1972 (Cmnd. 5109)[2] of the nine Prime Ministers declared their intention in paragraph 12, however:

To contribute, while respecting what has been achieved by the Community, to a progressive liberalisation of international trade by measures based on reciprocity and relating to both tariffs and non-tariff barriers.

To maintain a constructive dialogue with the United States, Japan, Canada and its other industrialised trade partners in a forthcoming spirit, using the most appropriate methods.

In this context the Community attaches major importance to the multilateral negotiations in the context of GATT, in which it will participate in accordance with its earlier statement.

To this end, the Community institutions are invited to decide not later than July 1, 1973, on a global approach covering all aspects affecting trade. The Community hopes that an effort on the part of all partners will allow these negotiations to be completed in 1975. It confirms its desire for the full participation of the developing countries in the preparation and progress of these negotiations which should take due account of the interests of those countries.

1. Ed. B. A. Wortley, Manchester University Press, 1972.
2. Reprinted in 10 *C.M.L.Rev.* (1973) 108–14.

Furthermore, having regard to the agreements concluded with the EFTA countries which are not members, the Community declares its readiness to seek with Norway a speedy solution to the Trade problems facing that country in its relations with the enlarged Community.

In order to promote détente in Europe, the Conference reaffirmed its determination to follow a common commercial policy towards the countries of Eastern Europe with effect from January 1, 1973 . . .

The enlarged European Economic Community (E.E.C.) will eventually, like the United States, have a common external tariff, and no internal tariffs, but this situation has to be built up during a transitional period. The machinery for this is to be found in the treaties establishing the *European Coal and Steel Community* (E.C.S.C.), the *European Atomic Energy Community* (E.A.E.C.) and the *European Economic Community* as amended by the 1972 Treaty of Accession (Cmnd. 4862; I and II).

The first two treaties are not likely to be of much *direct* concern to *most* practising lawyers, and for this reason receive only passing notice in this book.

In 1951 the European Coal and Steel Community, engendered by the great political imagination of Robert Schuman, did, however, set the pattern for a supranational economic authority. Many of its institutions and concepts were copied and adapted when the E.E.C. was set up in 1957.

Some of the case law of the Coal and Steel Community is still valuable when considering certain provisions of the E.E.C. Treaty and when we recall that since 1958 one and the same Court at Luxembourg has dealt with both these treaties and with the Euratom treaty.

The impact of the Coal and Steel Community is bound to be felt on the supply of coal and steel, on the prices for those commodities and generally on the policy of our two great nationalised industries. The European Atomic Energy Community will no doubt prove to be immensely important, since no one can foretell the impact of atomic energy in the future, but the treaty is of very specialised interest, more especially to our own State-controlled monopolistic atomic energy industry.

The E.E.C. Treaty is of very direct concern to solicitors and barristers.

II. THE MAIN COMMUNITY INSTITUTIONS

There now exist, in addition to the Common Court of Justice and the Common Assembly (1958), a single *Council of Ministers* (political) and a single *commission* (executive organ) for all three Communities.[3]

The institutions of the E.E.C. are dealt with by Dr White in chapters II and III. She treated the *Court of Justice* at some length in *An Introduction to the Law of the E.E.C.* (chapter V, p. 51). She brings this up to date and considers the Assembly, the Council of Ministers and the Commission, as well as important developments behind these formal structures. The *European Assembly* may become a legislative Parliament one day. At present it only has powers of discussion, and by Article 144 a power (by two-thirds majority of the votes cast, representing a majority of the members of the Assembly), to compel the resignation of the Commission and thus control the powerful civil service. Such a move was bruited in November 1972 (*The Times*, 17 November 1972) but was not successful.

The *Commission*, which consists of highly qualified officials whose task is to ensure the proper functioning of the Common Market within the terms of the Treaty, is the key to the whole structure. Article 155 reads:

In order to ensure the proper functioning and development of the common market, the Commission shall:

—ensure that the provisions of this Treaty and the measures taken by the institutions pursuant thereto are applied;
—formulate recommendations or deliver opinions on matters dealt with in this Treaty, if it expressly so provides or if the Commission considers it necessary;
—have its own power of decision and participate in the shaping of measures taken by the Council and by the Assembly in the manner provided for in this Treaty;
—exercise the powers conferred on it by the Council for the implementation of the rules laid down by the latter.

These powers may be tempered, as we have seen, by the Assembly and by the legal control of the Court of Justice of nine judges (one is British: *The Times*, 1 December 1972). The duty of the Court is to see that, in the application of the Treaty, the law is observed. The Court's orders are matters for each member State to accept and enforce (Article 164) Article 192 provides:

Enforcement shall be governed by the rules of civil procedure in force in the State in the territory of which it is carried out. The order for its enforcement shall be appended to the decision, without other formality than verification of the authenticity of the decision, by the national authority which

3. Cmnd. 4866, Treaty of 8 April 1965, and Cmnd 4867, Treaty of Amendments, 22 April 1970.

the Government of each Member State shall designate for this purpose and shall make known to the Commission, to the Court of Justice.

When these formalities have been completed on application by the party concerned, the latter may proceed to enforcement in accordance with the national law, by bringing the matter directly before the competent authority.

Enforcement may be suspended only by a decision of the Court of Justice. However, the courts of the country concerned shall have jurisdiction over complaints that enforcement is being carried out in an irregular manner.

The term 'law' relates to the law of the E.E.C., which in turn operates under general international law.

The *Council*, which co-ordinates the general economic policies of member States, operates a weighted system of voting, the four larger States having ten votes each and the other five members proportionately fewer.

There is a Committee of *Permanent Representatives* to assist this Council, and this may become politically very important because of the undoubted influence of its politician membership on Community institutions (see chapter II, p. 19).

III. OBJECTIVES

The objectives of the elaborate legal machinery of the E.E.C. are to create an area in Europe with a 'harmonious development of economic activity, a continuous and balanced expansion, an increase in stability, an accelerated raising of the standard of living, and closer relations between the States belonging to it' (Article 2 of the E.E.C. Treaty), i.e. it is intended to protect the common man in the Common Market place.

More detailed arrangements to achieve these ends are set out in Article 3 of the Treaty:

For the purposes set out in Article 2, the activities of the Community shall include, as provided in this Treaty and in accordance with the timetable set out therein:

(a) the elimination, as between Member States, of customs duties and of quantitative restrictions on the import and export of goods, and of all other measures having equivalent effect;

(b) the establishment of a common customs tariff and of a common commercial policy towards third countries;

(c) the abolition, as between Member States, of obstacles to freedom of movement for persons, services and capital;

(d) the adoption of a common policy in the sphere of agriculture;

(e) the adoption of a common policy in the sphere of transport;

(*f*) the institution of a system ensuring that competition in the common market is not distorted;

(*g*) the application of procedures by which the economic policies of Member States can be co-ordinated and disequilibria in their balances of payments remedied;

(*h*) the approximation of the laws of Member States to the extent required for the proper functioning of the common market;

(*i*) the creation of a European Social Fund in order to improve employment opportunities for workers and to contribute to the raising of their standard of living;

(*j*) the establishment of a European Investment Bank to facilitate the economic expansion of the Community by opening up fresh resources;

(*k*) the association of the overseas countries and territories in order to increase trade and to promote jointly economic and social development.

IV. THE SIX PARTS OF THE TREATY

The Treaty is drafted so as to set out its objects and then to show how these objects may be implemented.

Part 1 of the E.E.C. Treaty deals with the general objects to which I have just alluded, i.e. the creation of a common market with the object of benefiting consumers. *Part 2* deals with the free movement of goods, the progressive elimination of tariffs and quotas.[1] These are matters of great practical importance to men of business; their administration is a matter for the government departments concerned.

Part 2 includes the complicated arrangements in respect of agricultural products, which are dealt with by Mr Jaconelli in chapter XII. Part 2 also provides for the free movement of persons and services and will include eventually the right to establish a business or to work in any part of the Community. Mr Foster deals with some of these problems in chapter XIII. It is noteworthy that at the October 'Summit' the heads of member States (Cmnd. 5109),

invited the institutions, after consulting labour and management, to draw up, between now and January 1, 1974, a programme of action providing for concrete measures and the corresponding resources particularly in the framework of the social fund, based on the suggestions made in the course of the conference by Heads of State and Heads of Government and by the Commission.

This programme should aim, in particular, at carrying out a co-ordinated policy for employment and vocational training, and improving working conditions and conditions of life, at closely involving workers in the progress of firms, at facilitating on the basis of the situation in the different countries the conclusion of collective agreements at European level in

4. See Treaty of Accession, 1972, Arts. 31–43, as regards new member States.

appropriate fields and at strengthening and co-ordinating measures of consumer protection.

One aspect of the right of establishment, already alluded to, and of greatest importance to lawyers, is the impact of the Treaty on English company law. This is dealt with by Mr Flanagan in chapter x. Mr Davies of the Department of Trade and Industry paved the way for this in chapter IV of *An Introduction to the Law of the E.E.C.* on what were then *proposed* changes in company law, 'Company law and the Common Market: the first step', i.e. the step rendered necessary by Article 58(2) of the E.E.C. Treaty and the directive thereunder to approximate English company law to E.E.C. laws in order to protect members of companies and third parties dealing with companies.

Part 2 of the E.E.C. Treaty also deals with the free transfer of capital. This is a particularly thorny problem for the United Kingdom, for two reasons: first, because we have had most severe restrictions on the transfer of capital outside the sterling area, now a somewhat restricted area which includes the United Kingdom, the Channel Islands and the Republic of Ireland, but which until 1972 was vastly more extensive in the Commonwealth; second, because until recently sterling was very widely held as a world reserve currency. Article 67 of the E.E.C. Treaty provided for the progressive abolition of all restrictions and of any discrimination on the movement of capital for persons resident in member States. Directives have already been issued under this article.

Walsh and Paxton state (*Into Europe*, 1972, p. 151) that the first directive in 1960 was to establish among the six members of the E.E.C.

(1) unconditional freedom of capital movements connected with the freeing of trade goods, of services, and of the movement of persons, and also with the free exercise of the right of establishment;
(2) unconditional and irreversible freedom for sale and purchase of stocks and shares quoted on the Community's stock exchanges;
(3) conditional freedom with regard to the issuing and placing of stocks and shares on capital markets, and for the purchase of unquoted stocks and shares. *Any member country might, however, maintain or re-impose existing restrictions if their abolition was likely to hinder the achievement of its economic policy objectives.*

There was a special exchange of letters on monetary questions on 22 January 1972 between the U.K. and the E.E.C., organising the 'orderly and gradual run-down of the official sterling balance' and on monetary policy generally, then, as a result of the October 1972 European 'summit', it was agreed in paragraph 1 that:

The necessary decisions should be taken in the course of 1973 so as to allow the transition to the second stage of the economic and monetary union on January 1, 1974, and with a view to its completion not later than December 31, 1980.[5]

Paragraph 4 provides (*inter alia*) for 'a reduction in the role of national currencies as reserve instruments'.[6]

These matters are very much specialist banking questions, and the Treaty of Accession, whereby the United Kingdom, Ireland and Denmark are permitted to accede to the E.E.C. Treaty, provides for consultation on these matters (Article 120). The United Kingdom is, by Article 124, given a period of transition after accession before the 'liberalisation of direct investments in Member States'.

One day, when the position becomes settled, we may need to publish a special legal and economic symposium on the monetary questions, on budgetary problems, and on the position of the European Investment Bank. That will be for the future. Meantime, Mr Davey deals with the impact of Community taxation policy, so far as it is reflected in value added tax, in chapter XI. All the matters in Part 2 of the E.E.C. Treaty will become of direct importance to lawyers when they lead to disputes to be settled by negotiation, arbitration or litigation.

Part 3 of the E.E.C. Treaty deals with the policy of the Community. Chapters VII and VIII deal with the rules on competition, including State aid, which are probably among the most important practical matters for the average lawyer.

The problem raised by monopolies and restrictive practices are indeed perennial ones and of vital importance to the consumer.

The protection of the consumer is no new ploy. Holdsworth, in his *History of English Law*, vol. IV, p. 350, observes that in the Case of Monopolies (1602), 11 Co. Rep. 84b:

The Court followed the principles of medieval common law that *prima facie* trade must be free . . . freedom could only be curtailed by definite restrictions known to and recognised by the Common Law . . . but public policy demanded that the Law should permit exceptions,

especially where an invention has created a new industry or where the public interest required licensing. This is similar to the situation

5. *Sunday Times*, 22 October 1972.   6. *Ibid.*

with regard to monopoly in the Common Market today. Monopolies and monopolistic mergers need special justification if they are to be allowed.

Chapters VII and VIII, then, bring up to date the law on monopolies and restrictive practices first discussed in *An Introduction to the Law of the E.E.C.* These chapters are supplemented by Dr Kay in chapter IX. He deals with patents, trade marks, and industrial property, which, by their nature, are limited though permitted monopolies.

Mergers of firms, if controlled in the interest of the consumer, may lead to selective efficiency. The October 1972 'summit' (Cmnd. 5109) proposed the

. . . elimination of technical barriers to trade as well as the elimination, particularly in the fiscal and legal fields, of barriers which hinder closer relations and mergers between firms, the rapid adoption of a European company statute, the progressive and effective opening up of public sector purchases, the promotion of a European scale of competitive firms in the field of high technology, the transformation and conversion of declining industries, under acceptable social conditions, the formulation of measures to ensure that mergers affecting firms established in the Community are in harmony with the economic and social aims of the Community, and the maintenance of fair competition as much within the Common Market as in external markets in conformity with the rules laid down by the Treaties.

Inventive technology and economic efficiency must be married in the interest of the consumer.

Part 4 of the E.E.C. Treaty deals with the complicated and somewhat specialised matter of association with the Community of overseas countries and territories which are not full member States. This is discussed by Dr Cukwurah in chapter XV.

Part 5 of the E.E.C. Treaty deals with the Community institutions, Dr White's subject in chapters II and III. The conditions for accession (Article 237) and other general and final provisions are in *Part 6* of the E.E.C. Treaty.

The increase of full member States from six to nine was brought about by the Treaty of Accession of 1972 (Cmnd. 4862, I and II).

V. THE TREATY OF ACCESSION, 1972

Article 2 of this treaty provides that

from the date of accession, the provisions of the original Treaties and the acts adopted by the institutions of the Communities shall be binding on the new Member States and shall apply in those States under the conditions laid down in those Treaties and in this Act [i.e. of accession].

Once a new State has ratified the Treaty of Accession it will be bound by it in international law, and the fact that Norway has not joined will not affect the obligations of the other members, since Article 2 of the Treaty of Accession, paragraph 3, reads as follows:

If, however, the States referred to in Article 1(1) [the new members] have not all deposited their instruments of ratification and accession in due time, the Treaty shall enter into force for those States which have deposited their instruments.

One of the difficulties of the Community not so much experienced in other large economic units such as the United States, China and the U.S.S.R. is caused by the coexistence of different languages within the Community.

The language problem is of particular importance when common legislation and treaties are drafted, or when existing internal laws have to be approximated under Articles 100–102 of the E.E.C. Treaty. This problem was dealt with by Mr Akehurst in chapter III of *An Introduction to the Law of the E.E.C.* The official languages of the original community were French, German, Italian and Dutch. The arrangements made in the Treaty of Accession of 1972 aimed at bringing into the Community, Ireland, Norway, Denmark and the United Kingdom. Article 3 reads as follows:

This Treaty, drawn up in a single original in the Danish, Dutch, English, French, German, Irish, Italian and Norwegian languages, all eight texts being equally authentic, will be deposited in the archives of the Government of the Italian Republic, which will transmit a certified copy to each of the Governments of the other signatory States.

The Treaty of Accession also provides, in *Article 155*, that:

The texts of the acts of the institutions of the Communities adopted before accession and drawn up by the Council or the Commission in the Danish, English and Norwegian languages shall, from the date of accession, be authentic under the same conditions as the texts drawn up in the four original languages. They shall be published in the Official Journal of the European Communities if the texts in the original languages were so published.

Irish is not included here. Norwegian will no longer be so necessary. From the point of view of legal systems, Danish lawyers will represent a link with the Scandinavian systems, and the Irish will help to consolidate the common law approach so important in Community relations with the U.S. and the Commonwealth.

VI. THE EUROPEAN COMMUNITIES ACT, 1972

The Treaty of Accession was not ratified by the U.K. until it had first passed the *European Communities Act*, 1972. The effect of the Act is dealt with by Mrs Hoggett in chapters v and vi, which consider the constitutional implications of our entering the E.E.C. The White Paper on this topic, prepared by the former 'Wilson' government and accepted by the recent 'Heath' government, was set out in full as appendix 1 to *An Introduction to the Law of the European Economic Community*.

The explanatory and financial memorandum issued with the European Communities Bill also indicates that the object of the government was to give force of law in the United Kingdom to present and future Community law, which under the Community treaties is directly applicable in member States.

Section 3 of the *European Communities Act*, 1972, makes it clear that the effect of the Community treaties or any instruments made under them are questions of law and, if they are not settled by the European Court, are to be settled in accordance with its principles.

Section 2(1) of the Act is very wide and reads as follows:

All such rights, powers, liabilities, obligations and restrictions from time to time created or arising by or under the Treaties, and all such remedies and procedures from time to time provided for by or under the Treaties, as in accordance with the Treaties are without further enactment to be given legal effect or used in the United Kingdom shall be recognised and available in law, and be enforced, allowed and followed accordingly; and the expression 'enforceable Community right' and similar expressions shall be read as referring to one to which this sub-section applies.

To Mrs Hoggett falls the task of commenting on this section.

The Act also makes provision for subordinate legislation to implement Community obligations and for the exercise of rights under the treaties. This would include legislation harmonising laws under Articles 100–102 of the E.E.C. Treaty. The impact of this new subordinate legislation in relation to judicial review is dealt with in chapter iv by Professor Street, a member of the Crowther (now Kilbrandon) Commission on the Constitution, who is also familiar with Continental administrative law.

The *European Communities Act* 1972, provides for budgetary matters, for the new customs duties which will eventually be uniform as regards non-members of the Community, and for the disappearance of customs duties within the Community; see sections 1–5 of the Act.

Agriculture is provided for by section 6 of the Act, and special arrangements are made for sugar in section 7 and for cinema films in section 8. Of particular interest to businessmen and company lawyers is section 9, which is, as we have indicated, considered in chapter x by Mr Flanagan, who takes up the recent changes it makes in our company law, notably the softening of the *ultra vires* rule in its application to the powers of companies and of directors in the interests of *bona fide* dealings.

The Restrictive Trade Practices Act, 1956, will continue in England, but by section 10 of the Act it will be brought into line with the requirements of the Treaty. (See now the *Esso* case, [1973] 3 All E.R. 1057.)

The E.E.C. Treaty may result in the imposition of certain fines and penalties on British businessmen who violate Treaty law. This was possible even before Britain joined the Community, since any British assets in the territory of the Community were at risk, as we saw in the case involving I.C.I. These penalties are not criminal matters. The only criminal matters dealt with in the Act are those contained in section 11, which deals with perjury and official secrets. The European Economic Community only makes essential alterations in domestic law,[7] i.e. so far as it is necessary to make the Community work. It does not take the place of the ordinary criminal and civil law of the country; nor does it have any startling impact on the theory of sovereignty.[8] We have already accepted the creation of the United Nations, with its 'sanctions', and we recognise the overriding jurisdiction of the Commission and the Court of Human Rights at Strasbourg set up under the European Convention on Human Rights. And we have long tolerated many governmental functions being conducted by international institutions, especially those concerned with communications, transport and health. The operation of the Berne postal convention and the work of the World Health Organisation in combating disease, the regulations made by international bodies concerned with air, sea and land transport are so well established as to call for no comment, nor do they evoke surprise. They are part of the 'give and take' of international life. Some conflicts of laws are inevitable in any international commercial arrangements and they will continue, but they must not be exaggerated.

7. For a useful discussion, see B. M. Dickens, *The E.E.C. and the General Practitioner,* 1972, p. 22. Art. 222 states, 'The Treaty shall in no way prejudice the rules in Member States governing the system of property ownership.'

8. See B. A. Wortley, *Jurisprudence,* 1967, Manchester University Press.

Law cannot easily be unified on a world-wide basis.[9] In chapter xiv Mrs Kloss deals with some of the conflicts in relation to Community law. For the present, the legal system with the greatest impact on Community law is that of France, a pioneer country in administrative law. Dr Cukwurah deals with important implications which the E.E.C. Treaty has for 'associated States' in chapter xv.

9. See B. A. Wortley, *Jurisprudence*, 1967, Manchester University Press, chapter 11.

Chapter II

THE MAIN INSTITUTIONS OF
THE COMMUNITIES (I)

Gillian White

This and the following chapter seek to give an outline account of the main institutions of the European Communities. For an understanding of the legal framework which created the Community organs and within which they operate, it is not necessary to make an exhaustive catalogue of the relevant treaty provisions, or to analyse in depth their application and interpretation to date. What follows is an attempt to focus on the essential features of the system which it is believed will be informative for lawyers in the United Kingdom as they meet and seek to understand the end products of the legislative and executive process, or as they look for possible judicial remedies against Community actions which may be flawed with illegality.

I. THE LEGISLATIVE AND EXECUTIVE DIARCHY—
COUNCIL AND COMMISSION

The first mention of the institutions in the E.E.C. Treaty, Article 4, is significant in that it confers on the four organs—the Assembly, the Council, the Commission and the Court of Justice—the function of carrying out 'the tasks entrusted to the Community'. This refers back to the fundamental purposes of the E.E.C., namely 'to promote throughout the community a harmonious development of economic activities, a continuous and balanced expansion, an increase in stability, an accelerated raising of the standard of living and closer relations between the States belonging to it'.[1] Particular activities which the Community is to undertake for the achieving of these purposes are set out in Article 3. But the point to notice is that these tasks have been given by the member States to *the Community* to perform, and the four institutions therefore act as the organs of the

1. Article 2. Cf. Arts. 2 and 3 of the E.C.S.C. Treaty and Arts. 1 and 2 of the Euratom Treaty.

Community. The Community has a legal personality distinct from the personalities of the member States[2] and has the capacity to conclude treaties with other States and with international organisations.[3] The principle of legality or, to put it another way, the concept of *ultra vires* is also expressed in Article 4, and it clearly would have applied even had it not been written into the Treaty:

> Each institution shall act within the limits of the powers conferred upon it by this Treaty.

There are provisions stipulating the general functions and powers of the Council, Commission and Assembly,[4] but one must also look to the particular articles under which a measure or decision is taken in order to discover the precise relative powers of these organs in any given instance. The Court's task is to ensure that the law is observed in the interpretation and application of the Treaty, and it has been given a variety of jurisdictions to enable it to do this.[5]

Law-making powers are divided between the Council and the Commission, with the Assembly known officially as the European Parliament since 1962 having the right to be consulted about draft measures in many cases but possessing no right to propose legislation.

The general provisions setting out the respective powers of the Council and the Commission are Articles 145 and 155. Article 145 provides:

> To ensure that the objectives set out in this Treaty are attained, the Council shall, in accordance with the provisions of this Treaty:
>
> —ensure co-ordination of the general economic policies of the Member States;
> —have power to take decisions.

Article 155 provides:

> In order to ensure the proper functioning and development of the common market, the Commission shall:

2. Articles 210 and 211.

3. Articles 113, 114, 228, 238. The same applies to the other two communities, E.C.S.C. and Euratom. Treaty-making capacity does not come into being over the whole range of economic matters covered by the treaties until the Community has adopted a common policy on the particular subject, e.g. road transport. See *Commission* v. *Council*, case 22/70, [1971] C.M.L.R. 335.

4. Articles 145, 155, 137.

5. See my chapter on the Court in *An Introduction to the Law of the European Economic Community*. A short note on developments relating to the Court since that chapter was written appears at section VI, chapter III of the present volume.

—ensure that the provisions of this Treaty and the measures taken by the institutions pursuant thereto are applied;

—formulate recommendations or deliver opinions on matters dealt with in this Treaty, if it expressly so provides or if the Commission considers it necessary;

—have its own power of decision and participate in the shaping of measures taken by the Council and by the Assembly in the manner provided for in this Treaty;

—exercise the powers conferred on it by the Council for the implementation of the rules laid down by the latter.

The Council has the right to determine basic policy, but only upon 'proposals' from the Commission, a most valuable and politically important right vested in that body which will be discussed shortly. The Commission can be entrusted by the Council with executive functions in relation to particular Community measures, for example the application of Articles 85 and 86 of the E.E.C. Treaty under Council Regulation No. 17,[6] subject to appeal to the Court by any company or firm to which a decision under this regulation is addressed, or which is directly and individually concerned with a decision.[7]

The Council consists of representatives of the member States at ministerial level. Much preparatory work is done by sub-committees of officials, in consultation with the staff of the Commission, and there is also the Committee of Permanent Representatives, which has come to play a vital role in preliminary discussion of draft proposals from the Commission before they are formally presented to the Council.[8] But in the Council itself the States are represented by members of their governments. Which particular member of a government attends is determined by the nature of the agenda. Ministers of Agriculture, Transport and Finance attend regularly, but 'the natural and usual Minister who represents a member on the Council is its Foreign Minister'.[9] Meetings of the Council can be convened by the President (the presidential office is held for six months by each member in turn),[10] or on request of any member, or of the Commission.[11]

6. 6 February 1962, *Journal Officiel*, No. 13 of 21 February 1962, p. 204; set out as Appendix 3 in *An Introduction to the Law of the E.E.C.*, p. 118.

7. See chapter VIII below.

8. Merger Treaty, 1965, Cmnd. 4866, Art. 4, and Lasok and Bridge, *An Introduction to the Law and Institutions of the European Communities*, London, 1972, pp. 113–15.   9. *Ibid.*, p. 110.

10. Merger Treaty 1965, Art. 2, as amended by Accession Treaty, 1972, Art. 11.   11. Merger Treaty 1965, Art. 3.

II. AN INDEPENDENT COMMISSION

The Commission presents a complete contrast to the Council. It is a collegiate body of thirteen members[12] who act in the interests of the Community as a whole and who are given the necessary independence from the governments by the treaties themselves. After the governments have signified their agreement with the names of commissioners put forward by other member governments[13] they can play no further part in the work or policy-making of the Commission. The relevant provisions are common to the three Communities and are contained in Articles 10, 12 and 13 of the Merger Treaty of 1965. Article 10(2) provides that the commissioners 'shall, in the general interest of the Communities, be completely independent in the performance of their duties'. They are forbidden to seek or take instructions from any government or any other body. Furthermore, the member States undertake 'to respect this principle and not to seek to influence the members of the Commission in the performance of their tasks'. Article 10(2) goes on to prohibit commissioners from engaging in any other occupation during their term of office[14] and to prescribe the giving of a solemn undertaking to respect the obligations arising from their office both during and after its term.

The Court of Justice may compulsorily retire a commissioner who breaks this undertaking, or deprive him of his pension. The Court may also compulsorily retire a commissioner who no longer fulfils the conditions required for the performance of his duties[15] or who has been guilty of serious misconduct. Otherwise, commissioners have security of tenure,[16] subject only to a liability that the whole Commission may be dismissed by the Parliament in a vote of no confidence.[17] Such a motion was tabled for the first time before the Parliament in November 1972 but was withdrawn on December 12. The draft motion [18] would have censured the Commission for failing to fulfil its commitment of April 1970 to submit proposals within two years for the strengthening of the Parliament's control over the budget, a control which is minimal at present.[19] The Parliament

12. Two from each of the four larger States, France, Germany, Italy and the United Kingdom, and one from each of the five other member States.

13. See Art. 11 of the Merger Treaty. Art. 10 says that commissioners shall be chosen on grounds of their general competence and that 'their independence is beyond doubt'.   14. Four years, renewable.

15. See note 13 above.   16. Merger Treaty, Art. 12(3).

17. Article 144, E.E.C.   18. *The Times*, 13 December 1972.

19. See Art. 203, E.E.C., as amended by the Budgetary Treaty of 1970, and Lasok and Bridge, *op. cit.*, pp. 132–3.

adopted a compromise resolution which took note of the Commission's view, shared by Parliament, that the 1970 commitment had been largely overtaken by the summit conference of October 1972. The summit communiqué[20] confirmed this commitment, declared the desire of the nine governments to 'strengthen the powers of control of the European Parliamentary Assembly' and called for proposals from the Community institutions and from member States on measures relating to the distribution of competences and responsibilities among the institutions and member States which will be necessary to the proper functioning of an economic and monetary union. The heads of State or government also invited the Council and the Commission 'to improve the relations' of both bodies with the Assembly.

III. THE ROLE OF THE COMMISSION

Whatever may emerge as a result of this political initiative, the present legal structure within which the Community institutions seek to achieve the objectives of the treaties is one in which the Council and the Commission share the competence to take binding decisions, to make Community law[21] and to apply it. The Parliament has questioning, publicising and consultative functions but at present no law-making powers[22] and only limited control over part of the Community budget. The Council and the Commission are intended to balance the interests and claims of the individual member States, as expressed by their governments on the one hand, and those of the Community as a whole as expressed by the independent Commission on the other. Interested groups of all kinds can and do make representations to the Commission on policy proposals affecting them.

The Commission has been given the crucial right of initiative in almost every matter of general policy under the treaties setting up Euratom and the European Economic Community.[23]

Taking the E.E.C. Treaty, the following are among the articles

20. Cmnd. 5109.

21. See further chapters v and vi below.

22. Parliament can propose initiatives to the Commission, but the Commission is not bound by any resolution of the Parliament. See the Vedel report, Supplement No. 4 to *Bulletin of the European Communities*, 1972, and extracts in *The New Politics of European Integration*, ed. Ionescu, London, 1972

23. The earlier Treaty of Paris, 1951, creating the Coal and Steel Community, distributes the competences as between Council and High Authority (now Commission) rather differently, but both institutions have to play a part in decision-making.

under which the Council can act *only* on a proposal from the Commission (the list is not exhaustive but serves to illustrate the variety of subject-matters on which the Commission has the right of initiative):

Article 8. Changes in the length of the second and third stages of the transitional period [for the establishment of the Common Market].

Article 14. Reductions in custom duties of the member States *inter se.* These two provisions have no further application but were important in the development of the Common Market.

Articles 20, 21. Establishment of the common external customs tariff (C.E.T.).

Article 28 (and Article 33 in the Treaty of Accession). Alterations to or suspensions of duties in the C.E.T.

Article 43. Determination of the common agricultural policy and establishment of common marketing organisations for agricultural products.

(Article 52 in the Treaty of Accession authorises the Council, on a proposal from the Commission, to permit derogation from the common price for particular agricultural products in the new member States).

Article 49 of the E.E.C. Treaty. Legislation on the free movement of workers.

Article 51. Social security measures needed to achieve this freedom.

Article 54. Abolition of restrictions on freedom of establishment for firms, companies and individuals.

Article 87. Legislation to implement Arts. 85 and 86 (on competition).

Since the E.E.C. Treaty is largely an outline or framework treaty, laying down general principles and objectives but not containing, in most cases, detailed implementation provisions, the Commission's prerogative of initiating policy programmes and draft legislation assumes considerable importance. The Commission is present when the Council meets to consider the Commission's proposals, which will by then have been discussed by the Parliament, and in the Economic and Social Committee if the Treaty so requires,[24] as well

24. The Economic and Social Committee consists of 144 representatives of various branches of economic and social activity, 'in particular, representatives

as in the Committee of Permanent Representatives. The Commissioner most closely concerned with the particular proposal attends the Council and takes part in the discussion, assisted by members of the Commission's staff. This has been described as giving the Community a tenth seat at the Council table. The Commission has no vote in the Council, of course. Emile Noël, the Secretary General of the Commission, has stressed the uniqueness of this legislative and executive diarchy. He writes: '. . . the teaming of the Commission and Council in double harness provides the driving force, and perhaps the most original feature, of the whole institutional set-up'.[25] Noël and Henri Etienne, who is a head of division in the Commission, have elaborated this comment in another article:[26]

The Community process of decision therefore comprises an element of proposal and one of acceptance—and the system of the treaties is designed to keep these components independent of each other and place them on a near equal footing. It is here that the Community procedure differs profoundly from diplomatic procedure and likewise from that of the traditional intergovernmental organisations, whose secretariats more often than not have only a limited power of independence and political initiative.

IV. MODIFICATIONS TO THE TREATY PATTERN OF
LAW-MAKING

It is now appropriate to refer to certain deviations from the legislative procedure envisaged in the original E.E.C. Treaty. Some commentators have seen these as threats to the Commission's right of initiative and hence as a shift in the power balance away from the Commission, representing the Community as a whole, in favour of the Council, representing the individual States.[27] It is perhaps wise at this stage

of producers, farmers, carriers, workers, dealers, craftsmen, professional occupations and representatives of the general public' (Art. 193). The members are appointed by the Council for four-year terms. There are twenty-four United Kingdom members. They are appointed in their personal capacity and must not be bound by any instructions from their government or any other body. (Art. 194). Opinions of Parliament or the Economic and Social Committee must be referred to expressly in Community legislation to which they relate, when the Treaty requires such opinions (Art. 190). If no such reference is made, the legislation is liable to annulment by the Court under Art. 173, on ground of infringement of the Treaty.

25. 'How the European Community's institutions work', *Community Topics*, No. 37, 1971, p. 3.

26. 'The Permanent Representatives' Committee and the "deepening " of the Communities', in Ionescu (ed.), *op. cit.*, at p. 99.

27. E.g. Schindler on the Management Committee procedure, 8 *C.M.L.Rev.* (1971) 184. Cf. Bertram, 5 *C.M.L.Rev.* (1967–68) 246. See further, p. 21 below, on management committee procedure.

to suspend judgment until we have had a chance to observe the enlarged Community in operation, for whatever constitutional developments or distortions may have occurred in the Community of the Six, it is clear that different concentrations of political and economic influence will arise in the Community of Nine, and different decision-making practices are likely to emerge in consequence.[28]

The Committee of Permanent Representatives (C.P.R.) was created in 1953 in response to an apparent need for an intermediary body between the High Authority (Commission) of the E.C.S.C. and the Council of Ministers. It was called the Co-ordinating Committee ('Cocor') of senior officials of the six States, and undertook preparatory work on policy proposals and legislation for the Council. The Rome treaties establishing the E.E.C. and Euratom institutionalised this committee and upgraded it into a Committee of Permanent Representatives of member States.[29] These permanent representatives have the status of ambassadors. The C.P.R. co-ordinates, on behalf of the Council, the work of committees of senior officials which receive Commission memoranda and proposals initially. The Commission is represented at all meetings of Council working parties, committees and the C.P.R. itself, thus securing the continuance of the dialogue between the Commission's staff and national officials. If the C.P.R. and the Commission's representative are all agreed on a minor matter, the decision will be adopted in the Council itself without debate. Any important proposal is discussed in detail in the Council. The role of the C.P.R. is further recognised, with an awareness that it is perceived in some quarters as a threat to the Commission's powers, in the celebrated Luxembourg Accords of 1966. These Accords, the precise legal status and effect of which are controversial,[30] brought to an end the crisis in the Community over the financing of the Common Agricultural Policy and the proposed extended powers of control for the Parliament. France had boycotted Council meetings for some six months in 1965. Among

28. *Accord* Lasok and Bridge, p. 117.

29. Article 151, *E.E.C.*, Art. 121, Euratom. See now Art. 4 of the Merger Treaty, 1965.

30. Mathijsen, *A Guide to European Community Law*, London, 1972, p. 134; Lasok and Bridge, *op. cit.*, pp. 120–1. The Solicitor General said, in discussion of what is now section 1(4) of the European Communities Act, that the Luxembourg 'document' was not an agreement: 'It does not become an agreement when it is recording the differing views of the parties merely because it takes the form of a declaration.' (*H.C. Deb.*, vol. 833, col. 617, 15 March 1972.) Text of the Accords in Sweet and Maxwell's *European Community Treaties*, 1972, p. 234.

the recorded agreements reached at the extraordinary Council session of 28 and 29 January 1966 in Luxembourg was the following, under the heading 'Relations between the Commission and the Council':

Before adopting any particularly important proposal, it is desirable that the Commission should take up the appropriate contacts with the Governments of the Member States, through the Permanent Representatives, without this procedure compromising the right of initiative which the Commission derives from the Treaty.

Another possible modification may be derived from Article 152 of the E.E.C. Treaty. This may be open to abuse by a Council determined to wrest the Commission's right of initiative away from it on particular subjects. Or Article 152 may simply be applied as a sensible *modus operandi* with no intention or effect of altering the respective powers of the two bodies. The article provides:

The Council may request the Commission to undertake any studies which the Council considers desirable for the attainment of the common objectives, and to submit to it any appropriate proposals.

However, Article 235 gives residuary powers to the Council, acting unanimously on a proposal from the Commission and after consulting the Parliament, to 'take the appropriate measures' if action is needed to attain one of the objectives of the Community and 'this Treaty has not provided the necessary powers'. When Article 152 is read with Article 235, any threat to the Commission's prerogative can be met by a sufficiently resolute Commission, which can properly insist upon its right to initiate any actual decisions and legislation, as distinct from preparatory studies undertaken at the request of the Council under Article 152.

The management committee procedure consists of the interposition into the decision-making process of a committee on which the member States are represented by officials and whose chairman represents the Commission, but has no vote. These management committees control the exercise by the Commission of decision-making powers delegated to it by the Council, particularly in agricultural matters. If the Commission's draft measures receive the approval of a qualified majority of forty-one votes, weighted in accordance with Article 148(2), the measures enter into force immediately and do not require Council action. But if the Commission's draft is not approved by the management committee the matter goes to the Council, which has a period of one month in which it may rescind or vary the Commission's measure. In the meantime the measure will have come into operation.[31] Thus the Council's delegation of power is conditional upon the Commission's proposed measures being approved by the management committee on which the governments are represented.

There have been very few occasions on which draft measures have had to be referred to the Council under the management committee procedure,[32] and more than a thousand regulations and decisions have been adopted in this way. The European Court upheld the legality of the procedure in 1971 when it was challenged by several German import–export firms in the cereal trade.[33] The Court said that it

allows the Council to transfer considerable powers to adopt implementing measures to the Commission subject to the reservation that in a given case the Council can take back the power of decision, but this procedure does not adulterate the Community structure and the institutional balance of powers.

31. Unless the Commission decides to suspend its operation for a month after notifying the disagreement to the Council.

32. Noël, *loc. cit.*, p. 7; Lasok and Bridge, *op. cit.*, p. 144.

33. *Internationale Handelsgesellschaft m.b.H., Frankfurt/Main* v. *Einfuhr- und Vorratstelle für Getreide und Futtermittel* (the German Agricultural Intervention Board), case 11/70; also cases 25/70 26/70, and 30/70; [1972] C.M.L.R. 255.

Chapter III

THE MAIN INSTITUTIONS OF
THE COMMUNITIES (II)

Gillian White

I. VOTING IN THE COUNCIL

All three treaties provide for decisions to be taken by the Council, either by unanimous vote, or by simple majority of member States, or by a qualified majority of votes weighted in accordance with the relevant provisions. In the Coal and Steel treaty[1] votes of members are weighted according to the proportions of the total coal and steel output of the Community produced in the several States. In the E.E.C. and Euratom treaties votes are weighted according to a numerical formula which is contained in Article 148(2) of the E.E.C. Treaty,[2] as amended by the Accession Treaty (Article 14) and further amended by Article 8 of the Council decision of 1 January 1973, making adjustments consequent upon Norway's decision not to join the Communities.[3] The 'Big Four' States have ten votes each; Belgium and the Netherlands five each; Denmark and Ireland three each; and Luxembourg two votes. Where the treaties require the Council to act *only* on a proposal from the Commission, Council acts need a qualified majority of forty-one votes out of a total of fifty-eight. This means that two of the Big Four or any group of member States wielding a total of eighteen votes, can block a decision, and all the smaller States together have eighteen votes; other combinations with veto power are one of the Big Four with the three smallest (Denmark, Ireland, Luxembourg), or one of the Big Four with either Belgium or the Netherlands plus either Denmark or Ireland. It is important to note that the Big Four alone possess forty votes only, and so cannot form a qualified majority without the support of at least one other member.

Where the Treaty does *not* require a proposal from the Commission, the qualified majority is still forty-one votes, but these must be

---

1. Article 28. 2. Article 118(2), Euratom.
3. *Off. Journal*, vol. 16, No. L 2, p. 1, 1 January 1973.

cast by at least *six* members. In other words, the Big Four need the support of at least *two* other members before they can outvote the smaller States. The reasoning behind this difference is that the Commission's participation by introducing proposals is considered to secure a degree of protection for the smaller members, since the Commission acts independently and in the interests of the Community as a whole. This protection is lacking when the Treaty empowers the Council to act without a proposal from the Commission, but, as we have seen, there are not many such provisions.[4]

The Luxembourg Accords of January 1966 modified the practice of the Council, and the Treaty provisions for action by simple majority or qualified majority have been virtually ignored.[5] The Accords state, under the heading 'Majority voting procedure':

i. Where, in the case of decisions which may be taken by majority vote on a proposal of the Commission, very important interests of one or more partners are at stake, the Members of the Council will endeavour, within a reasonable time, to reach solutions which can be adopted by all the Members of the Council while respecting their mutual interests and those of the Community, in accordance with Article 2 of the Treaty.

ii. With regards to the preceding paragraph, the French delegation considers that where very important interests are at stake the discussion must be continued until unanimous agreement is reached.

iii. The six delegations note that there is a divergence of views on what should be done in the event of a failure to reach complete agreement.

iv. The six delegations nevertheless consider that this divergence does not prevent the Community's work being resumed in accordance with the normal procedure.

Successive British governments have placed considerable emphasis on this power of veto apparently secured for each member State by paragraphs i–iii of the Accords.[6] The legal validity of the Accords is, as we have said, dubious. They purport to change the voting provisions of Article 148 by an instrument which is not a formal amendment of the Treaty under Article 236, which requires a conference and ratification of any amendments by all members in accordance with their constitutional requirements. However, the political significance of the Accords is considerable. Any prospect of the Court being asked to rule upon their validity is so remote as

4. See p. 17 above.
5. See Vedel report, pp. 26–7.
6. Legal and Constitutional White Paper, 1967 (appendix 1 in *An Introduction to the Law of the E.E.C*), Cmnd. 3301, para. 14; *The U.K. and the European Communities*, 1971, Cmnd. 4715, paras. 30, 70. Mr Rippon in *H.C. Deb.*, vol. 831, col. 274, 15 February 1972.

to be academic.[7] The balanced comment of M. Noël illuminates the probable effects in practice of this 'agreement to disagree'. He wrote in 1971:

The general interest of the Community must of necessity take account of any essential interest of one of its members . . . The close union of the six nations which the Community exists to bring about would in any case not be feasible if one of those nations suffered grave injury to its essential interests. Moreover, the system of deliberation in the Council . . . is calculated to achieve the broadest possible measure of agreement. Conversely, even where unanimity is the rule, no member of a Community can disregard the general interest in assessing his own: unanimity in a Community cannot be equated with an absolute right of veto. Thus, in a living Community, abuse of majority voting—and probably abuse of unanimity too—is a theoretical risk which, with the Community's inner bonds drawing ever closer as it moves forward, is becoming less and less likely to materialize, while the possibility of majority decisions renders the whole system more flexible and more dynamic.[8]

The Commission has proposed a scheme for future operation of the voting rules in the enlarged Communities, but space precludes discussion of this here.[9] It is important to note that the Treaty itself requires unanimity for any amendment by the Council to a Commission proposal.[10] If the members are not agreed, therefore, they can only adopt or reject the proposal *in toto*: it can be amended only by the Commission. However, the practice of unanimity since the Luxembourg Accords has clearly removed most of the force from this provision. In view of the elaborate preparatory machinery of sub-committees, working parties and the C.P.R., the Commission is unlikely to table proposals which it fears will meet with rejection.

II. THE PRODUCT OF THE LEGISLATIVE PROCESS

The only matter which falls within the scope of this account of the main institutions is to draw attention to the provision in the E.E.C.

7. Cf. Mathijsen, *op. cit.*, p. 135.
8. Noël, *loc. cit.*, pp. 8–9, Cf. Sir Derek Walker-Smith, who regards the veto as of no substance, at any rate if sought to be exercised on a view of the vetoing State's important national interests which is not shared by other members: *H.C. Deb.*, vol. 831, cols. 318–19, 15 February 1972. The Vedel committee expressed concern at the effect of the practice of unanimity upon the actions of the Commission: 'The dose of innovation which could and normally should be included in its proposals is likely to be sacrificed in the search for solutions which will meet with unanimous approval' (p. 27).
9. See Lasok and Bridge, p. 121.
10. Article 149, E.E.C.; Art. 119, Euratom. The E.C.S.C. structure is different.

Treaty which must be familiar by now to most British lawyers, namely, Article 189.[11] This empowers the Council and the Commission to make Community law and policy, in accordance with the Treaty and by selecting whichever of five types of instrument is most appropriate for the particular purpose. Community law, an expression which of course comprises the treaties themselves, can take the form of regulations or directives or decisions, under Article 189. Regulations are of general application and take immediate effect in their entirety as law in all member States, with no intervention or confirmation by their governments or legislatures.[12]

Directives are legally binding on any member State or States to which they are addressed only as to the object to be achieved. The States are free to choose the form and method of securing this object within their own legal and administrative systems. Decisions are addressed to individual governments, enterprises or other bodies, and are binding in their entirety upon the addressees. Community policy under Article 189 takes the form of recommendations or opinions which are not binding. One should also have in mind the proposals' of the Commission in which its policy initiatives are conveyed to the Council and which are not binding at that stage, being draft legislation which requires enactment by the Council. The E.E.C. Treaty contains many instances of the possible use of recommendations. For example, if there had been a risk that the progressive abolition of customs duties in force between the original Six would be unattainable in the time or to the extent laid down in Articles 13 and 14, the Commission had to 'make all appropriate recommendations to Member States' (Article 14(6)). In devising and implementing the Common Agricultural Policy the Council is empowered by Article 43(2) to make recommendations as well as to make regulations, issue directives or take decisions. In the Treaty's chapter on services, Articles 59–66, member States may go further in liberalising the right to provide services than directives made under Article 63 require, if their general economic situation and the situation of the economic sector concerned permit this. In such a situation the Commission is to make recommendations to the member States concerned. A final example concerns dumping; Article 91 of the E.E.C. Treaty and Article 136 in the Treaty of Accession. The Commission is first to address recommendations to

11. Article 161, Euratom. Cf. Arts. 14 and 15, E.C.S.C.
12. See s. 2(1), European Communities Act, 1972, and Mrs Hoggett's chapter v below.

26

the person or persons guilty of dumping practices, if it so finds, upon application by a member State or by any other interested party, that is, by any company or firm whose business was being harmed. If the dumping practices continue, the Commission is to authorise the injured State to take protective measures upon conditions determined by the Commission.[13]

It may be worth repeating that recommendations and decisions can also be made pursuant to secondary Community law.[14] An important example for lawyers is the power of the Commission under Regulation No. 17 of the Council, the first regulation implementing Articles 85 and 86, to address recommendations and decisions to undertakings in order to terminate any infringements of those articles,[15] the effect of which is further adumbrated by Professor Wortley in chapter VIII.

There are fewer express references to opinions in the Treaty. In the title on social policy, Article 118 gives the Commission the task of promoting co-operation between member States in matters such as employment, labour law and social security. The Commission is to make studies and deliver opinions on these matters, in consultation with the governments and before delivering opinions; it must consult the Economic and Social Committee. Article 126 empowers the Council to decide, unanimously, upon any new tasks that are to be given to the European Social Fund,[16] but it may do so only after receiving the opinion of the Commission, and after consulting the Economic and Social Committee and the Parliament.

These examples have been given purely for purposes of illustration. Clearly, there is no question of the legal power of either Council or Commission to issue directives, make regulations, take decisions, make recommendations or give opinions being restricted to cases in which these forms are stipulated by the treaties. Article 189 itself is couched in general terms and empowers the institutions, in achieving the objects of the Community, to use whichever form of law or

13. See chapter VII below.   14. See p. 15 above.
15. See Art. 3(3) of Reg. 17 (recommendations) and Arts. 3(1), 6, 7, 8, 14(3), 15, 16 (decisions) and Art. 3 (power to give negative clearance; the exercise of this power amounts to the taking of a 'decision', e.g. the first such decision, concerning the agreement between *Grosfillex* (a French manufacturer) and *Fillistorf* (a Swiss dealer), [1964] C.M.L.R. 237.
16. This fund is established by Art. 123, E.E.C., for the object of improving employment opportunities. It is to be used mainly for helping governments to pay the resettlement or retraining costs of workers who are wholly or partly unemployed as a result of conversion of industries to other production. The fund is administered by the Commission; see Arts. 123–8, E.E.C.

policy-making is appropriate to the matter in hand. The sole restriction is the obligation to comply with any Treaty provisions which prescribe a particular form or which require prior consultation of the Parliament, the Economic and Social Committee or other body.

III. DEMOCRATIC CONTROL?[17]

The very limited role which the European Parliament plays in the law-making and decision-making process needs no further emphasis. The European Parliament is not yet directly elected by voters in the member States, although there is provision for this to happen in the future.[18] The Vedel committee recommended that Parliament be given powers of co-decision with the Council and Commission over an increasing range of subjects over a period of years, but these recommendations have not been implemented.

For the time being, therefore, the national parliaments are the effective repositories of democratic control over the Community institutions, the degree of effectiveness varying according to national constitutional provisions and practices.[19] At Westminster each House of Parliament set up a Select Committee on European Community legislation. Each committee has issued two reports.[20] The government responded to the first report of the Commons committee by arranging for the issue of departmental memoranda explaining draft *Council* legislation, and for ministerial statements to be made to the House on Council proceedings.[20a] The second report recommended the creation of a new scrutiny committee of the House to receive Community proposals referred to it by the Minister with overall responsibility for Community affairs and by a Law Officer.[20b] The committee would inform the House of any proposals of legal or political importance, indicating any changes in United Kingdom law that would be involved. Any proposal reported as of major importance should be sent to the Commons 'for consideration and debate well before the expected decision of the Council of Mini-

17. See generally the Vedel report, pp. 32–3 and 36 ff.

18. Article 138, E.E.C., and Art. 139(1) in the Act of Accession, 1972.

19. See Niblock, *The E.E.C. National Parliaments in Community Decision-making* (Chatham House), P.E.P., London, 1971.

20. H.C. 143 (1972–73) and 463–I, 463–II (1972–73); H.L. 67 and 194 (1972–73).

20a. *H.C. Deb.*, 16 April 1973, cols. 550–618.

20b. The committees said that there should be *one* Minister with this responsibility and an additional Law Officer: H.C. 463–I, paras. 46, 49, 50.

sters'.[21] The Lords committee recommended (second report) the creation of a Lords' Select Committee to consider Community proposals, to obtain information about them and to report those which, in its view, raise important questions of policy or principle; it suggested that the Select Committee should have a law sub-committee to consider *inter alia* whether regulations impliedly repealed existing law, and whether any amendment to existing law was desirable (even where not obligatory) to comply with any regulation.

The government has not yet taken a position on these recommendations, nor has either House taken decisions on the second reports. British Ministers will remain responsible to the U.K. Parliament for their actions in the Council, but it may be impossible in practise to undo what the Council has enacted into Community law if it proves unacceptable to the British Parliament.

IV. THE FINANCING OF THE COMMUNITIES

The Communities are financed from two sources at present, in pursuance of the provisions of an important Council decision of 1970.[22] Member States have to contribute to the budget in fixed proportions,[23] and the Communities have been allocated 'resources of their own' by this decision. These 'own resources' comprise the total revenue from Community agricultural levies, collected by each member State's authorities in accordance with the relevant Council and Commission decisions and regulations,[24] together with a proportion of the revenue from common customs tariff duties, that is, duties on non-agricultural imports entering the Community from non-member territories. The proportion of this revenue which becomes the Communities' own resources is governed by a formula contained in Article 3, paragraph 1, of the 1970 decision. The formula provides for the proportion to increase progressively from January 1971, when this system of financing began, to January 1975, when the *whole* of this revenue will constitute the Communities' own resources. It is further provided[25] that from 1 January 1975 the Communities' budget is to be financed entirely from the Communities' own resources, and the member States will then cease to 'pay a subscription' but will be under a continuing obligation to

21. *Ibid.*, para. 72.
22. Decision of 21 April 1970, *Off. Journal*, No. L 94, 28 April 1970; Cmnd. 4867, p. 19.
23. Article 3, paras. 2 and 3 of this decision.
24. See Mr Jaconelli's chapter XII below.
25. Article 3(2) and Art. 4 of the 1970 decision.

collect the revenue from agricultural levies and the external customs tariff on behalf of the Communities.[26]

The legal position created by this obligation is thus strikingly different to that which normally arises from the United Kingdom's membership of an international organisation, and is a salient feature of the distinctive and incipiently federal nature of the European Communities. In the debate on what became section 2(3) of the European Communities Act in the House of Commons, the Chief Secretary to the Treasury explained the effect of the Council decision on 'own resources'. He said:

This means, and can only mean, that the sums concerned, although collected in the first instance by Member States, belong, from the moment at which the payment arises, to the Communities. The payments 'flow through the Exchequers of Member States to the Community budget'.[27]

It was not a question of the British government collecting sums due from manufacturers and traders, and then from time to time paying a subscription due to the Communities:

The payments belong from the outset to the Communities, and it is merely for convenience that collection is to be undertaken through the existing machinery in each Member State. The Communities' entitlement to the money is absolute from the moment a claim on the importer for the levy or duty is established.[28]

The Minister pointed out that, in consequence, it would not be appropriate to use a charge to Votes, which is the method used for British subscriptions to other international organisations. The 'own resources' system was incompatible with any arrangements which allowed Parliament to intervene through a Vote procedure. Accordingly, section 2(3) of the European Communities Act provides that

There shall be charged on and issued out of the Consolidated Fund or, if so determined by the Treasury, the National Loans Fund the amounts required to meet any Community obligation to make payments to any of the Communities. . .

Article 6 of the 1970 Council decision, which creates the obligation to collect the 'Community resources' described above, constitutes a 'community obligation' within section 2(3). The article provides that 'Member States shall make these resources available to the Commission'.

26. Article 6. The replacement of contributions of member States by 'own resources' is referred to in Art. 201 of the E.E.C Treaty.
27. *H.C. Deb.*, vol. 838, col. 844, 8 June 1972.
28. *Ibid.*, col. 845.

It is also clear from section 5(4) and section 6(5) of the Act that revenues from Community customs duties and from Community agricultural levies do not at any moment comprise part of the revenues of the Crown.

The Council foresaw in 1970 that the income from these duties and levies arising in the member States would not be sufficient in 1975 to ensure that the Communities' budget was in balance.[29] Consequently, a further category of 'own resource' was provided for, namely, so much of the revenue from value added tax in the member States as is obtained 'by applying a rate not exceeding 1 per cent to an assessment basis which is determined in a uniform manner for member States according to Community rules'.[30]

This rate is to be fixed each year. There are provisions derogating from the above in case the rules determining the uniform basis for assessment of V.A.T. have not yet been applied, on 1 January 1975, by all the member States. No Community rules for the basis of assessing V.A.T. have yet been adopted.[31]

So far as democratic control over the Communities' budget is concerned, a very limited power has been given to the European Parliament by the 1970 Budgetary Treaty to propose modifications to the budget during the period from January 1971 to December 1974. From 1975 the Parliament will be able to override the wishes of the Council and impose modifications to the budget. However, it should immediately be pointed out that the power to prevail over the Council relates only to expenditure which is *not* 'necessarily resulting from the Treaty or from acts adopted in accordance therewith'.[32] In relation to expenditure which does necessarily result from the Treaty or from Community secondary legislation—a category which includes the major expenditure of the Communities, particularly the financing of the Common Agricultural Policy, and payments to farmers from the Agricultural Guidance and Guarantee Fund—the Council has the last word on the budget. The Parliament could control only some 3–4 per cent of total Community expenditure, namely some of the administrative expenditure and a few items of operating expenditure. The above exposition accords with the Council's interpretation of the relevant provisions of the

29. Article 20 of the Merger Treaty (as amended by Art. 10 of the 1970 Budgetary Treaty) requires the annual budget of the Communities to be in balance.

30. Article 4(1) of the 1970 decision.

31. See Mr Davey's chapter XI below.

32. Article 203(4), (5) and (6), E.E.C. Treaty (as amended by the Budgetary Treaty, Art. 4). For the position up to January 1975 see Art. 203a.

Budgetary Treaty, which are not at all clear. The Parliament and the Commission have taken the view that, from 1975, Article 203(6) confers on the Parliament 'at the end of the proceedings and in case of serious objection [the right] to reject the whole draft budget in order to secure fresh budgetary proposals'.[33]

This whole problem was rigorously examined by the Vedel committee, which concluded that, for a number of reasons, 'purely budgetary powers are a weak means of influence'. The Committee proposed that the Parliament should acquire 'a power of co-decision in legislative matters' and were firmly of the view that 'it is this reform which . . . will give real significance to the budgetary power of the Parliament.'[34] A similar view, in relation to the powers of the British Parliament, was expressed in the House of Commons by the Chief Secretary to the Treasury during the debate on the Communities' 'own resources' system. He said: 'The reality of the power of the House of Commons to control expenditure has long since ceased to reside in what has become a quite theoretical right to reject estimates.'[35] The Minister drew attention to the fact that payments out of the Consolidated Fund made under section 2(3) of the European Communities Act are subject to the scrutiny of the Expenditure Committee, the Public Accounts Committee and of the Comptroller and Auditor General.

It is clear, however, that democratic control must be sought through the Communities' institutions and evolving procedures rather than by means of the powers of the parliaments of individual members. These revenues belong to the Communities and are raised and spent on the basis of Community law. The national parliaments should not lose sight of the problems raised by the present lack of controlling power in the European Parliament, but it is submitted that progress ought to be made along the road of increasing the effectiveness and powers of that body, rather than along the road of seeking to remove powers from the Communities and restore them to national parliaments. At any rate, it is highly probably that the British Parliament will not be content with the *status quo*, and will be endeavouring to secure greater democratic control, both through pressure on British Ministers to take some initiatives in the Council and through the efforts of the British members of the European

33. Resolutions of 11 March 1970, 5 and 13 May 1970; Special report, Eur. Parliament, Doc. 42 (1970–71). See Vedel report, p. 54.
34. Vedel report, p. 55. See Commission proposals, *Bulletin*, supplement 9/73.
35. *H.C. Deb.*, vol. 838, col. 848, 8 June 1972.

Parliament, in collaboration with their colleagues from the other national parliaments.

V. OTHER INSTITUTIONS

Finally, it may be helpful to mention some of the other institutions which the treaties created or which are to be established as a result of decisions taken at the 'summit conference' of October 1972.

The treaties established advisory bodies which have to be consulted by the Commission in the course of formulating its final proposals on many matters. These bodies, the Economic and Social Committee for E.E.C. matters, and the Coal and Steel Consultative Committee, bring in representatives of economic and social activity and of the relevant industries and trade unions.[36] Numerous other committees have been created to assist the Council and Commission in their work, but, with the exception of the Committee of Parliamentary Representatives,[37] none of these bodies has been formally recognised in the treaties.

The European Investment Bank is endowed by the E.E.C. Treaty[38] with separate legal personality. Its functions and powers are contained in a statute annexed to the Treaty. Subscriptions from member States are prescribed by this statute for the original Six,[39] and by Protocol No. 1 to the Accession Treaty for the three new members.[40] The Bank may grant loans or guarantee the financing of projects to develop the less developed regions of the Community, to modernise undertakings or develop new activities needed because of the establishment of the Common Market; or projects of common interest to several member States. Projects in the last two categories may be assisted by the Bank only if they are of such a nature or extent that they cannot be wholly financed by means available within the State.

The European Monetary Co-operation Fund was established by Council regulation on 6 April 1973[40a] with separate legal personality. It is directed by a board of governors composed of the members

36. Articles 193–5, 197, E.E.C. Treaty, and Art. 21, Accession Treaty; Arts. 18 and 19, E.C.S.C. Treaty, and Art. 22, Accession Treaty.

37. See p. 20 above. See also Nielson, 'European groups and the decision-making processes: the Common Agricultural Policy', in *The New Politics of European Integration*, ed. Ionescu, 1972, p. 215.

38. Article 129.   39. Article 4.

40. As amended by Arts. 35 and 36, Council decision of 1 January 1973 to take account of Norway's not joining the Communities (see note 3 above).

40a. Regulation (EEC) 907/73, *Off. Journal*, L 89, 5 April 1973. For the fund's capacity as a legal person see Art. 6 of its statutes.

of the Committee of Governors of the Central Banks of Member states. The purposes of the fund are to promote (a) the proper functioning of the progressive narrowing of the margins of fluctuation of the members' currencies *inter se*; (b) intervention in Community currencies on exchange markets; and (c) settlements between central banks leading to a concerted policy on reserves. The statutes of the fund, annexed to the regulation, provide that the board is to achieve these aims by action in accordance with the general economic policy guidelines drawn up by the Council and with Council directives adopted unanimously. The Commission has recently reported to the Council on the difficulties confronting the fund in the absence of effective co-ordination of members' domestic monetary policies.[40b]

A Regional Development Fund has not been set up at the time of writing. It would be financed from the Community's own resources.[41] It is to be expected that the fund will have separate legal personality, although it could operate within the Commission, and be administered by it, as is the case with the Agricultural Guidance and Guarantee Fund[42] and the Social Fund.[43]

VI. THE COURT OF JUSTICE OF THE COMMUNITIES: RECENT DEVELOPMENTS

This note is intended as a supplement to the writer's chapter on the European Court in *An Introduction to the Law of the European Economic Community* (1972). The main developments which need to be noted by lawyers in the United Kingdom are the changes consequent upon the enlargement of the Communities, and the provisions which have been made in United Kingdom law to enable the country's courts to co-operate with the European Court, as intended by the treaties. Some other developments of general interest have occurred, particularly in recent decisions which have thrown more light on the working of Article 177 of the E.E.C. Treaty.

Composition of the Court. The Court has been enlarged, by decision of the Council, to nine Judges instead of seven. There are now four

40b. Monetary organisation of the Community, *E.C. Bulletin, Supplement.* 12/73 (report to Council presented 28 June 1973).

41. Summit communiqué, October 1972, para. 5 (Cmnd. 5109); and see chapter VII below.

42. See the booklet *The Common Agricultural Policy* (1972) issued by the Commission and obtainable from its Information Office, 22 Chesham Street, London s.w.1. 43. See note 16 above.

Advocates General, in place of two prior to the enlargement.[44] The present composition of the Court is: Judge Lecourt (President); Judges Mertens de Wilmars, Donner, Kutscher, Monaco, Pescatore, Soerensen, Mackenzie Stuart and O'Dalaigh. The Advocates General are MM. Roemer, Mayras, Trabucchi and Warner. For a decision of the full Court, as distinct from a chamber, seven Judges must sit.

Procedure of the Court. English and Danish are now Community languages and can therefore be used in the Court as the language of procedure, according to the rules for deciding which language is to apply in a particular case.[45] Simultaneous translation are provided for hearings, and the Court staff translate all documents in a case into the other languages. Irish is not a Community language, although, as we have seen, there is an authentic Irish text of the treaties and of the Treaty of Accession.

Other procedural provisions are unaffected by the enlargement of the Communities. These are contained in the protocol on the statute of the Court annexed to the E.E.C. Treaty, and in rules of procedure adopted by the Court from time to time under Article 188 of the Treaty.

Evidence. Article 26 of the Court's statute and the Evidence (European Court) Order, 1972,[46] provide that evidence of witnesses or experts may be taken in the United Kingdom if the Court requests.

Enforcement of Community judgments and decisions. The relevant treaty provisions—Articles 187 and 192, E.E.C.; Articles 44 and 92, E.C.S.C., and Articles 18, 159 and 164, Euratom—have not been modified or added to by the Treaty of Accession. The necessary provision has been made by order under section 2(2) of the European Communities Act, 1972 to give effect to these treaty provisions. The European Communities (Enforcement of Community Judgments) Order[47] provides for the registration in the High Court in England or Northern Ireland, and in the Court of Session in Scotland, of Community judgments to which the Secretary of State has attached an order for enforcement. The amended Order 71 of the rules of the Supreme Court lays down the procedure for giving effect to

44. Council decisions of 1 January 1973, *Off. Journal*, vol. 16, No. L 2, pp. 1 and 29.
45. *An Introduction to the Law of the E.E.C.*, p. 51.
46. S.I. 1972 No. 1722, made under s. 4(1) of the Oaths and Evidence (Overseas Authorities and Countries) Act, 1963.
47. S.I. 1972 No. 1590.

Community judgments in the United Kingdom.[48] 'Community judgment' is defined by the Enforcement Order as 'any decision, judgment or order which is enforceable under or in accordance with' the above-mentioned treaty provisions. Thus decisions of the Commission under Council Regulation No. 17 imposing fines on enterprises which are in breach of the competition provisions of the Treaty are enforceable under the order. The Secretary of State has no discretion in attaching an order for enforcement; he simply has to satisfy himself as to the authenticity of the Community judgment. Application for registration in the High Court or Court of Session can be made by the 'person' entitled to enforce the particular judgment or order. The Commission represents the Communities and is a 'person' for this purpose. Once registered, the Community judgment is equivalent to a High Court judgment or order for all purposes of execution. Only the European Court may suspend enforcement, under Article 192(4). The national courts have no power to do so, but they have jurisdiction to hear and determine any complaint of irregularity in the enforcement process. Article 5 of the order gives effect to this by providing for the registration in the High Court of any order of the European Court suspending enforcement of a registered Community judgment.

When a sum of money is payable under a Community judgment, the judgment is to be registered for such sum in sterling as, on the basis of the exchange rates prevailing on the date when the Community judgment was originally given, is equivalent to the sum payable.

References under Article 177. Rules have been made for the Supreme Court, Crown Court, Court of Appeal, Criminal Division and county courts, but not yet for magistrates' courts or any tribunals.[49] The rules made so far are straightforward, providing for reference to the European Court by the High Court, Crown Court or Court of Appeal on its own motion, or upon application by a party to proceedings in those courts. The proceedings will normally be adjourned while the European Court gives its preliminary ruling on the point of Community law referred to it. But the Crown Court or Court of Appeal, Criminal Division, is empowered to determine that the proceedings before them should not be adjourned. This is clearly a desirable provision, particularly for criminal courts,

48. Rules of the Supreme Court (Amendment No. 3), 1972, S.I. No. 1898.
49. See chapter v below by Mrs Hoggett.

and will enable witnesses to be heard and argument on other points of law pursued, pending the European Court's reply on the questions of Community law. It is clear from the wording of Article 177 that references may, and under Article 177(3) must, be made by criminal courts on exactly the same basis as references by civil courts. If this were not so, and the European Court had no jurisdiction to give a preliminary ruling on a reference by a criminal court, Community law could be applied differently by different member States in their national criminal courts.[50]

On the difficult questions capable of arising on the interpretation of Article 177(3) in the context of the English courts, the new Order 114 provides no guidance. The courts themselves will have to determine the circumstances in which the Court of Appeal or lower courts or tribunals constitute a court 'against whose decisions there is no judicial remedy under national law'.[51]

The European Court has decided that where there is an appeal in the national court against the order making a reference to it, and the appeal has the effect in the national law of suspending execution of the order of the lower court,[52] the European Court, which may already have received the reference, will refrain from giving a preliminary ruling until the national appeal court has given judgment. But it will not suspend its proceedings on the reference in any other respect. In particular, it will hear argument and the Advocate General will prepare and deliver his submissions.[53] However, it is unlikely that the European Court will be seised by receipt of an order made by the High Court in England which is then the subject of an appeal, since Order 114, paragraph 5, provides that the Senior Master shall not transmit a copy of the court's order to the European Court until the time for appeal against it has expired, or, if an appeal is made, until the appeal has has been been determined. The order does reserve the right of the High Court or the Court of Appeal to order transmission of the reference before the fourteen days have elapsed, but there is no such right if an appeal has already been entered.

The German Federal Finance Court has decided that the fact

50. The Advocate General made this point succinctly in *Pubblico Ministero* v. *S.p.A. Agricola Industria Latte (S.A.I.L.)*, [1972] C.M.L.R. 723, at 727, 740.

51. See Mrs Hoggett, chapter v below and p. 34 above.

52. R.S.C. Order 114, para. 6, provides for appeal against such an order made by the High Court. Appeal lies to the Court of Appeal without leave, within fourteen days of the order.

53. *Chanel S.A.* v. *Cepeha Handelmaatschappij N.V.*, [1971] C.M.L.R. 403.

that it was obliged to refer a Community law question to the European Court, because it fell within Article 177(3), did not prevent it from granting a stay of execution of an administrative decision. Further, it held that in the course of granting a stay the court was entitled and bound to make 'a summary examination' of relevant E.E.C. provisions.[54] In summary proceedings the Finance Court granted the plaintiff firm stay of execution of an order of the German Agricultural Intervention Board that it must repay an export subsidy granted to it on an export of powdered milk. The Finance Court referred certain questions of Community law to the European Court and at the same time granted this temporary stay of execution on the basis of its own examination of the Community regulations and decisions. This is a decision of obvious practical importance for courts in any member State.

With regard to decisions or other measures taken by the Community institutions, the treaties provide that actions or appeals brought to the European Court are not to have suspensory effect on the decision or measure challenged or appealed against.[55] Stay of execution of the Commission's decision may be granted in exceptional circumstances.[56] In *Firma Rheinmühler* (*The Times*, 15 January 1974) the Court decided that national rules of precedent did not preclude a reference under Article 177.

Extension of the Court's jurisdiction—conventions on companies and on enforcement of judgments. Finally, it should be noted that the United Kingdom has undertaken to accede to the conventions concluded by the original member States under Article 220 of the E.E.C. Treaty, and to the protocols which provide for their interpretation by the Court of Justice.[57] The two conventions, concluded in 1968, relate respectively to the Mutual Recognition of Companies and Bodies Corporate and to Jurisdiction and the Enforcement of Civil and Commercial Judgments.[58] The protocols were signed by the six members in the Council in June 1971.[59] All these instruments

54. *Re export subsidies for powdered milk,* [1972] C.M.L.R. 992.

55. Article 185, E.E.C.

56. [1972] C.M.L.R. 694. Cf. *Europemballage Corpn.* v. *Commission* [1972] C.M.L.R. 690.

57. Article 3(2) of the Treaty of Accession.

58. Companies Convention, *Bulletin of the E.C.,* 1969, supp. No. 2; Jurisdiction and Enforcement Convention, *ibid.*

59. Both protocols, *Bulletin of the E.C*, 1971, supp. No. 7; also in 8 *C.M.L. Rev.* (1971) 491 (English translation by M. R. Mok, the author of a useful brief note on the protocols at *ibid.*, p. 485).

are in force between the original six member States. The United Kingdom has not yet acceded to either convention. Indeed, a committee under the chairmanship of Lord Kilbrandon has been set up by the Lord Chancellor to advise on any adjustments which it may be necessary or desirable to negotiate with the original members with a view to enabling the United Kingdom to become a party to the Convention on Jurisdiction and Enforcement of Judgments.[60]

VII. CONCLUSIONS

In the age of Castlereagh, Metternich, Talleyrand and the Concert of Europe men spoke of 'the public law of Europe', meaning the system of constitutional, political and legal principles and rules established by the Congress of Vienna in 1815. In many respects the public law of Europe was a synonym for what we now know as international law. The European Communities, of which the first to be created—the Coal and Steel Community—is twenty years old, represent considerable steps towards the economic and political integration of the member States. They also created, as an essential element in achieving the degree of integration desired by the treaties, a constitutional structure of some novelty and considerable complexity through which the new 'public law' of part of Western Europe is to be made and applied. This is a new legal order, quite distinct and different from international law, and applicable only to the member States and their citizens,[61] not to the whole of Europe. The United Kingdom, with the common law tradition of England, Wales and Northern Ireland and the 'traditional civilian imprint' of Scots law,[62] ought to be able to contribute positively and beneficially to the development of the new legal order. The wider the understanding of its nature and functioning among British lawyers, the greater will be the likelihood of Britain making a valuable contribution.

60. 116 *S.J.* (1972) 260. On the present position regarding the enforcement of English judgments in the six original member States see Thirlway in 116 *S.J.* (1972) 891. On the Companies Convention see chapter x by T. Flanagan below, and on the Jurisdiction Convention see chapter xiv by Mrs D. Kloss below.
61. See Mrs Hoggett, chapter vi below.
62. Blom-Cooper and Drewery, *Final Appeal: a Study of the House of Lords in its Judicial Capacity*, Oxford, 1972, p. 375.

Chapter IV

ADMINISTRATIVE LAW AND JUDICIAL REVIEW IN THE E.E.C.

Harry Street

European Community law gives rise to substantially the same problems concerning judicial review of administrative action as English administrative law. The law is based essentially on the judicial control of executive action developed by the Conseil d'Etat in France. First, it is necessary to classify the various forms of act which can emanate from the organs of the European Economic Community.

I. CLASSIFICATION OF ACTS

Article 189 provides:

In order to carry out their task the Council and the Commission shall, in accordance with the provisions of this treaty, make regulations, issue directives, take decisions, make recommendations or deliver opinions.

REGULATIONS

A regulation shall have general application. It shall be binding in its entirety and directly applicable in all Member States.[1]

Regulations are the most important source of law under the Treaty. Their relationship to the Treaty is subordinate in the same sense as delegated legislation is made under a United Kingdom statute. In each, validity depends on its being within the power of the parent legislative document. Regulations have mandatory effect; they must be observed by member States. They have the force of law in the territories of those States without any further implementation by the legislature of those States. This is what is meant by saying that a regulation is 'directly applicable'. It further means that it creates rights and obligations, not only for the States but for all their citizens

1. Article 189.

too. Regulations are designed to operate uniformly throughout the Community; hence the reference to 'all States'. A regulation cannot be overridden by any subsequent legislation inconsistent with it. Of course, many regulations will be in general terms and will contemplate that national laws will work out the details in their own way; the free movement of workers is an example. Regulations are published in the *Official Journal* of the Community.

DIRECTIVES

A directive shall be binding, as to the result to be achieved, upon each Member State to which it is addressed, but shall leave to the national authorities the choice of form and methods.[2]

Directives are used where the Commission is agreed on the general objective of policy and the results which have to be attained but is content to let each member State work out for itself the choice both of forms and means. The normal occasion for their use will be where the Community policy makes necessary the modification of existing national legislation or the enactment of new provisions. Value added tax was introduced in this way. Normally a directive sets a time limit within which it must be implemented in the States. The impact on individuals of a directive is clearly less direct than that of a regulation. Yet a directive may be so specific and detailed as to leave little choice to the States about how they will transform it into law; for practical purposes, then, the citizen will be closely affected by such a directive.

DECISIONS

A decision shall be binding in its entirety upon those to whom it is addressed.[3]

A decision may be addressed either to member States or to individuals; it binds only the addressee, and 'binds in its entirety'— that is to say, there is no discretion in the way it is to be carried out. 'Decision' here does not mean a document pronouncing the conclusion of a dispute after some judicial process. It is an administrative act implementing Community law, for example by granting an exception or an authorisation.

2. Distinguish recommendations under the E.C.S.C. Treaty, which under Art. 14 thereof have binding force.
3. Article 189.

Recommendations and opinions shall have no binding force.[4]

Not all the functions of the Community are legislative. Sometimes it will wish to advise a State to act in a certain way; on other occasions it will give an opinion when requested. The Treaty recognises these functions but provides that they shall have no binding force. Indirectly, however, they may produce legal consequences. For example, Article 91 provides that the Commission shall authorise a member State injured by dumping to take protective measures against the originator of the dumping who had disregarded a previous recommendation to end the practice.

II. PROCEEDINGS FOR ANNULMENT

Article 173 begins:

The Court of Justice shall review the legality of acts of the Council and the Commission other than recommendations or opinions.

The third paragraph adds:

The proceedings provided for in this Article shall be instituted within two months of the publication of the measure, or of its notification to the plaintiff, or, in the absence thereof, of the day on which it came to the knowledge of the latter, as the case may be.

English lawyers will need to accustom themselves to this short limitation period, characteristic of European administrative law, and in contrast with our six-year period for challenge in an action for a declaratory judgment, or even the six-month period on certiorari. The only comparison is the exceptional six-week period for challenging compulsory purchase orders under town and country planning and housing legislation. The article is admirably clear in indicating the time from which the period runs: the date of publication or notification, or, in the absence of publication or notification, the time when the plaintiff knew of it.

The Court has jurisdiction to hear challenges by a member State, the Council or the Commission to the legality of regulations, directives and decisions. The right of challenge by others is much more restricted, as the second paragraph provides:

4. Article 189.

Any natural or legal person may, under the same conditions, institute proceedings against a decision addressed to that person or against a decision which, although in the form of a regulation or a decision addressed to another person, is of direct and individual concern to the former.

This paragraph was interpreted by the Court in *Re Noordwijks Cement Accoord*.[5] Enterprises which in breach of the Treaty participate in cartels are liable to heavy fines. In general, however, cartels amounting to restriction arrangements contrary to Article 85(1) which have been notified to the Commission cannot be fined as long as the Commission has not pronounced on their validity, and on the possibility of their being exempted[6] under the relevant regulation, e.g. Council regulation No. 17 on restrictive practices. That exemption for notified cartels is subject to one exception: if after a provisional enquiry the Commission is of the opinion that a particular cartel is incompatible with E.E.C. laws and that there are no grounds for exempting it, the Commission can communicate this opinion to the parties concerned and thereby remove the safeguard against fines (unless they modify their cartel). The plaintiffs appealed against such a communication, to which the Commission pleaded that the court had no jurisdiction to adjudicate on a mere opinion of the Commission. The Court held that it had jurisdiction. An act of the Commission which alters the legal position of the addressee, and which binds him, is a decision even if the Commission intended it to be an opinion only, and even though the legislative text which prescribes it describes it as an opinion. This decision is especially welcome since the Treaty has no equivalent to prohibition or injunction whereby administrative action can be stayed beforehand, so that if the decision had been otherwise the cartel would have either had to dissolve or run the serious risk of heavy fines. The implications of this case are obscure; it may, for instance, give jurisdiction over a recommendation which is a declaration of intention to perform some act in certain eventualities, on the ground that it would be a disguised decision. On the other hand, where the opinion is negative, e.g. states that Article 85 does not apply to a notified cartel, it is a refusal to condemn and presumably never challengeable because it has no positive legal effect.

The weak position of an individual with regard to directives must be noted. He cannot challenge the directive itself, no doubt on the view that his concern is with its implementation by member States. Nor has he any means of challenging in the Community

Court allegedly inadequate State measures executing such a directive. His recourse then would be to a municipal court—not a valuable right in England, where, it will be recalled, mandamus never lies against the Crown for failure to carry out duties imposed on it. The difficulties of the individual in this connection have been eased by one decision in 1970.[7] A firm challenged before a municipal court the continued imposition by Germany of a tax on goods carried into the country by road, after a Community decision that value added tax was to replace other taxes, supplemented by a directive to Germany requiring it to be implemented. The Community Court held that 'the provisions of the decision and of the directive, taken together, produce direct effects in the relations between the Member States and their citizens and create for the latter the right to invoke them before the courts'.

LOCUS STANDI

Member States have an unrestricted right to appeal. There have been many decisions which clarify the standing of the individual to challenge acts of the Commission. In *Confédération des Producteurs etc.* v. *E.E.C. Council*[9] a French association of fruit and vegetable producers appealed against a regulation which would have deprived their members of the benefit of restrictions on imports of agricultural products from member States. The regulation affected all agricultural producers within the Community, whether or not members of this association. The individual members of the association were concerned individually, but not the association. The Treaty contemplates proceedings by affected persons to whom administrative acts are addressed, not by trade associations to whom some may belong. The plaintiffs' appeal was therefore dismissed for lack of standing. In *Plaumann* v. *E.E.C. Commission*[10] a decision of the Commission addressed to the German government refused a request by Germany for permission partially to suspend customs duties on the import of mandarins and clementines from non-member States. One of thirty affected German importers appealed. Holding that it had no jurisdiction to determine his appeal, the Court said:

Persons other than those to whom the decision was addressed can justifiably claim to be concerned individually only if the decision affects them because

7. *Grad* v. *Finanz-Amt. Traunstein*, [1971] C.M.L.R. 1.
9. [1963] C.M.L.R. 160.
10. [1964] C.M.L.R. 29.

of certain characteristics which are particular to them or by reason of a factual situation which is, as compared with all other persons, particularly relevant to them, and by reference to which they may be individually described in a way similar to that of the addressee of the decision. In this case the applicant is affected by the Decision in his capacity as an importer of clementines, that is to say by reason of a commercial activity which may be carried on by anyone at any time.

In *Glucoseries Réunies* v. *E.E.C. Commission*[11] a decision authorised the French government to impose duties on imported glucose. The plaintiff challenged this decision on the ground that he was the only Belgian exporter affected. His case was dismissed because the decision was general in application and might therefore affect exporters from other member States. In *Alcan* v. *E.E.C. Commission*[12] a decision shared out a global aluminium quota among member States, and also set aside a reserve. By a further decision the Commission refused the Belgian–Luxembourg Union an additional quota from the reserve. Affected aluminium refining companies appealed. It was held that they had no standing; even though the decision was in effect negative, it created a power in favour of member States, and not in favour of possible individual beneficiaries from decisions about the quota.

In the important case of *Toepfer* v. *E.E.C. Commission*[13] some of the earlier decisions were distinguished. A decision subjecting maize imports to a levy affected only those German importers who had previously applied for import licences. The Commission was in a position to know, at the date of its decision, that the decision affected only the interests and legal positions of those importers. They were identified, so that the decision was of direct and individual concern to each of them. Any one of them had the right to appeal against the decision. In the subsequent case of *Cie Française Commerciale et Financière S.A.* v. *E.E.C. Commission*[14] there was a regulation which fixed cereal subsidies in the light of the devaluation of the franc. One affected firm sought to challenge its validity and pointed out that its consequences were not uniform and affected persons in different ways, and that the number or identity of affected persons could be established. None the less the court ruled that the appellant was not able to challenge. So long as the regulation takes effect in terms of an objective situation of fact or law, defined by the instrument in relation to its ends, it is a regulation of general application only.

11. [1964] C.M.L.R. 596.   12. [1970] C.M.L.R. 337.
13. [1966] C.M.L.R. 111; followed and applied in *Bock* v. *E.E.C. Commission*, [1972] C.M.L.R. 160.   14. [1970] C.M.L.R. 369.

It may be said that these decisions rest on fine distinctions. This is inherent in the subject matter: English administrative law has just the same difficulty in deciding issues of *locus standi*. Contrast, for example, *Buxton* v. *Minister of Housing and Local Government*[15] (an adjoining landowner whose land was seriously damaged by chalk quarrying was not allowed to challenge the grant of planning permission) with *R.* v. *Hereford Corporation ex parte Harrower*[16] (electrical contractor ratepayer could have mandamus ordering Hereford corporation to invite tenders for their electrical contracts).

GROUNDS FOR JUDICIAL REVIEW

These are set out in Article 173 as follows: 'the Court of Justice shall review the legality of acts of the Council and the Commission other than recommendations or opinions' for 'lack of competence, infringement of an essential procedural requirement, infringement of this Treaty or of any rule of law relating to its application, or misuse of powers.'

1. *Lack of competence*. This is substantially the same as *ultra vires* in English law, of which *Vine* v. *National Dock Labour Board* is a typical example.[17] A statute empowered the Board to make disciplinary decisions affecting dockers; this task was delegated to a committee of a local board. Their decision to dismiss plaintiff was *ultra vires*, for the National Board had no power to delegate that power to the local committee. *Meroni* v. *High Authority* is a sufficient illustration of the rule.[18] Brussels institutions made decisions to impose levies on the plaintiff. The High Authority had delegated this power to the institutions. The plaintiff successfully challenged the levies on the ground that the High Authority had no authority to delegate the decision-making power.

2. *Infringement of an essential procedural requirement*. In English law failure to observe a procedural requirement may make the administrative act *ultra vires*. This rule is reinforced by the implication that bodies which act 'judicially' must observe the rule of *audi alteram partem*. The application of these rules is difficult in practice, especially because of uncertainty whether a particular specific requirement is mandatory and how far standards of procedural fairness

15. [1961] 1 Q.B. 278. 16. [1970] 3 All E.R. 460.
17. [1957] A.C. 488, H.L. 18. [1958] 4 *Recueil* 9.

may be implied. Exceptionally, as in town and country planning and housing legislation, a statute may expressly provide that those substantially prejudiced by breach of a procedural requirement may successfully challenge an order, for example a compulsory purchase order.

The Treaty provision corresponds precisely to the *vice de forme* of French administrative law. A decision of the Court on an act of the Euratom Commission illustrates its approach to the term 'essential'.[19] The issue was whether an official was to be given a permanent appointment. One member of the board was absent while some of the evidence was taken but was later given a minuted summary of it. This did not invalidate the decision; the procedural irregularity must have a direct bearing on the substantive decision. One would expect a stricter approach to *audi alteram partem* in an English court, with its emphasis on 'justice must be seen to be done'.

Most of the case law under this head has centred on Article 190 of the E.E.C. Treaty:

Regulations, directives and decisions of the Council and of the Commission shall state the reasons on which they are based and shall refer to any proposals or opinions which were required to be obtained pursuant to this Treaty.

This article goes much further than English law, where reasons for subordinate legislation are never required to be stated. The Court's interpretation of the article has taken it beyond English law in other respects, too. Section 12 of the Tribunals and Inquiries Act, 1971, is the one general statutory requirement to give reasons, but it has been held not to require a tribunal to summarise the evidence or to state the findings of fact on which the decision is based. Contrast that approach with *Federal Republic of Germany* v. *E.E.C. Commission*.[20] The Commission would allow Germany to import from outside the Community only two-ninths of the quantity of cheap wines which it wished to use for the production of 'Brennwein'. The only reason given by the Commission was that 'information that has been gathered' indicated 'that the production of wines of this nature within the Community is amply sufficient'. The difficulties of stating facts when so many decisions are, like this one, economic, are obvious. That did not deter the Court from annulling the decision on the ground that it was in breach of Article 190 and thereby

---

19. *Weighardt* v. *Euratom Commission*, [1966] C.M.L.R. 1, decided on Art. 162 of the Euratom Treaty, which is in the same words as the corresponding Art. 196 of the E.E.C. Treaty.　　　　　　　　　　20. [1963] C.M.L.R. 347.

infringed an essential procedural requirement. The Commission had to state the most important legal and factual considerations on which its decision was based and which are necessary for an understanding of the lines of reasoning that led to the decision. The Court will insist on so much being stated, and yet will not expect the Commission to expound its economic predictions, as distinct from data.

3. *Infringement of the Treaty or of any rule of law relating to its application.* This covers not only the Treaty and amendments but also any treaty of accession. Unlike the previous head, any infringement is enough, even though unimportant.

There has been speculation about the meaning of 'rule of law'. There is an affinity with the *violation de la loi* of French administrative law. This is an important question because this has been the most expansive ground for review by the Conseil d'Etat in the last twenty-five years. Just as the English courts' development of 'natural justice' has expressed judicial resolve to impose judicial standards on bodies exercising judicial functions, so has the Conseil d'Etat evolved rules of due administration for all governmental bodies. It has done what many English administrative lawyers believe Parliament ought to do—formulate a code of administrative conduct for government departments in their dealings with citizens. The possibility canvassed is that the Court might eventually utilise this part of the article as a means of declaring on issues of fundamental rights and maintaining standards of administrative fairness within the Community.

4. *Misuse of powers.* This has its equivalent in English law: abuse of discretion or power, taking into account extraneous factors, ignoring proper considerations. The effectiveness of such a head of review is difficult to predict; so much depends on how thoroughly a court probes motives, and how ready it is to infer bad faith on the part of bureaucracy. English experience has been that, in actions against central government at least, plaintiffs have very little chance of success under this head. *Détournement de pouvoir* appears to the outsider to have been a more effective ground of review by the Conseil d'Etat, although nominally it covers virtually the same area. One might have expected Community experience to resemble more closely the French, but so far this has not happened. It appears that only one of the many challenges to the Court under this head of the

Treaty has yet succeeded. In the *Chinese mushrooms* case[21] Germany wished to prohibit the import of mushrooms from China. Article 115 enacts:

In order to ensure that the execution of measures of commercial policy taken in accordance with this Treaty by any Member State is not obstructed by deflection of trade, or where differences between such measures lead to economic difficulties in one or more of the Member States, the Commission shall recommend the methods for the requisite cooperation between Member States. Failing this, the Commission shall authorise Member States to take the necessary protective measures, the conditions and details of which it shall determine.

Germany obtained an authorisation under that article after Bock applied for an import permit and refused him permission. Bock challenged the legality of the authorisation by the Commission. The Court held that Article 115 derogates from the free movement of goods which is at the heart of the Common Market and must be narrowly interpreted and upheld. The plaintiff sought to import 0.26 per cent of Germany's 1969 imports of mushrooms. It was not necessary within Article 115 to extend the authorisation to cover a pending application for so small an amount; the Commission therefore acted in excess of its powers.

It is too early to say how difficult it will be to convince the Court that a discretionary power has been used to achieve some object other than that for which it was conferred. It might be crucial to know how closely the Court reviews the fact-finding and economic conclusions of the challenged institutions.

EFFECT OF ANNULMENT

Article 174 reads:

If the action is well founded, the Court of Justice shall declare the act concerned[22] to be void.

In the case of a regulation, however, the Court of Justice shall, if it considers this necessary, state which of the effects of the regulation which it has declared void shall be considered as definitive.

The Court in *Consten and Grundig* v. *E.E.C. Commission*[23] annulled part only of a decision. The Commission decided that a sole agency contract from Grundig products violated the Treaty's restrictive practices laws. Finding that only parts of the contract were so

21. *Werner A. Bock K.G.* v. *Commission,* [1972] C.M.L.R. 160.
22. See Art. 173 above for the 'act' referred to.
23. [1966] C.M.L.R. 418.

illegal, the Court annulled only those parts of the decision where it upheld the finding of breach of the restrictive practices provisions. In chapter VIII Professor Wortley stresses that one consequence of the *Consten–Grundig* case has been a greater suppleness in the practice of the Commission. After due notification of an agreement that might have features offending against Article 85 on unfair competition in the Common Market, the Commission may now permit the re-notification of a modified agreement on terms acceptable to its rules. (See below, p. 92.)

Whether the *Consten–Grundig* case means that the Court is always free, despite the absence of any direct authority in the Treaty, to extend Article 174 to decisions, or whether it is referable only to contracts (there is an English analogy in severing covenants in restraint of trade) remains to be seen.

An annulment is negative in effect. Article 176 provides:

The institution whose act has been declared void or whose failure to act has been declared contrary to this Treaty shall be required to take the necessary measures to comply with the judgment of the Court of Justice.

English administrative law has been beset over the last few years with teasing and, many would say, sterile discussions about whether acts are void or voidable, and whether void decisions are a nullity.[24] Whether Community law is free of these problems is not clear. Should the court allow a challenge out of time on an allegation of *ultra vires*? Some think the answer may come from the French theory of *nullité de plein droit*, that some administrative acts may be tainted by such serious legal defects as to be void *ab initio*.

III. APPEALS AGAINST INACTION

Article 175 provides:

Should the Council or the Commission, in infringement of this Treaty, fail to act, the Member States and the other institutions of the Community may bring an action before the Court of Justice to have the infringement established.

The action shall be admissible only if the institution concerned has first been called upon to act. If, within two months of being so called upon, the

---

24. De Smith, *Judicial Review of Administrative Action*, second edition, *passim*.

institution concerned has not defined its position, the action may be brought within a further period of two months.

Any person may also bring proceedings subject to the same conditions where 'an institution of the Community has failed to address to that person any act other than a recommendation or an opinion'.[25] The article does not enable an individual to complain to the Court of the failure of a member State to implement a Community directive.

In *Borromeo Arese* v. *E.E.C. Commission*[26] the Commission had not complied with the plaintiffs' request to withdraw an allegedly illegal measure. When the plaintiffs relied on this article before the Court, the Court said that it must take into consideration that Article 173 provides a remedy where measures are illegal. It added that

to accept, as requested by the plaintiffs, that interested parties could ask the institution responsible for said act, to revoke it, and in case of inaction, refer this omission to the Court of Justice, would result in opening proceedings which would run parallel to those of Article 173 without being submitted to the conditions laid down in the Treaty.

IV. DEFENCE OF ILLEGALITY

Article 184 reads:

Notwithstanding the expiry of the period laid down in the third paragraph of Article 173, any party may, in proceedings in which a regulation of the Council or of the Commission is in issue, plead the grounds specified in the first paragraph of Article 173, in order to invoke before the Court of Justice the inapplicability of that regulation.

A party may be too late or not have the standing to challenge a regulation. In subsequent proceedings before the Court he may wish to raise its illegality. This article enables him to do so (*l'exception d'illégalité*). The Court is then free to declare the regulation in question inapplicable to him in those proceedings, but its general validity may remain unimpaired.[27]

English law recognises a similar form of collateral attack. For example, a person charged with breach of a bye law could plead that it was *ultra vires*, and an action of trespass would lie against

25. Article 175.
26. [1970] C.M.L.R. 436.
27. Cf. *Meroni* v. *High Authority* [1958] 4 *Recueil* 9.

someone who in acquiring land relied on an item of subordinate legislation now found to be made without authority. In English law *vires* can be challenged in any court collaterally, not merely in one which has jurisdiction to entertain a direct challenge.

Chapter V

THE IMPACT OF COMMUNITY LAW UPON THE LAW OF THE UNITED KINGDOM (I)

Brenda M. Hoggett

The object of this chapter is to discuss in general terms the legal effect in the United Kingdom of adherence to the law of the European Economic Communities, in preparation for the more detailed study of some aspects of that law which follows. Our present concern, therefore, is with the provisions of Part I of the *European Communities Act*, 1972, and with the nature of the system of law which it seeks to implement.

At first sight, Community law has the appearance of a system of international law: its primary sources are the treaties themselves, which establish the international institutions controlling the Communities' affairs and impose obligations upon the member States towards one another and towards the Communities. In this they resembled previous treaties establishing international organisations, but they also included some novel features which were to have far-reaching effects. Nevertheless, in 1963 the Court of Justice was referring to the treaties as creating a 'new legal order in international law.'[1]

For reasons which will later appear, the terms of the treaties are nowhere to be found in the European Communities Act; the alternative devices which give them legal effect[2] refer simply to 'the Treaties' and it is therefore essential to refer at the outset to the definition given in section 1(2) of 'the Treaties' or 'the Community Treaties'. These are of three kinds: the 'pre-accession treaties', which are listed[3] and include those setting up the three Communities, those relating to their common institutions and making budgetary changes, and those already made in pursuance of a Community power to make treaties in its own right;[4] next are the enlargement agreements; and finally the definition includes post-accession treaties made either by the Communities, with or without

1. *N.V. Algemene Transport- en Expeditie Onderneming van Gend en Loos* v. *Nederlandse Tariefcommissie*, [1963] C.M.L.R. 105, at p. 129.
2. Principally s. 2(1).   3. In the First Schedule, Part I.
4. E.g. under the E.E.C. Treaty, Articles 113 and 238.

any of the member States, or by the United Kingdom if made ancillary to any Community treaty. Any post-accession treaty to which the United Kingdom becomes a party *must* be specified in an Order in Council which has previously been approved in draft by both Houses of Parliament before it is included in the definition.[5] Post-accession treaties which are made *by the Community alone*, however, *may* be specified by Order in Council in order to provide conclusive proof of their inclusion, but there is no absolute necessity for Parliamentary approval.[6] The distinction is a necessary one, because were any such agreement to produce binding effects in the law of the United Kingdom, it would in any event be given automatic effect by another section of the Act.[7] This provision for future treaties is but one example of the way in which the Act seeks to take account of the future development of the Communities, and the European Court has already shown a dynamic attitude towards the extension of their treaty-making powers.[8]

The word 'treaty' employed in the definition includes 'any international agreement', together with its annexes and protocols.[9] It should not, therefore, include every declaration made in connection with accession, some of which are unilateral in form;[10] the view has also been expressed[11] that it does not include the Luxembourg Accords of 29 January 1966, whereby the member States agreed to differ on the question of unanimity. Thus in theory an agreement entered into by the Community under Articles 113 and 114[12] by a qualified majority of member States, even if in defiance of those Accords, might be included in the definition and have to be given effect in this country. It is perhaps fortunate that the political realities of the Communities' management make this unlikely.

Notwithstanding its origin in treaties, it was from the first contemplated that the legal Community created should have some unusual features taking it beyond ordinary inter-governmental institutions. A starting point for the study of those features lies in the provisions of the treaties granting powers to Community institutions

5. Section 1(3); e.g. S.I. 1972 No. 1993.
6. Section 1(3).   7. Section 2(1).
8. *Commission of the European Communities* v. *Council of the European Communities*, [1971] C.M.L.R. 355 (the *ERTA* case).
9. Section 1(4).
10. E.g. the Declaration by the government of the United Kingdom on the definition of 'nationals'.
11. By Her Majesty's government.
12. Of the E.E.C. Treaty, to which all treaty references apply unless otherwise stated. On the Accords see Dr White, chapter III above.

to issue subordinate instruments of binding effect. The powers of the merged institutions differ in extent under each of the three treaties, but those under the E.E.C. Treaty are the most far-reaching, and this discussion will be confined to them. The terms of Article 189 have already been referred to in earlier chapters to exemplify the powers of the Commission and the Council[13] and to illustrate the control exercised by the European Court over the legality of such measures.[14] They must, however, be mentioned again, firstly because they form an integral part of the system of law to which the Act gives effect, and secondly because they illustrate much more clearly than do the treaties themselves the 'municipal' character of Community law. By the term 'municipal' is meant a system of law which applies directly in member States, and thus produces direct effects upon the legal rights and obligations of every individual person.

The power to issue directives does not on the face of it present a great innovation, for directives are addressed solely to member States and, while binding upon them as to the result to be achieved, leave the choice of form and methods, and thus the task of producing any necessary internal legislation, to them.[15] Nevertheless, even directives have been held by the European Court to produce direct effects upon the legal rights of individuals if the appropriate conditions are fulfilled.[16] About the nature of regulations, on the other hand, there has never been any doubt. These have general application, are binding in their entirety, and are directly applicable in each member State, having there the force of law without the national legislature having either the need or the right to intervene.[17] They are already very numerous, the more important being made by the Council, and the more minor, regulatory and frequently temporary ones being made by the Commission. The third compulsory power under Article 189 is to take decisions. These are binding only upon those to whom they are addressed, but they may range from important decisions affecting the Community's institutions or addressed to member States, to those which impose sanctions upon individuals for breach of Community regulations.[18]

13. Chapter III by Dr White.   14. Chapter IV by Professor Street.
  15. E.g. Directive 151/1968 on companies; for a discussion of its implementation in the Act, see chapter X by T. Flanagan; perhaps the most far-reaching power to issue directives is that under Art. 100 on the approximation of laws.
  16. *Grad* v. *Finanzamt Traunstein*, [1971] C.M.L.R. 1. See chapter IV above.
  17. E.g. Council Regulation No. 17, *J.O.* 204/62, on competition, discussed in chapter VIII below.   18. *Ibid.*

Decisions which are addressed to member States may, like directives, produce direct effects upon the rights of individuals if the appropriate conditions are fulfilled.[19] What, then, are the novel features of Community law which these powers indicate? In the first place, there is the duty upon member States to accept in advance the binding nature of subordinate instruments and the fact that these instruments will apply directly within their territory.[20] It is from this fact that concern must be expressed over the obvious fact that neither the Council nor the Commission bears much resemblance to a democratically controlled legislature. The House of Commons may be able to exercise some control through the Ministerial responsibility of the individual representative on the Council, but it has already been recognised that that responsibility may be limited where the Council is acting as a collegiate body; and one of the cardinal features of the Community is the independence from national control of the members of the Commission, who are responsible only to the Parliament and to the Court of the Community. Thus the United Kingdom Parliament will have to adapt itself to examining and commenting upon proposals for regulations during the consultative process before they are made, and Her Majesty's government must accept an obligation to keep Parliament informed of developments within the Community.[21]

The second novel feature is that no national lawyer can afford to ignore the existence of Community law, because of its potential effect, without any intervention from Westminster, upon the legal position of his clients. It was always clearly contemplated, and not merely as a result of Article 189, that the treaties might result in the imposition of legally enforceable penalties upon individuals.[22] It was also clear that, as regulations applied directly, they might protect or improve the legal position of individuals: indeed, in many cases that would be their object. Thus the Community's rules against unfair competition may help one enterprise while hindering another. Thus, again, a Community scheme to regulate the supply of dairy products may provide for compensation out of Community

19. See note 16 above.

20. *Legal and Constitutional Implications of United Kingdom Membership of the European Communities*, 1967, Cmnd. 3301, para. 22.

21. See Dr White's discussion of proposals contained in reports of Select Committees of each House of Parliament, pp. 28–9 above.

22. Imposition of penalties upon individuals is provided for directly by the Treaty of the European Coal and Steel Community.

funds for the slaughter of cows.[23] However, many of these provisions contemplate benefits being available to individuals before the Community's own institutions. The third novel feature of Community law is its involvement of *national* courts in the system.

Here a slight digression must be made to consider the link provided for in the treaties between national courts and the European Courts. Under Article 177 of the E.E.C. Treaty,[24] any national court or tribunal before which a question is raised as to the interpretation of the Treaty, or the validity and interpretation of acts of Community institutions, may request the European Court to give a preliminary ruling should it consider one necessary to enable it to give judgment. In England rules governing references by the Supreme Court, the Crown Court and county courts have now been made.[25] In several cases points of Community law have arisen,[26] and some tentative conclusions may be drawn about the attitude of English judges towards the making of references.

First, the High Court appears mindful of the limitation of the power to refer cases in which a ruling from the European Court is necessary to enable judgment to be given. When a point of Community law has been raised, and the judge has investigated it, if he has seen no chance of its assisting the party concerned he makes no reference. Thus when the defendants resisted the grant of an interlocutory injunction to prevent their passing off their own product as a well known brand of German lager beer on the ground that this might infringe Article 36 of the E.E.C. Treaty the judge examined the authorities and, feeling confident that the grant of an injunction would in no way infringe the Treaty, refused a referral.[27] Second, the court will not make a reference until substantial issues of fact and of national law have been determined. This is to avoid the cost and delay involved in a reference which ultimately proves valueless; there may well be few references in the interlocutory stages of a case.

23. See *Orsolina Leonesio* v. *Ministry of Agriculture and Forests of the Italian Republic*, [1973] C.M.L.R. 343; see also *Commission* v. *Italian Republic*, [1973] C.M.L.R. 439.

24. Similar provisions are Art. 150 of the Euratom Treaty and Art. 41 of the European Coal and Steel Community Treaty.

25. See Dr White, above, p. 36.

26. The first cases were *Aero Zipp Fasteners Ltd and Lightning Fasteners Ltd* v. *YKK Fasteners (U.K.) Ltd*, [1973] C.M.L.R. 819, *Esso Petroleum Co. Ltd* v. *Kingswood Motors (Addlestone) Ltd*, [1973] 3 All E.R. 1057, *Löwenbräu München* v. *Grunhalle Lager International Ltd*, [1974] C.M.L.R. 1, and *Van Duyn* v. *Home Office*, *The Times*, 15 February 1974.

27. *Löwenbräu München* v. *Grunhalle Lager International Ltd*, note 26 above.

In the first case in which a reference was made, both the above criteria were satisfied.[28] The point of Community law raised, which was the whole basis of the plaintiff's case, 'might well be arguable', to put it no higher; there were no substantial issues of fact and there was no issue at all of national law. In the circumstances a reference was clearly appropriate, and there was nothing to be gained by waiting until the hearing of the action.

Article 177 applies to all courts and tribunals, however lowly their status. Despite any lack of procedural rules, magistrates' courts and administrative tribunals should be entitled to make references by virtue of section 2(1) of the Act, which gives legal effect to all powers, remedies and procedures which the Treaty requires to be recognised without national enactment.

A further point is that a question raised under Article 177 in a case pending before a national court or tribunal 'against whose decisions there is no judicial remedy under national law' *must* be referred to the European Court. Every court of last resort must make such references, even perhaps where a ruling is *not* 'necessary to enable it to give judgement', although a second reference need not be made if the European Court has already ruled on the same question.[29]

The House of Lords is therefore under a duty to refer questions; but an interesting problem arises when the Court of Appeal is in fact the court of last resort. It is never so in a civil case until leave to appeal has been refused, but once that has happened the case is no longer 'pending'. Presumably, however, leave to appeal may be sought from the House of Lords, in which event can the case then be said to be 'pending' before them? Order 114 does not solve this problem.

Still more difficult problems arise with lower courts and tribunals, which may well be the court of last resort on the facts, although it will be extremely rare that there is 'no judicial remedy' against their decisions, either by way of appeal on a point of law or by way of certiorari or the like. Yet it will generally be in the best interests of clients if the tribunal can be persuaded to refer the problem at the earliest possible moment rather than wait for a complex appeal mechanism to oblige it to be done.[30]

28. *Van Duyn* v. *Home Office*, note 26 above.
29. E.g. *Da Costa en Schaake*, [1963] C.M.L.R. 224.
30. E.g. correspondence in *The Times* newspaper, 11 and 13 January 1973, and the *Birra Dreher* case, *ibid.*, 4 March 1974.

The concept of reference to higher authority of some essential legal issue, although unusual in English courts, should not be regarded too suspiciously, for two reasons. Firstly, the European Court when dealing with such references has always been scrupulous to separate the question of Community law from any question of national law; nor is it concerned whether the question is phrased badly, but will rewrite it if necessary; and secondly, the Court has never sought to dictate to the national court how it should decide the particular case before it.[31]

Despite this scrupulousness, it has been through the medium of Article 177 references that the full impact of Community law upon national law has emerged, and it is for this reason that Article 177 may be regarded as the lynchpin of the system.

The detailed implications for English law will be discussed later, but a preliminary outline of the main principles governing the Court's approach to the effect of Community law in national courts must be given. The first step was the realisation by the Court that if individuals were as much the subjects of the new legal order created by the treaties as were States, then they might enjoy rights as well as liabilities. The logic of the new Community required that its rules be applied uniformly throughout its territories, but what was to be done if a member State failed to comply? One solution would be for the Commission,[32] or a member State,[33] to take proceedings against the offender in the European Court. But a much more effective solution has been to hold that certain provisions of the Treaty, and of subordinate instruments, take direct effect in each member State, so as to grant the individual who is aggrieved by their non-observance the right nevertheless to enforce them before his own national courts.

At first this was a question of giving an individual the right to claim in his national courts that if his government had done something contrary to Community law he might in certain circumstances be entitled to a remedy.[34] But it soon became clear that, in order to

31. This has been made clear throughout the cases and was acknowledged by the judge in *Van Duyn* v. *Home Office*, note 28 above.

32. Under Art. 169; cases have been brought against each of the original six member States except Germany, the greatest number being against Italy. A comparison of the effectiveness of such proceedings with that of the concept of direct effect may be gained from the 'Art Treasures' cases: *Re export tax on art treasures, E.E.C. Commission* v. *Italy*, [1969] C.M.L.R. 1, and *S.A.S. Eunomia di Porro E.C.* v. *Ministry of Public Instruction of the Italian Republic*, [1972] C.M.L.R.4.

33. Under Art. 170; there have been no examples.

34. See the cases cited on pp. 69–71 below.

give proper effect to the Community, these rights should be effective even where the Community rule was in conflict with a rule of national law: thus it might be said that such rights were enforceable not only against the governments but also against the legislatures of member States.[35] The primacy of Community law which was thus established indicated quite clearly that the individual competence of member States in Community fields was limited.[36] International treaties have usually sought to limit the individual discretion of the States which accede to them, but it is unusual to find them so doing in a way which compels, or seeks to compel, the national courts of those States to enforce some of those limitations.

An example of the extensive limits which the European Court might be prepared to place upon national governments is to be found in the *ERTA* case,[37] although it is not immediately obvious how any national court might be expected to give effect to this particular limitation. The Court indicated that once a common policy had been agreed upon some matter within the Community's objects, then the Community might be able to conclude international agreements to further that common policy, despite the lack of a specific power so to do in the Treaty, and furthermore that individual member States might no longer be able so to do.

Thus the new legal order created by the treaties has elements of both international and municipal systems, and the task of implementing it in the United Kingdom was a formidable one. One advantage enjoyed over the original six member States was that the full nature of Community law has now become much more apparent, and every effort has been made in the European Communities Act to give effect to it. In order to consider the methods employed, it is simpler to divide Community law into two categories, although they are by no means mutually exclusive.

On the one hand, there are those provisions which impose an obligation upon member States to implement them through national measures, while on the other hand there are those provisions which apply directly in member States without the need for any national implementation. Provisions of Community law may cut across these two categories in at least two ways: firstly, a regulation may be directly applicable under Article 189 but may in fact require further action by a member State to give it effect. This is

---

35. *Costa* v. *E.N.E.L.*, [1964] C.M.L.R. 455.
36. E.g. *Molkerei-Zentrale Westfalen/Lippe G.m.b.H.* v. *Hauptzollamt Paderborn*, [1968] C.M.L.R. 187, at p. 217.   37. [1971] C.M.L.R. 335.

an example of what is meant when a distinction is drawn between 'directly applicable' and 'directly effective' Community law; a regulation is always directly applicable, but may in fact have no direct effect upon the rights and obligations of individual persons. Secondly, the very concept of Community rights generally presupposes that some obligation has been placed upon a member State which that State has failed to fulfil. Thus there are two sub-sections in the Act, each designed to provide for one of these categories, but both of which may be applicable in any one legal situation. It will also be necessary to consider those provisions of the Act which are designed to solve the problem of conflict between Community law and national law.

Chapter VI

THE IMPACT OF COMMUNITY LAW UPON THE LAW OF THE UNITED KINGDOM (II)

Brenda M. Hoggett

I. COMMUNITY LAW REQUIRING NATIONAL IMPLEMENTATION

The obligation of a member State to implement Community objectives may result from the treaties themselves, or from subordinate acts, be they directives, decisions, or regulations. While there is nothing to prevent some of these being put into effect by Act of Parliament, they are so numerous and complex that means have had to be devised of allowing them to be implemented as quickly as possible, while giving some scope for Parliamentary discussion and control. Apart from specific powers given in the Act, this is effected by section 2(2), which gives a general power to legislate by Order in Council, or for a designated[1] Minister or department to legislate by regulation, for the purpose of implementing the Community obligations[2] of the United Kingdom or enabling the community rights of the United Kingdom to be enjoyed.

Legal and Parliamentary controls are placed upon this power by the Second Schedule of the *European Communities Act*, 1972. This forbids its use for four purposes: the imposition or increase of domestic taxation, the making of instruments with retrospective operation, the sub-delegation of legislative (as opposed to administrative) powers, and the creation of new criminal offences with penalties greater than the fairly substantial limits prescribed. Parliamentary control is provided for either by approval in draft or by annulment by negative resolution. It is thought that the flow of instruments made under the subsection will not be too heavy, and that the Select Committee on Statutory Instruments, if remodelled in line with recent recommendations, should be able to

---

1. By an Order in Council, which may place limits on the extent to which this power may be used by the designated Minister or department.

2. This means any obligation created or arising by or under the treaties, whether or not it is enforceable under s. 2(1); First Schedule, Part II.

provide adequate Parliamentary scrutiny.[3] On the other hand, Community directives sometimes leave little scope for national discretion, and it might be a more effective means of Parliamentary control if their implications were to be included in the machinery established to consider other Community proposals.[4]

Section 2(2) assists in the national implementation of Community law in two further ways. Firstly, the power to legislate by Order in Council or by regulation is stated, in the first part of section 2(4), to include any provision for the same purposes 'as might be made by Act of Parliament', subject, of course, to the limitations imposed by the Second Schedule. Thus these delegated powers may be used for the repeal and amendment of previous legislation where this is necessary to comply with obligations or to exercise rights; in addition, despite the limitation upon using these powers to sub-delegate legislative functions, they may nevertheless be used to amend existing ones or to extend them to similar purposes to those for which they were originally conferred.[5] The use of delegated legislation to amend or repeal previous statutes has been frowned upon since the report of the Committee on Ministers' Powers,[6] but it should be of undoubted assistance in the resolution and prevention of conflicts between Community law and national law.

Secondly, section 2(2) permits any person exercising statutory powers or duties from another source to have regard to the objects, obligations or rights of Community law. Doubtless such powers might sometimes be appropriate to the actual implementation of a Community obligation of the United Kingdom, but on many other occasions persons exercising them will have to do so with the Community's requirements in mind, perhaps in order to avoid conflicts. In either case, the subsection ensures that the exercise of such power should not be challenged in the courts as having been made with the wrong objects or taking irrelevant considerations into account,[7]

3. *Report of the Joint Committee on Delegated Legislation, 1971–72*, H.L. 184/H.C. 475.

4. See the discussion by Dr White of proposals contained in reports of Select Committees of each House of Parliament, pp. 28–9 above.

5. Second Schedule, para. 1(2).

6. Where it was referred to as the 'Henry VIII' clause, 1932, Cmnd. 4060, para. 15(III) and (IV).

7. E.g. *Westminster Corporation* v. *L. & N.W. Rly. Co.*, [1905] A.C. 426 (unsuccessful attempt to attack the building of an underground public lavatory on the ground that the power to build public lavatories did not include the power to build a subway which could be used by pedestrians generally) and *Roberts* v. *Hopwood*, [1925] A.C. 578 (successful attack upon 'Poplarism' on the ground that the

both well known grounds for judicial review in administrative law.

The normal processes of judicial review in the United Kingdom would, of course, apply to the exercise of powers under section 2(2). It should thus be possible for an English judge to hold that a statutory instrument made under the subsection was invalid because of failure to implement a Community obligation correctly. This possibility might lead to considerable confusion in regard to those instruments purporting to repeal or amend previous legislation in order to fulfil Community obligations, a field in which certainty is particularly important. It will, however, assist in ensuring that this new 'Henry VIII clause' is not abused.

The Act contains three other provisions required by constitutional law in order to assist national authorities in carrying out their obligations to the Communities. One provides for the payment out of the Consolidated Fund of moneys required in respect of Community obligations towards the Communities themselves, or other member States, or the European Investment Bank, thus providing a substantial exception to the usual necessity for annual appropriation;[8] other expenses incurred by Ministers or government departments will, however, be defrayed out of moneys provided by Parliament.[9]

The other two are designed to allow the subordinate parliaments of the United Kingdom, Islands and Gibraltar to legislate for Community purposes despite the normal statutory or constitutional limitations which would prevent their so doing. Thus the legislatures of the Islands and Gibraltar are for Community purposes relieved of both the doctrine of repugnancy to imperial statutes and the prohibition on legislation with extra-territorial effect.[10] The subsection allowing the Northern Ireland parliament to legislate upon matters within its scope for Community purposes despite its normal exclusion from treaty matters[11] has now been repealed and replaced by a similar provision for the new Assembly.[11a]

---

local authority took irrelevant considerations of socialist philanthropy and feminist ambition into account when deciding the amount of wages to be paid to employees). See chapter IV above by Professor Street.

8. Chapter III by Dr White above.

9. Section 2(3); the obligations and liabilities which are made enforceable by s. 2(1) will also be of relevance in the fields of taxation and appropriation as a greater proportion of the Community's budget is derived from taxes.

10. Section 2(6).　　　　　11. Section 2(5).

11a. Northern Ireland Constitution Act, 1973, Second Schedule, para. 3.

COMMUNITY LAW AND THE U.K.

II. COMMUNITY LAW DIRECTLY APPLICABLE OR EFFECTIVE WITHOUT NATIONAL INTERVENTION

In view of the dualist approach of our law towards the incorporation of rules made in international treaties, means had to be found both of enacting all the existing directly applicable and effective provisions of Community law and also of giving automatic effect to all such future provisions. The formula chosen by the *European Communities Act*, 1972, section 2(1) was a single subsection in all-embracing terms:

All such rights, powers, liabilities, obligations and restrictions from time to time created or arising by or under the Treaties, and all such remedies and procedures from time to time provided for by or under the Treaties, as in accordance with the Treaties are without further enactment to be given legal effect or used in the United Kingdom shall be recognised and available in law, and be enforced, allowed and followed accordingly; . . .[12]

There are many advantages enjoyed by this deceptively simple arrangement over the alternative suggestion of, for example, an enormous Bill enacting all the present law and leaving the implementation of future provisions to the national authorities,[13] or even over the more obvious solution of scheduling the treaties to an enacting Bill which granted power to the Community to legislate for the future. For existing law, this formula minimises the risk of conflict arising between the Community rules and the statute putting them into effect. Adherence to the Community requires that such a conflict should not be allowed to arise, yet, despite the goodwill of the judiciary in interpretation,[14] some discrepancy would have been quite possible in an attempt to translate Continental treaties and regulations into a United Kingdom legislative idiom. Any possibility of Parliamentary amendment would, of course, have increased this risk.

For the future, the formula emphasises the independent life in this country of the 'new legal order', both by its refusal to refer to the delegation or transfer of legislative powers to the Community, and by its insistence that, in order to discover its laws, courts and lawyers must turn not to United Kingdom legislation but to the

12. Section 2(1).
13. *H.C. Deb.*, fifth series, vol. 831, cols. 641–2; the suggestion made by the leader of the Opposition would appear to conflict with the United Kingdom's obligations under Art. 189.
14. *Salomon* v. *Commissioners of Customs and Excise*, [1967] 2 Q.B. 116. *Post Office* v. *Estuary Radio Ltd*, [1968] 2 Q.B. 740.

treaties, regulations, directives and decisions themselves. This necessity is reinforced by the provisions of section 3 of the Act, requiring that for the purposes of any legal proceedings all questions relating to Community law shall be treated as questions of law,[15] and that judicial notice be taken of its sources;[16] furthermore, all such questions are, if not referred to the European Court, to be decided in accordance with its jurisprudence.[17]

Thus the attention of the judiciary is immediately directed towards the court whose radical attitude to the development and primacy of Community law has already been mentioned. One important advantage of the 'all-embracing' formula employed by section 2(1) is that any more specific enactment might have failed to take account of some future decision of the European Court, for example extending the concept of direct effect to another article of the Treaty, or further restricting the competence of individual member States, both of which have happened in hitherto unforeseen ways.[18]

Subsection 2(1) is not, however, without its difficulties. In the first place, there is the possibility of an English judge refusing to follow, for example, a Commission regulation on the ground that it was *ultra vires* the Treaty, and therefore was not 'created . . . under the treaties'. Yet the clear intention of the treaties is that questions as to the validity of acts of the Communities should be dealt with only by the European Court.[19] There could thus be a conflict between the duty of the English judge only to give effect to regulations which are created under the Treaty and his equally strong duty to observe the obligations and restrictions contained in the treaties. The practical solution is, as we have seen, a reference to the European Court under Article 177 of the Treaty, where a ruling on validity could be given which the English court would be bound to follow.

The provisions of section 2(1) and section 2(2) of the Act will frequently overlap, as, for example, where a directly applicable Community regulation also imposes an obligation upon the United Kingdom to take action. But one part of section 2(2) provides for overlap in a somewhat ambiguous way: the power to make delegated legislation may be used, says section 2(2)(b), 'for the purpose of dealing with matters arising out of or related to any such obliga-

15. Section 3(1).   16. Section 3(2).   17. Section 3(1).
18. Both the *ERTA* (above, p. 60) and the *Grad* (above, p. 155) decisions were regarded as something of a surprise within the Community.
19. E.E.C. Treaty, Art. 173.

tion or rights or the coming into force, or the operation from time to time, of subsection (1) above'. The words 'any such obligation or rights' clearly refer to the Community obligations and rights of the United Kingdom, which are previously referred to in section 2(2)(a), rather than those of individuals, and no difficulties would appear to arise from the power to deal with 'matters arising out of or related to' them. However, it requires a somewhat nice exercise in construction to determine the precise meaning of the remainder of section 2(2)(b). Does it merely permit the use of delegated legislation to deal with 'matters arising out of or related to . . . the coming into force, or the operation from time to time' of the all-embracing formula of section 2(1)? Or does it permit 'dealing with . . . the coming into force, or the operation from time to time' of section 2(1)? In other words, does the phrase 'matters arising out of or related to' govern all that follows, or simply govern the first part of what follows? The distinction is important, for a power to use delegated legislation to deal with minor and consequential matters arising out of or related to section 2(1) gives far less discretion to a government to interfere with the operation of that 'all-embracing' formula than would the latter interpretation. Fortunately, the position of the first comma in section 2(2)(b) suggests that the former is the correct interpretation.

Section 2(1) therefore provides for the automatic recognition in the courts of the United Kingdom of enforceable rights, powers, liabilities, obligations and restrictions of Community law. Some general indication of what these are has already been given, but it will be necessary to devote more detailed attention to them. In particular, it would appear that the words 'in the United Kingdom' following the words 'as . . . are without further enactment to be given legal effect or used' must be given a wide interpretation if all eventualities are to be covered.

III. 'ENFORCEABLE COMMUNITY RIGHTS, POWERS, LIABILITIES, OBLIGATIONS AND RESTRICTIONS'

Liabilities and obligations may rest directly upon individuals, as a result, for example, of the Community's rules upon competition, under which penalties may be imposed upon individuals and enterprises by the Community itself. Unlike certain Continental countries, the United Kingdom has no national supreme court for the protection of constitutionally guaranteed human rights which such procedures might possibly infringe,[20] and thus the enforcement of penalties should present little legal difficulty. Nevertheless, this does involve another departure from the traditional concept of the rule of law, in so far as it permits the imposition of enforceable penalties without trial before the ordinary courts according to the ordinary principles of English law. It is not unknown for financial obligations, and even penalties, to result from decisions of bodies other than the courts,[21] but hitherto these bodies have been applying obligations existing under United Kingdom law and subject to the supervisory jurisdiction of the United Kingdom courts.

However, there are many safeguards built into the Community system. The validity of the Community rule may itself be challenged in the European Court;[22] the Community's procedures for the imposition of penalties involve extensive investigations of a quasi-judicial nature; and advantage is taken of the power given in, for example, the E.E.C. Treaty,[23] to provide for a right of appeal to the European Communities Court, at which stage the validity of the rule itself may be challenged even though the normal short time limit for such challenge has passed.[24] On the other hand, the European Communities Court may not have allayed the fears of those member States who consider that the Communities' law-making powers may infringe their constitutionally guaranteed human rights; for its assurance that implicit in the treaties is respect for and acceptance of those human rights which are fundamental to its members' legal systems, and which it is therefore within the province of the European Communities Court to protect, was accompanied by an insistence that no considerations of national constitutionality must be allowed to affect the validity in national law of a provision of Community law.[25]

Once a final Community decision is made imposing a penalty upon an individual from which there has been no successful appeal to the Court, the treaties require that it be enforced through the medium of civil execution in that individual's State.[26] No challenge of the merits of the decision, nor stay of execution, may be granted

20. International protection is, of course, provided through the United Kingdom's ratification of the European Convention on Human Rights.

21. E.g. the Special Commissioners' powers with regard to income tax.

22. Article 173.   23. Article 172.   24. Article 182.

25. *Internationale Handelsgesellschaft m.b.H.* v. *Einfuhr- und Vorratsstelle für Getreide und Futtermittel*, [1972] C.M.L.R. 255, at p. 282. It seems unlikely that the Bundesverfassungsgericht would agree: 5 *C.M.L.Rev.* 483.

26. E.E.C. Treaty, Art. 192; E.C.S.C. Treaty, Art. 92; Euratom Treaty, Art. 164.

by the national authority, but local discretion as to the means of civil execution is permitted. Among the first instruments made in pursuance of section 2(2) powers was the order providing for the registration and enforcement in the High Court and Court of Session of such Community decisions and judgments.[27]

It must also by now be apparent what sort of obligations and restrictions are being placed upon the courts of the United Kingdom as a result of Community law. Section 2(1) imposes enforceable Community obligations and restrictions upon Her Majesty's government, and attempts to impose these upon the Parliament of the United Kingdom, for Community obligations and restrictions are the logical corollaries of the European Court's concept of 'enforceable Community rights' for individuals.

This concept stemmed both from the need for uniform operation of the Community from State to State and from the recognition that individuals as well as States were the subjects of the new legal order created. It has been adumbrated in a series of cases under Article 177 where individuals have asked their national courts to give effect to some provision of Community law and the national court has sought the guidance of the European Court.

The leading case[28] arose when Dutch importers claimed that they were not liable to pay an increased duty upon their product which they alleged had resulted from the government's reclassification of it, because the increase of customs duties upon trade between member States is clearly prohibited under Article 12 of the E.E.C. Treaty. The national customs tribunal before whom they appeared referred the question to the European Court for a preliminary ruling under Article 177.

The European Court, in accordance with its practice upon such rulings, did not seek to decide the merits of the particular case before the Dutch tribunal, nor to dictate to that tribunal how the problem should be solved. It stated clearly, however, that certain of the obligations created by the treaties could operate automatically to create a right in an affected individual not to have that obligation disregarded by his national authorities. Article 12, for example, created a right in the individual not to have the import duties upon his products raised, and that was a right which the national tribunal

27. S.I. 1972 No. 1590; see also R.S.C. (Amendment No. 3) Order 1972, S.I. No. 1898 Order 71 (Part II). See further the note on the European Court by Dr White, chapter III above.

28. *N.V. Algemene Transport- en Expeditie Onderneming van Gend en Loos* v. *Nederlandse Tariefcommissie*, [1963] C.M.L.R. 105.

must find a means to respect and enforce. The Court then went on to elucidate the meaning of Article 12 in order to assist the Dutch tribunal in its decision as to whether the customs duty on the plaintiff's product had in fact been increased in a way which contravened the Treaty; in the event, it was never called upon to do so, because the Dutch tax administration conceded the plaintiff's claims and the proceedings were withdrawn.

That case was a reasonably cautious beginning, for it applied the concept to an unequivocal obligation placed upon member States to refrain from innovation once the Treaty had been concluded. The next step was to apply it to provisions which unequivocally prohibited innovation after a particular date, in accordance with a timetable established under the Treaty. An example is the prohibition of the introduction of new quantitative restrictions upon trade between member States once a product has been liberalised in accordance with the provisions of Article 31.[29] A more substantial advance was the recognition of an individual's right to take advantage of a member State's obligation to abolish something, provided again that that obligation is sufficiently precise and arises from a determinable date. The clearest example[30] is provided by the claim by an Italian company in a Turin court for the return of duty paid upon the export to West Germany of a valuable picture, duty which had been levied under an Italian law of 1939 despite the provision of Article 16 that customs duties between member States were to be removed at the latest by the end of the first stage in the establishment of the Common Market. It is this case which illustrates how much more effective is this concept of enforceable Community rights than is the power of the Commission to take action against a member State; for while the Italian government was able to disregard the direction of the European Court that the failure to repeal the law of 1939 was a breach of the Treaty,[31] it is less able to disregard decisions in its own courts that the duty is not payable.

It is now becoming possible for individuals to claim rights resulting from failure by member States to implement obligations to do something more positive than to abolish customs duties, always

29. *Salgoil S.p.A.* v. *Foreign Trade Ministry of the Italian Republic*, [1968] *C.M.L. Rev.* 478.
30. *S.A.S. Eunomia di Porro E.E.* v. *Ministry of Public Instruction of the Italian Republic*, [1972] C.M.L.R. 4.
31. *Re export tax on art treasures: E.E.C. Commission* v. *Italy*, [1969] C.M.L.R. 1; for the latest instalment see [1972] C.M.L.R. 699.

provided that the obligation is so precise as to leave no discretion to the national authority. Thus[32] an Italian widow sought to oblige the Italian government to secure the appropriation of funds in order to pay its share of the premium to which she was entitled under E.E.C. regulations for having slaughtered her few cows. The European Court held that her right to enforce the obligation must be upheld by the national court.

The last case is also an illustration of a right which may arise from a subordinate instrument of Community law.[33] Even directives and decisions which are addressed solely to a member State may have this effect, provided that the obligation which they impose is in sufficiently unequivocal terms for the concept to operate.[34] It has now become apparent that the criterion for deciding whether a provision of Community law has this effect is not whether that provision imposes a negative or a positive obligation, nor is it the type of instrument creating it: the criterion is whether or not the obligation leaves no real discretion to the member State as to the way in which it is to be implemented, so that the national court in enforcing it will not have to guess what the legal effects of correct implementation will be.[35]

These, therefore, are examples of 'enforceable Community rights', to which effect is so comprehensively given by section 2(1) of the Act. As must already be apparent, such rights have as their corollary the existence of enforceable Community restrictions upon the individual discretion of member States. The inescapable logic of this new legal order, which takes effect in both international and national law, is that in cases of conflict between its provisions and those of a member State the former must prevail. Provided, therefore, that national courts are prepared to give Community law its proper effect, it must place restrictions upon the powers not only of national governments but also of national legislatures.

IV. CONFLICT BETWEEN COMMUNITY LAW AND NATIONAL LAW

The need to provide against such conflicts has been recognised for some time, and a variety of means of so doing have been suggested.

32. *Orsolina Leonesio* v. *Ministry of Agriculture and Forests of the Italian Republic*, [1973] C.M.L.R. 343.
33. Council Regulation 1975/69 and Commission Regulation 2195/69.
34. *Grad* v. *Finanzamt Traunstein*, [1971] C.M.L.R. 1, above, p. 55.
35. E.g. see the submissions of the Advocate General in *Alfons Lutticke G.m.b.H.* v. *Hauptzollamt Sarrelouis* [1971], C.M.L.R. 674. It is obviously also necessary that

BRENDA M. HOGGETT

The White Paper on *The Legal and Constitutional Implications of United Kingdom Membership of the European Communities* suggested that the overriding of existing inconsistent United Kingdom law 'need not be left to implication'.[36] Thus Part II of the Act does indeed deal with those aspects of national law which require immediate amendment as a result of accession, and the powers granted by section 2(2) to amend and repeal previous inconsistent legislation in order to solve subsequent conflicts have already been discussed.[37]

As far as conflicts which may arise as a result of the government's failing to detect or remove inconsistencies are concerned, the Act provides, in the second part of section 2(4), that 'any enactment passed or to be passed . . . shall be construed and have effect subject to the foregoing provisions of this section'. Principal among those foregoing provisions is, of course, the all-embracing formula of section 2(1),[38] which directs that the courts observe all directly applicable and effective Community law.

Together, these subsections should be effective impliedly to repeal any pre-accession national law which conflicts with pre- or post-accession Community law. Although the idea may take a little time to become accustomed to, they should also be sufficient to repeal any enactment made after the coming into force of the Act which conflicts with a new provision of Community law which is made after that enactment. If rights and obligations 'from time to time' arising under the treaties are to be recognised under section 2(1), they must take precedence over any previous inconsistent national enactment; this is one of the reasons for the inclusion of the words 'to be passed' in the words quoted from section 2(4).[39]

The problem which has most exercised writers on the subject, however, is that of conflict between Community law and a subsequent national enactment. The view of the European Court was clearly stated in the celebrated case of *Costa* v. *E.N.E.L.*,[40] in which the plaintiff claimed that he was not liable to pay a small electricity

the obligation of the member State should have clearly arisen at the relevant time: the obligation must, therefore, require no further action from any institution of the Community to perfect it.

36. 1967, Cmnd. 3301, para. 23. See *An Introduction to the Law of the E.E.C.*, p. 101.
37. See p. 63 above.
38. To these must be added the submission to the European Court required by s. 3(1).
39. It is also a reason for employing the s. 2(1) formula instead of delegating legislative power to the Community; the use of *delegated* powers to repeal post-accession enactments could have caused much difficulty.
40. [1964] C.M.L.R. 425.

bill because the body which was demanding it had been set up by a statute passed in 1962, which he alleged was invalid as it contravened certain articles of the E.E.C. Treaty. The European Court, to which the case was referred by the Italian judge, held that if a provision of Community law created individual rights and if some subsequent provision of national law contravened those rights, then the national court must give effect to the primacy of Community law.

The European Court did not seek either to apply the Treaty to the facts of the individual case before it or to dictate to the Italian court the methods whereby it might disregard a subsequent statute passed by its own legislature. In fact, the Italian Constitutional Court found itself unable to declare that the statute establishing the nationalised electricity industry was invalid, for Italy had acceded to the Community by means of an ordinary and not a constitutional law, and therefore the principle of *lex posterior derogat priori* was applied.[41] The Milan judge of merits, however, was able to give judgment for the plaintiff.[42]

The original six members of the Communities have adopted various solutions to the problem, with differing and ever-developing degrees of success,[43] but perhaps the most startling example of devotion to the European ideal comes from Belgium,[44] where the Cour de Cassation granted the plaintiff relief in the teeth of a statute expressly passed to indemnify the government from the consequences of having collected import duties under royal decrees which contravened Article 12 of the E.E.C. Treaty.

In the United Kingdom, however, the very idea runs counter to two cherished concepts of constitutional law, that Parliament cannot bind its successors[45] and that no court can impugn the validity of a statute.[46] The question whether a later statute might seek expressly

41. [1964] C.M.L.R. 425.

42. [1968] C.M.L.R. 267, Giudice Conciliatore di Milano.

43. For a discussion see, for example, Brinkhorst and Schermers, *Judicial Remedies in the European Communities*, chapter 3.

44. *Minister for Economic Affairs* v. *S.A. Fromagerie Franco-Suisse 'Le Ski'*, [1972] C.M.L.R. 330.

45. *Ellen Street Estates Ltd* v. *Minister of Health*, [1934] 1 K.B. 590; *Vauxhall Estates Ltd.* v. *Liverpool Corporation*, [1932] 1 K.B. 733.

46. *Edinburgh and Dalkeith Railway* v. *Wauchope* (1842), 8 Cl. & F. 710; *Lee* v. *Bude and Torrington Junction Railway Company* (1871), L.R. 6 C.P. 576; *British Railways Board* v. *Pickin*, [1974] 1 All E.R. 609. On the other hand, the Belgian Cour de Cassation, in the *Fromagerie Franco-Suisse* 'Le Ski' case, note 44 above, did not hold the national statute invalid but held that the conflicting rule of Community law overrode it where the two were inconsistent, a distinction which an English court might find hard to grasp.

to repudiate our obligations under the treaties and remove the United Kingdom from the Communities is of comparatively little importance, since such a move would, like previous revolutions, be respected by the judiciary if it accorded with political realities. The real question is what attitude the judges will be prepared to take to such minor and inadvertent lapses as will almost inevitably occur, or where the government of the day seeks to delay or even to defy some particular requirement of the Communities.

The fact that the generally enthusiastic Europeans of the Six have failed to avoid such conflicts tends to indicate that to rely mainly upon the goodwill of Parliament and upon the use of Parliamentary machinery will not suffice.[47] Others, while accepting that the general principles of Parliamentary supremacy cannot be challenged, have sought to provide practical legal solutions. The only perfectly safe method would be to include, in every subsequent statute, a formula that its provisions must be given effect subject to the provisions of Community law.[48] In view of the extensive potential effect of Community law, it would probably be unsafe to confine such a formula to the most likely fields of legislation.[49] But these solutions also rely upon the goodwill of Parliament in inserting the formula, and would not be effective against deliberate evasions and delays.

What the Act has done is to attempt to provide a solution which will not be dependent on Parliament's future attitude to the Communities. In the first place, the provisions of subsections 2(4) and 2(1) already quoted should be as effective as an interpretation Act to secure primacy for Community law in many cases of doubt. But in order to succeed in a suggestion that Community law should prevail in a case of obvious conflict with subsequent law, counsel would probably be obliged to argue that the Act has modified the very principle of Parliamentary supremacy.

Attacks upon the immutability of the conventional doctrine are not new: it has been pointed out that if the doctrine itself was largely the work of some academic lawyers others have been making up for it ever since.[50] Some very convincing points have been made,[51] not least that it is strange to extol the flexibility of the

47. E.g. Cmnd. 3301, para. 23; 6 *C.M.L.Rev.* 7 (Martin), pp. 23–5; 35 *M.L.R.* 375 (Trinidade).   48. 6 *C.M.L.Rev.* 50 (Hunnings).
49. Professor H. W. R. Wade, *The Times*, 18 April 1972.
50. Marshall, *Constitutional Theory*, p. 35.
51. E.g. 5 *C.M.L.Rev.* 112 (Professor Mitchell); see also Heuston, *Essays in Constitutional Law*, pp. 16–20; de Smith, *Constitutional and Administrative Law*, pp. 77–82.

British constitution while adhering to a fundamental principle of alarming and virtually unproven rigidity. It may claim the support of a handful of cases concerning relatively minor statutes,[52] but whenever confronted with the realities after an Act of 'transcendent constitutional importance' the judges have disregarded it.[53] On the other hand, it may be argued that these latter cases relate to surrender of legal control over territory outside the United Kingdom, and not the surrender of legislative power within the Kingdom; it might also be noted that the cases dealing with conflict between a statute giving effect to an international treaty,[54] or the general principles of international law, and a later inconsistent statute have not been encouraging.[55]

Nevertheless, the courts have never before been confronted by a statute with the three important characteristics of the European Communities Act: firstly, it expressly attempts both to prevail over subsequent legislation and to impose restrictions upon national competence in Community matters; secondly, it is of obvious fundamental importance to the whole structure of the legal system of the United Kingdom; and thirdly it clearly attempts, in section 2(1) and section 3(1), to give to the national courts a jurisdiction to do whatever is required by the principles of Community law and the European Court. It is in this last respect that the Act may be most compelling.[56]

There is one further argument towards this result, which is that where a statute of such fundamental constitutional importance provides for certain of its provisions to be alterable, it must thereby be entrenching the remainder. Section 2(4), in its last part, expressly provides that the Second Schedule may be altered by subsequent Act of Parliament, a provision which is otherwise quite unnecessary. Is this a further attempt to entrench the fundamental sections of the Act?

In any event, the primacy of Community law is dependent either upon the goodwill of Parliament or upon the goodwill of the judiciary, for the very doctrine of Parliamentary supremacy, if it is more than an academic theory, is a description of the way in which

52. Cited on p. 73, notes 45 and 46 above.
53. *A.G. for Ontario* v. *A.G. for Canada*, [1947] A.C. 127; see also *British Coal Corporation* v. *The King*, [1935] A.C. 500.
54. *I.R.C.* v. *Collco Dealings Ltd*, [1962] A.C. 1.
55. *Mortenson* v. *Peters* (1906), 14 S.L.T. 227; *Cheney* v. *Conn*, [1968] 1 W.L.R. 242; *Post Office* v. *Estuary Radio Ltd*, [1968] 2 Q.B. 740.
56. Cf. *MacCormick* v. *Lord Advocate*, [1953] S.C. 396.

the courts deal with Acts of Parliament. One or two indications already exist, for there have been statements accepting the primacy of Community law in at least two cases,[57] and the judges have resolutely refused to commit themselves on the question of conflict with a subsequent enactment.[58] This may augur well for the future acceptance of Community law.

57. *Aero Zipp Fasteners Ltd and Lightning Fasteners Ltd* v. *YKK Fasteners (U.K.) Ltd,* [1973] C.M.L.R. 819, per Graham J. at p. 820; *Esso Petroleum Co. Ltd* v. *Kingswood Motors (Addlestone) Ltd,* [1973] 3 All E.R. 1057, per Bridge J. at p. 1064.

58. *Blackburn* v. *Attorney General,* [1971] 2 All E.R. 1380, per Lord Denning at p. 1393.

Chapter VII

MONOPOLIES

B. A. Wortley

I. STATE MONOPOLIES OF A COMMERCIAL CHARACTER

State monopolies of a commercial character may not prove easy to kill in the interests of the consumer. In a communist State they must inevitably exist, and the consumer is at the mercy of the State planners, who may order too much or too little of any commodity to suit the needs of the consumer. When there is a shortage of State-produced goods anything will sell; when there is a surplus it may well be wasted unless the price is reduced by official decree. The object of the creation of the E.E.C. is a large free market in which supply equals demand in conditions of objective fairness. Any monopoly must, if the needs of the consumer require it, be curbed. Thus Article 37(1) of the E.E.C. Treaty:

1. Member States shall progressively adjust *any State monopolies of a commercial character* so as to ensure that when the transitional period has ended, no discrimination regarding the conditions under which goods are produced and marketed exists between nationals of Member States.[1]

On 21 April 1970 the Council laid down Regulation No. 727/70 aiming at a Common Market organisation for raw tobacco.[2] According to the fifth Report of the Commission (pp. 100–1), the Commission informed the Council that from 1 January 1972 the French and Italian governments 'had notified the Commission of numerous,

1. This continues: 'The provision of this Article shall apply to any body through which a Member State, in law or in fact, either directly or indirectly supervises, determines or appreciably influences imports or exports between Member States. These provisions shall likewise apply to monopolies delegated by the State to others.' To implement this, Article 37(6) states: 'With effect from the first stage, the Commission shall make recommendations as to the manner in which and the timetable according to which the adjustment provided for in this Article shall be carried out.' State Monopolies are then to be 'progressively' adjusted to avoid discrimination between nationals of member States, by implication to reduce prices. What has been done?

2. The Commission's Fourth *General Report on the Activity of the Communities, 1970,* Brussels, 1971.

substantial measures for the adjustment of their manufactured *tobacco* monopolies'. The fifth Report continues:

As regards *spirits* monopolies, the German Government abolished quantitative restrictions on spirits and spirituous beverages and the French Government is preparing to abolish discriminations covered by the last Commission recommendation.

In the case of the *potash and basic slag* monopolies, the French Government put forward agricultural and regional arguments for considering solutions differing in some respects from those recommended by the Commission.

In Italy, the *lighter* monopoly has been abolished. The *flint, cigarette paper* and *salt* monopolies are to be abolished with effect from April 1972. Abolition of the *match monopoly* has also been announced.

Mr Mathijsen rightly indicates that progress is slow.[3]

Any State commercial monopolies of our own will be reviewed before the end of 1977;[4] the coal and steel production monopolies which exist here or elsewhere in the member States will be the concern of the European Coal and Steel Community, with which we are not directly concerned in this volume. The United Kingdom has already been reminded by the Commission of the obligation to end the freeze of steel prices.[5]

Public undertakings must also abide by the rules against discrimination and distortion of competition (Art. 90(1) of the E.E.C. Treaty). Article 90(2) does, however, provide an escape clause covering public utilities such as gas, water, electricity and transport, as well as 'revenue-producing' monopolies, 'in so far as the application of such rules does not obstruct the performance, in law or in fact, of the particular tasks assigned to them . . .'

II. STATE SUBSIDIES

State subsidies to manufacturers or traders may by distortion render competition unfair and be illegal under Article 92 so far as they affect 'trade between Member States'.

What is improper is the favouring of certain undertakings or the producers of certain goods. The E.E.C. *Bulletin* of 1972 reports a refusal of the Commission to accept State aid to a Belgian firm 'whose chances of showing a profit are very seriously in jeopardy'.

Section 92 does not relate to action by a State to maintain the *general infrastructure*, e.g. roads, railways, harbours, cities, or the

3. *A Guide to European Community Law*, 1972, pp. 96–7.
4. Article 44 of the Act annexed to the Treaty of Accession.
5. *The Times*, 3 February 1973.

general background of a nation, though there may be a case for harmonising these (Mathijsen, *op. cit.*, p. 99). Some countries are well endowed by nature, some are not. Some countries, like Holland, have improved on nature.

Inequalities resulting from nation-wide economic measures can be abolished only through approximation of legislation or taxation,[6] not through competition policy.

Aids to the general economic infrastructure must presumably be paid for by general State taxes or loans and they will presumably be compatible with the E.E.C. Treaty. *State aids* that 'shall be compatible' with the Treaty *have been defined in* Article 92(2). The fifth General Report of the E.E.C. Commission states:

they are aids having a *social character*, aids to make good the damage caused by *natural disaster*, and aids granted in Germany to areas affected by the division of the country. Although the treaty provides that these aids are 'compatible', it is the Commission's task to verify whether the conditions required for granting such aids are indeed fulfilled.

III. AIDS LIMITED TO PARTICULAR 'BACKWARD' REGIONS

The rules governing aids for backward areas will be relevant in relation to aid given by our government to our own development areas, as in the North-west.

Article 92(3) states:

The following may be considered to be compatible with the Common Market:

> (a) aid to promote the economic development of areas where the standard of living is abnormally low or where there is serious under-employment; . . .

Also compatible with the Common Market are projects of 'Common European interest' or to remedy 'serious disturbance in the economy of a Member State' (Article 92(3)(b)).

Under Article 92(3)(c) aid may be granted to develop 'certain economic activities' or 'certain economic areas'.

An example of aid allowed under 92(3)(c) is reported at p. 55 of the second General Report of the Commission (1968), which states:

The Commission is considering possible guide lines for a Community solution to the problem of aid to the film industry. Any such solution should

6. See Lasok and Bridge on approximation, Arts. 100–106, and tax, Arts. 95–99, pp. 280-5.

help to improve the industry's competitiveness, particularly on the markets outside the Community.

The Commission stated its views on a draft law notified in May 1968 by the Government of the Federal Republic of Germany, introducing aid arrangements for the film industry. It took the view that the law would establish a better equilibrium, in matters of aid, among the chief film producing countries in the Community by creating fresh scope for co-operation within the Community. The Commission raised no objection to the measures contemplated, considering that they might qualify for the waiver in Article 92(3)(c).

This type of aid given under Article 92(3)(c) must 'not adversely affect trading conditions to an extent contrary to the common interest'. No such limitation, points out the fifth report of the Commission, applies to aid to *backward* areas, e.g. under Article 92(3)(a).

Discrepancies between State aids given by member States to their own regions need to be ironed out if competition is to be fair.

Consequently, says the fifth report of the Commission (p. 100/1), to prevent one State outbidding another in its regional aid, endeavours to terminate out-bidding by authorities *granting* regional *aids* have led to the implementation of a co-ordination arrangement.

This arrangement is the subject of a memorandum in which the Commission informed the Council that from 1 January 1972 onwards it would apply certain principles to regional aid arrangements, within the limits of the powers vested in it by the Treaty. For their part, in response to a request from the Commission, the member governments, meeting in Council, adopted a resolution on 20 October 1971[7] stating their political readiness to conform to these principles.

Initially, the co-ordination arrangement will apply only to the 'central regions' of the Community, where the effects of outbidding are most disquieting. The arrangement has four main features:

(a) The scale of aid will be subject to a uniform 20 per cent ceiling; that is to say, not more than 20 per cent of capital expenditure (after deduction of taxation) under any individual scheme is to be covered by aids. It is intended that aids should tend to decline in central regions, and the level of the ceiling will be reviewed at the end of 1973.

(b) Aids are to be made 'transparent' in 1972 (that is to say, it must be possible to calculate maximum aid percentages by the same method as the one used to calculate the ceiling).

(c) The 20 per cent ceiling is to be an upper limit. The Commission will

7. See Mathijsen, p. 101.

ensure that actual aid percentages within this limit correspond to the seriousness of the relevant national problems.

(*d*) A method will be worked out for identifying the impact of regional aids on specific industries.

Regional aid in the Netherlands is now being recast (fifth E.E.C. *Bulletin*, 1972, p. 65) and certain proposals by Italy have been declared bad (*ibid.*, p. 66).

1 July 1973 is the date fixed for the application of the rules on regional aid to new member States (Article 154 of the Act annexed to the Treaty of Accession).[8] These rules are addressed to member States and give no rights directly to individuals.[9] However, by Article 93(2) of the E.E.C. Treaty the Commission or any interested State may refer the matter to the Court of Justice direct.

IV. DUMPING[10]

Dumping provisions are dealt with in Article 136 of the Act annexed to the Treaty of Accession, the official translation of which runs:

(1) If, before 31 December 1977, the Commission, on application by a Member State or by any other interested party, finds that dumping is being practised between the Community as originally constituted and the new Member States or between the new Member States themselves, it shall address recommendations[11] to the person or persons with whom such practices originate for the purpose of putting an end to them.

Should the practices continue, the Commission shall authorise the injured Member State or States to take protective measures [e.g. retaliatory duties or quotas], the conditions and details of which the Commission shall determine.[12]

(2) For the application of this Article to the products listed in Annex II to the E.E.C. Treaty, the Commission shall evaluate all relevant factors, in particular the level of prices at which these products are imported into the market in question from elsewhere, account being taken of the provisions of the E.E.C. Treaty relating to agriculture, in particular Article 39.

8. See *The Times*, 13 February 1973, on 'End-of-year assessment of E.E.C. aid to regions'.

9. *Flaminio Costa* v. *E.N.E.L.*, [1964] C.M.L.R. 425, cited by Lasok and Bridge, *op. cit.*, p. 280.

10. Defined in *An Introduction to the Law of the E.E.C.*, p. 69.

11. These, it will be recalled, are not binding on States.

12. See Campbell, vol. II, p. 604, for Regulation 459/68 of 5 April 1968.

B. A. WORTLEY

V. ABUSE OF DOMINANT POSITION

This aspect of distortion of competition is dealt with at p. 72 of
An Introduction to the Law of the E.E.C., Article 86. The official translation of Article 86 is now as follows:

Any *abuse by one or more undertakings of a dominant position within the Common
Market or in a substantial part of it shall be prohibited as incompatible with the
Common Market in so far as it may affect trade between Member States.*[13] Such
abuse may, in particular, consist in:

(a) Directly or indirectly imposing unfair purchase or selling prices or
other unfair trading conditions.
(b) Limiting production, markets or technical development to the prejudice of consumers.
(c) Applying dissimilar conditions to equivalent transactions with other
trading parties, thereby placing them at a competitive disadvantage.
(d) Making the conclusion of contracts subject to acceptance by the other
parties of supplementary obligations which, by their nature or according to commercial usage, have no connection with the subject of such
contracts.

In *An Introduction to the Law of the E.E.C.*, pp. 72–6, in 1971 it was
stressed that this article was aimed at abuses of monopolistic power,
and there was then no case where Article 86 was the *only* reason for
invalidating an agreement or understanding, for the matter of
'Continental Can' was then under review by the Commission, but
had not been decided by it.

In its decision in the *Continental Can* case, in 1972, the Commission
ruled that the

amalgamation of a dominant enterprise with a rival enterprise can be
abusive within the meaning of Article 86 if it restricts consumers' freedom
of choice in a manner incompatible with Treaty competition rules. Continental Can Company obtained a controlling interest in the largest
German maker of packaging and metal containers, Schmalbach-Lubeca-
Werke, and then bought the largest maker of packaging equipment in
Benelux, the Dutch Thommassen & Drijver-Verblifa. This concentration
resulted in excessive restriction of consumers' freedom to choose certain
packaging equipment in substantial parts of the Common Market. Such
freedom must be reintroduced by 'deconcentration' measures. The Commission is continuing to supervise markets where there is a high degree of
concentration, so as to be able to identify similar cases of prohibited concentrations between enterprises. In fact, proposals were to be submitted to
the Commission by 1 July 1972. [*Bulletin* of the E.E.C., vol. 5, 1972, p. 64]

13. Our italics.

82

In the fifth General Report on the activities of the Communities (1972, p. 99) the Commission had stated its policy in applying Article 86:

In the year under review, action was taken under Article 86 of the E.E.C. Treaty for the first time. The Gesellschaft für musikalische Aufführungs- und mechanische Vervielfaltigungerechte (G.E.M.A.), German composers' copyright company which has a *de facto* monopoly on the German market, was forbidden to impose *abusive restrictions*[14] on the economic freedom of composers, authors or publishers. This means that G.E.M.A. cannot discriminate against nationals or other Member States, grant special concessions to its members or collect dues for musical works which have become public property. In future, imported sound recordings will attract the same dues as those made in Germany.

Clearance may be applied for because an enterprise or association of enterprises may, by Article 2 of Council Regulation No. 17 (see *An Introduction to the Law of the E.E.C.*, p. 118), request the Commission to find that there are no grounds for it to intervene in respect of a particular agreement or practice.[15] The practice here is not well developed as it is with Article 85, as we shall see.

The Commission may need evidence to consider whether grounds do or do not exist for its intervention, and to get evidence the Commission has exercised the power to fine a firm for a failure to submit a complete set of 'business papers' (fifth General Report, 1972, p. 95). Once Article 86 has been shown to have been infringed, the Commission will give instructions to end the agreement or practice (Regulation No. 17(3)) or may 'address to the enterprises or associations of enterprises concerned, recommendations designed to put an end to the infringement'. This allows room for manoeuvre.

It must be stressed that to offend against Article 86 a substantial part of the Common Market territory must be affected *and proved*.

The rapporteur on competition policy stated in the European Parliament (*The Times*, 13 February 1973) that

the enormous wave of concentrations which was spreading across the Community was a crucial problem for the E.E.C. The Commission was now testing the scope of Article 86 . . . the Community should decide how it was to dovetail British cartel policy into the Community's competition policy.

The commissioner for competition policy then added that 'a system of undistorted competition in a single market remained the best

14. Certain limited monopolies are 'permitted, to encourage inventions, patents and to protect trade marks. Dr Kay deals with these in chapter IX.
15. See the *Sirena* case, [1971] C.M.L.R. 260, and Dr Kay p. 106 below.

way of obtaining steadily increasing efficiency in industry'. And this is the aim of fair competition.

The Commission's ruling in the *Continental Can* case excited a good deal of comment. Taking up the theme of the Chatham House and P.E.P. paper *Concentration or Competition: a European Dilemma, The Times* of 16 November 1972 suggested that during the 1960's there was a need to create industrial and commercial units big enough to face the American challenge, *le défi américain*, but that, on the other hand, complete free trade was also an ideal of the E.E.C. Consequently, said *The Times*, the burden of proof of improper advantage should be a heavy one. One might add that any proof of the required 'abuse' must be heavy.

This view, in fact, appears to have been one which commended itself to the European Communities Court of Justice when it decided the *Continental Can* case in February 1973,[16] holding that the decision of the Commission had 'not sufficiently explained the facts and appraisals' on which it was based (p. 228). The case is very important for these reasons:

1. The Court has for the first time ruled against the Commission on competition.

2. The Court reiterated (according to *The Times* of 26 February 1973) the principle of Article 86 and noted that Article 85

would be pointless if Article 86 were to condone such agreements so long as they came about by means of company merger or takeover. . . There could be an abuse of a dominant position whenever a company already in such a position tended to strengthen it to a point at which potential competitors no longer existed . . . However, . . . the Commission had not in the present case specified in which field or fields the claimant companies were deemed to hold a dominant position, i.e. whether in the field of meat tins, in that of fish tins, in that of metal jar lids, or in all of these fields.[17]

Commenting on the decision defeating the Commission, *The Times* of 23 February 1973 observed:

. . . the Commission has already achieved most of what it wanted from the Court, namely an interpretation of Article 86 which would go a long way towards helping it prepare more detailed anti-monopoly legislation.

It is not clear at this stage which form this legislation will take. There would appear to be two possibilities. The Commission can go ahead with

16. *Europemballage Corporation and Continental Can Co. Inc.* v. *E.E.C. Commission,* [1973] C.M.L.R. 199.
17. *Ibid.,* at p. 224, which gives a different and more succinct version.

completely new legislation for a *notification*[18] procedure by companies contemplating mergers before they take place.

Alternatively, it could introduce legislation on the basis of Article 86, which would probably by its very nature not allow the Commission to *interfere* with any *takeovers or mergers* until after they have been concluded.[18]

It will remain to be seen whether, on the offering of further evidence, the Continental Can Company will be held to strengthen its position in the Common Market (e.g. by take-overs), will eliminate 'fair competition', and whether the Commission will produce rules to divide up monopolies.

This litigation in the court had the effect of halting the work of the Commission.[19] It may well have opened the way to proper and legitimate discussions between the firms and the Commission to safeguard the consumer. This, after all, has been the procedure in relation to the power to exempt or to modify agreements under Article 85, which is to be dealt with in chapter VIII.

18. Our italics.

19. However, in the case of *Istituto Chemioferapico Italiano SpA and Commercial Solvents Corporation* v. *The Commission, The Times*, 8 March 1974, the E.E.C. Court at Luxembourg upheld the Commission's power to fine in respect of an infringement of Art. 86 by refusing to supply raw materials.

Chapter VIII

COMPETITION

B. A. Wortley

I. COMMUNITY LAW AND ENGLISH LAW

Since the Schill lecture on this topic was given in 1971 (*An Introduction to the Law of the E.E.C.*, chapter VII) there have been many new developments in E.E.C. law. Let us look first at the British *European Communities Act*, 1972, which regulates any possible conflict between national legislation and the Treaty:

Section 10.—(1) Part I of the British Restrictive Trade Practices Act 1956 shall apply to an agreement notwithstanding that it is or may be void by reason of any directly applicable Community provision, or is expressly authorised by or under any such provision; but the Restrictive Practices Court may decline or postpone the exercise of its jurisdiction under section 20 of the Act, or may (notwithstanding section 22(2)) exercise its jurisdiction under section 22, if and so far as it appears to the court right so to do having regard to the operation of any such provision or to the purpose and effect of any authorisation or exemption granted in relation thereto, and the Registrar may refrain from taking proceedings before the court in respect of any agreement if and for so long as he thinks it appropriate so to do having regard to the operation of any such provision and to the purpose and effect of any such authorisation or exemption.

Under section 10(2) The Registrar under the British Act is to be given particulars of steps taken or of decisions, by the E.E.C. or the E.C.S.C.

We may, then, still apply our own law, even if an agreement is void under E.E.C. law or is authorised thereunder. However, it seems that if the E.E.C. permits an agreement to stand, we too should permit it. In the case of *E.E.C. Commission* v. *Italy* (case No. 39/92; first reported in *The Times* for 19 February 1973) member States were held by the Community Court not to be entitled to invoke rules of domestic law to justify non-implementation of Community regulations. The Court said:

... It cannot be accepted that a Member State should apply in an incomplete or selective manner provisions of a Community Regulation so as to render abortive certain aspects of Community legislation which it has opposed or which it considers contrary to its national interests . . . practical difficulties cannot permit a Member State unilaterally to opt out of observing its obligations.[1]

This view is widely shared by international lawyers and by the International Court of Justice at The Hague.[2]

II. PROHIBITIONS

It is vital to know what at first blush appears to infringe Article 85(1) and (2) of the E.E.C. Treaty, i.e. (our italics):

85(1). The following shall be prohibited as incompatible with the common market: all agreements between undertakings, decisions by associations of undertakings and concerted practices which may *affect trade between Member States* and which have as their object or effect the *prevention, restriction or distortion of competition* within the common market, and in particular those which:

(a) directly or indirectly fix purchase or selling prices or any other trading conditions;

(See the *Cement* case, [1973] C.M.L.R. 7, Court of Justice, trade association price rings (tied houses, see p. 99 below.)

(b) limit or control production, markets, technical development, or investment;

(See *Italy* v. *E.E.C. Council and Commission*, [1969] C.M.L.R. 39, Court of Justice (vertical agreements) horizontal agreements between traders.)

(c) share markets or sources of supply;

(See *Grundig* case, [1966] C.M.L.R. 418, Court of Justice, p. 49 above.)

(d) apply dissimilar conditions to equivalent transactions with other trading parties, thereby placing them at a competitive disadvantage;

(e) make the conclusion of contracts subject to acceptance by the other parties of supplementary obligations which, by their nature or according to commercial usage, have no connection with the subject of such contracts.

(2) Any agreements or decisions prohibited pursuant to this Article shall be automatically void.

1. Page 18 of cyclostat translation of case No. 39/72 by the Court.
2. *U.K.* v. *Iceland*, [1973] I.C.J. 3; and recall Mrs Hoggett's discussion in chapter VI above.

III. EXEMPTIONS

Avoidance under article 85(1) and (2) may be prevented if the conditions of article 85(3) are observed:

The provisions of paragraph 1 may, however, be declared inapplicable in the case of:
—any agreement or category of agreements between undertakings;
—any decision or category of decisions by associations of undertakings;
—any concerted practice or category of concerted practices;

which contributes to improving the production or distribution of goods or to promoting technical or economic progress, while allowing consumers a fair share of the resulting benefit, and which does not:

(a) impose on the undertakings concerned restrictions which are not indispensable to the attainment of these objectives:
(b) afford such undertakings the possibility of eliminating competition in respect of a substantial part of the products in question.

IV. NECESSITY OF NOTIFICATION

Let us look at attempts to implement Article 85 by regulations made under Article 87, since these save many agreements from being void automatically under Article 85(1). If the E.E.C. regulations for the time being are followed, doubtful agreements may be saved. These regulations require notification, and failure to notify is at one's peril.

In *An Introduction to the Law of the E.E.C.*, at pp. 118–28, there is set out the vital *Council Regulation No. 17* of 6 February 1962, as amended by Regulation 59 of 3 July 1962. These regulations related to agreements *which may* be caught by Article 85. They are very detailed as compared with the relatively scant attention given by regulations to Article 86 (monopolies). They set up the scheme of notification which (see *An Introduction to the Law of the E.E.C.*, p. 89) resulted in the Commission receiving between 1962 and 1971 (14 May) no fewer than 37,000 notifications under Article 85. There are now the additional agreements produced in three more member States to contend with! Even a gentlemen's agreement caught by Article 85(1) must be registered with the E.E.C. in Brussels. Failure to register, and therefore to publicise, may lead to very serious consequences.

To accommodate the three new member States, Regulation 17, as amended, provides that all existing notified arrangements in those three States should be notified within six months from the date of accession, and *new* agreements from the date they are effective, in order to be able to obtain, where proper, negative clearance of the agreements, i.e. permission to continue. The effect of Regulation 17 on *new* agreements has been explained by Mathijsen (at p. 93):

Consequently, if a *new* agreement becomes effective for instance on 1 January 1974 and the Commission is notified on 1 July 1974, a decision granting dispensation cannot become effective before this last date, which means that the agreement is to be considered void (E.E.C. Art. 85(2)) between 1 January 1974 and 1 July 1974.

Forms A and B for notifying should be applied for and completed.[3]

Notification is possibly the principal means whereby the Commission exercises its function to regulate competition, but it also carries out its own surveillance of markets and spot checks.[4] One also suspects that it does not close its eyes to the activities of the U.S.A. anti-trust authorities.

V. EXCEPTION TO NOTIFICATION UNDER REGULATION 17

Whilst, in general, Article 4(1) of the Council's Regulation 17[5] requires notification to the Commission of agreements caught by Article 85(1), exceptions are made by Article 4(2) of the Council regulations, and indeed 'Paragraph 1 shall not be applicable to agreements, decisions and concerted practices where' (our italics):

(1) *enterprises of only one Member State* take part and where such agreements, decisions and practices involve *neither imports nor exports* between Member States;

(2) *only two enterprises* take part and the sole effect of these agreements is:

    (a) to restrict the freedom of *one party* to the contract to fix prices or conditions of trading in the resale of goods which have been acquired *from the other party* to the contract, or

    (b) to impose restraint on the exercise of the rights of any person acquiring or using *industrial property rights*—particularly patents, utility models, registered designs or trade marks—or on the exercise of the rights of any person entitled, under a contract, to acquire or use manufacturing processes or knowledge relating to the utilisation or application of industrial techniques; . . .

3. *Cawthra, Restrictive Agreements in the E.E.C.*, 1972, hereafter referred to as Cawthra, pp. 121 ff.
4. Commission, Third General Report, 1969, p. 62.
5. Cawthra, pp. 42 ff., and *An Introduction to the Law of the E.E.C.*, p. 119.

Since the issue of Council Regulation 17 in 1962 there have been regular attempts to cope with the flood of notifications.

VI. BLOCK EXEMPTIONS FROM NOTIFICATION

Exemptions from notification have been offered (A) *to small businesses* on the basis of *de minimis non curat lex*, and (B) to *all businesses* on the basis that certain restrictive practices may actually be beneficial to the consumer. Block exemptions are intended to cut down unnecessary bureaucratic intervention. This was recognised by Bridge J. in the *Esso* case, [1973] 2 All E.R. 1057, see p. 76 above.

A. SMALL BUSINESSES

There are three cases.

1. By a Commission's announcement or notice of 27 May 1970 it was provided that 'certain agreements of minor importance' are so insignificant as not to be 'noticeable' and therefore do not fall within Article 85, i.e.[6] (our italics):

—when the products covered by the agreement do not represent, in the part of the Common Market in which the agreement produces its effect, more than *five per cent of the amount of business done with identical products* or with products considered by the consumer to be similar by reason of their properties, their price or their use, and

—when the *total annual turnover* of the undertakings taking part in the agreement does *not exceed 15 million units* of account or, in the case of commercial undertakings, 20 million units of account. . . .[7]

—when these agreements are not covered by the prohibition in Article 85(1) if, during two consecutive financial years, the shares of the market and the turnover thus determined allow an excess of less than 10 per cent.

Elaborate rules are then set out for the ascertainment of turnover.

2. By the Council's Regulations (E.E.C.) No. 2822/71 of 20 December 1971[8] it was provided that Article 4(2) of Regulation No. 17 requiring notification

should not apply to agreements, decisions and concerted practices where . . . by Article 4(3) they have as their sole object . . .

6. Campbell, supplement No. 2, 1971, vol. 1, p. 88; Cawthra, pp. 134 ff.
7. See *An Introduction to the Law of the E.E.C.*, p. 81; one unit was then (1 January 1972) 10p.
8. Cawthra, p. 142.

(c) specialisation in the manufacture of products, including agreements necessary for the achievement thereof:
—where the products which are the object of specialisation do not, in a substantial part of the Common Market, represent more than 15 per cent[9] of the volume of business done in identical products or those considered by the consumers to be similar by reason of their characteristics, price and use, and
—where the total annual turnover of the participating undertakings does not exceed 200 million units of account.

That was the Christmas present for 1971.

3. For 1972 there was also a Christmas present, i.e. Commission Regulation No. 2779/72 dated 21 December 1972. This was mentioned shortly in *The Times* of 2 January 1973; it was not then known at H.M.S.O. in Manchester, but has been kindly made available to us by the legal department of the Foreign and Commonwealth Office in the French text of the *Journal officiel* No. L292/23–25. Article 1 of this provides that Article 85(1) on restrictive practices shall not apply to specialisation arrangements until 31 December 1977. Article 3 says that Article 1 shall not apply when (a) the products which are the subject of specialisation do not exceed 10 per cent of the volume of business done with identical or similar products . . . and (b) where the turnover of the enterprises concerned does not exceed 150 million units of account. Again special rules are given for arriving at the turnover. By Article 6 there is a retroactive effect of exemption from the date when these conditions are fulfilled, but this cannot be before the date of notification for agreements that had to be notified[10] before 18 January 1972.

B. ALL BUSINESSES ARE EXEMPT FROM THE FOLLOWING RESTRICTIONS, WHICH MAY BE TERMED BENEFICIAL

There are four cases:

1. *Patent licensing exemptions.* These are dealt with by Dr Kay in chapter IX. See notice of the Commission of 24 December 1962 (Cawthra, p. 65).
2. *Transport exemptions* are mentioned by Mr Jaconelli in chapter XII (Cawthra, p. 93).
3. *Exclusive dealing exemptions.* In the notice of 24 December 1962 the Commission stated that

9. I.e. by the rules applying to then member States.
10. I.e. by the rules applying to then member States.

contracts made with commercial agents in which those agents undertake for a *specified part* of the territory of the Common Market,

—to negotiate transactions on behalf of an enterprise, or

—to conclude transactions in the name and on behalf of an enterprise, or

—to conclude transactions in their own name and on behalf of this enterprise,

are not covered by the prohibition laid down in Article 85, paragraph 1, of the Treaty.

It is essential in this case that the contracting party, described as a commercial agent, should, in fact, be such, by the nature of his functions, and that he should neither undertake nor engage in activities proper to an independent trader in the course of commercial operations. [Cawthra, p. 62]

Such a person is an agent in the true sense, i.e. more of an employee (permanent or temporary) than an independent dealer.

Agency was also dealt with in the famous Regulation 67/67 of the Commission,[11] put out after the *Consten–Grundig* case, [1966] C.M.L.R. 418,[12] which permitted duly notified agreements which infringed Article 85 to be renegotiated: see *An Introduction*, p. 88. This has now been extended by Regulation 2591/72 of 8 December 1972 (not in Cawthra). Article 1 of Regulation 67/67(1) is as follows:

Article 85(1) of the Treaty shall not apply to agreements to which *only two undertakings* are party and whereby:

(a) one party agrees with the other to supply only to that other certain goods for resale within a defined area of the common market; or

(b) one party agrees with the other to purchase only from that other certain goods for resale; or

(c) the two undertakings have entered into obligations, as in (a) and (b) above, with each other in respect of exclusive supply and purchase for resale.

Paragraph 1 [hereof?] shall not apply to agreements to which undertakings from one Member State only are party and which concern the resale of goods within that Member State.

However, the exemptions accorded by Article 1(1) shall not apply where[13] according to Article 3 of Reg. 67/67:

(a) manufacturers of competing goods entrust each other with *exclusive dealing* in those goods;

(b) the contracting parties make it *difficult* for intermediaries or *consumers*

11. Cawthra, pp. 89–93; our italics.
12. Facts in Dr Kay's chapter ix below.
13. Cawthra, pp. 90–1; our italics.

to obtain the goods to which the contract relates from other dealers within the common market, in particular where the contracting parties:

1. exercise *industrial property* rights to *prevent dealers or consumers* from obtaining from other parts of the common market or from selling in the territory covered by the contract goods to which the contract relates which are properly marked or otherwise properly placed on the market;
2. exercise other rights or take other measures to prevent dealers or consumers *from obtaining* from elsewhere goods to which the contract relates or from selling them in the territory covered by the contract.

Article 2(1) sets out the only acceptable restrictions on exclusive dealers, i.e.

Apart from an obligation falling within Article 1, no restriction on competition shall be imposed on the *exclusive dealer* other than:

(a) the obligation not to manufacture or distribute, during *the duration* of the contract *or until one year after* its expiration, goods which compete with the goods to which the contract relates;
(b) the obligation to refrain, outside the *territory covered by the contract*, from seeking customers for the goods to which the contract relates, from establishing any branch, or from maintaining any distribution depot.[14]

Article 2(2) permits the following:[15]

Article 1(1) [giving exemptions] shall apply notwithstanding that the exclusive dealer undertakes all or any of the following obligations:

(a) to purchase complete ranges of goods or minimum quantities;
(b) to sell the goods to which the contract relates under trade marks or packed and presented as specified by the manufacturer;
(c) to take measures for promotion of sales, in particular
—to advertise
—to maintain a sales network of stock of goods
—to provide after-sale and guarantee services
—to employ staff having specialised or technical training.

4. *Joint research and development.* Council Regulation 17 excluded the need to notify agreements

(a) To develop uniform standards.
(b) For joint research accessible to all parties.

By Council Regulation No. 2821/71 of 20 December 1971 (Cawthra, p. 137) the Commission may by regulation declare that Article 85(1)

14. Cawthra, p. 90; our italics.   15. *Ibid.*

is not applicable 'to categories of agreements between undertakings, decisions and concerted practices the object of which is standards, research and specialisation . . .'[16]

By a notice (not in Cawthra), No. IV/308/72-E) exemptions grantable are further spelled out by the Commission.

As a result of this Notice, as a general rule, it should no longer be useful for enterprises to obtain negative clearance, as defined by Article 2 of Regulation No. 17,[17] for the agreements listed, nor should it be necessary to have the legal position established through a Commission decision on an individual case. This also means that notification with this end in view will no longer be necessary for agreements of this type. . . .

The Commission takes the view that the following agreements do not restrict competition.

1. Agreements having as their *sole object*:

   (a) An exchange of opinion or experience.
   (b) Joint market research.
   (c) The joint carrying out of comparative studies of enterprises or industries.
   (d) The joint preparation of statistics and calculation models. . . .

2. Agreements having as their *sole object*:

   (a) Co-operation in accounting matters.
   (b) Joint provision of credit guarantees.
   (c) Joint debt-collecting associations.
   (d) Joint business or tax consultant agencies. . . .

3. Agreements having as their *sole object*:

   (a) The joint implementation of research and development projects.
   (b) The joint placing of research and development contracts.
   (c) The sharing out of research and development projects among participating enterprises. . . .

Some of the more important categories are:

4. Agreements which have as their *sole object* the joint use of production facilities and storing and transport equipment.

These forms of co-operation do not restrict competition because they are confined to organization and technical arrangements for the use of the facilities. There may be a restraint of competition if the enterprises involved do not bear the cost of utilization of the installation or equipment themselves or if agreements are concluded or concerted practices applied regarding joint production or the sharing out of production or the establishment or running of a joint enterprise.

16. Cawthra, p. 139.
17. *Journal officiel*, No. 13, 21 February 1962.

5. Agreements having as their *sole object* the setting up of consortia for the joint execution of orders, where the participating enterprises do not compete with each other as regards the work to be done or where each of them by itself is unable to execute the orders.

Where enterprises do not compete with each other they cannot restrict competition between them by setting up consortia. This applies in particular to enterprises belonging to different industries but also to firms in the same industry to the extent that their contribution under the consortium consists only of goods or services which cannot be supplied by the other participating enterprises. It is not a question of whether the enterprises compete with each other in other sectors so much as whether in the light of the concrete circumstances of a particular case there is a possibility that in the foreseeable future they may compete with each other with regard to the products or services involved. If the absence of competition between the enterprises and the maintenance of this situation are based on agreements or concerted practices, there may be a restraint of competition.

But even in the case of consortia formed by enterprises which normally compete with each other there is no restraint of competition if the participating enterprises cannot execute a specific order by themselves. This applies in particular if, for lack of experience, specialized knowledge, capacity or financial resources, these enterprises, when working alone, have no chance of success or cannot finish the work within the required time-limit or cannot bear the financial risk.

Nor is there a restraint of competition if it is only by the setting up of a consortium that the enterprises are put in a position to make an attractive offer. There may, however, be a restraint of competition if the enterprises undertake to work solely in the framework of a consortium.

6. Agreements having as their *sole object*:

(*a*) Joint selling arrangements.
(*b*) Joint after-sales and repairs service, provided the participating enterprises are not competitors with regard to the products or services covered by the agreement.

As already explained in detail under heading 5, co-operation between enterprises cannot restrict competition if the firms are not in competition with each other. There are other cases of less importance.[18]

VII. PROCEDURE

If a client is clearly exempt from notification, nothing need be done. If not, action should be speedy. Matters which are not *clearly*

18. '7. Agreements having joint advertising as their *sole object* . . .
   8. Agreements having as their *sole object* the use of a common label to designate a certain quality, where the label is available to all competitors on the same conditions.'

exempt from notification should be notified to the Commission on forms A and B 'as a precaution only'. If you consider Article 85(1) to be inapplicable, you must say so; if you want, in addition, a declaration of inapplicability under Article 85(3) you must say so, giving reasons. Forms A and B are to be found in Cawthra at pp. 121–5.

It is only when Article 85(1) has been infringed and there is no defence under Article 85(3) that there may be legal consequences. Even here, as we have seen, if the agreement has been duly notified, there will be a *locus poenitentiae* in which the *notified* agreement that would otherwise be void can be put right by arrangement with the Commission to modify. If this cannot be done, there is a liability not only to avoidance but also to fine.

Decisions of the Commission may be attacked in the Court if they are *ultra vires* as Professor Street has shown (above, chapter IV). This is why, technically, any exemption 'is without prejudice to any interpretation by the Court of Justice of the European Communities'.

If a firm were *bona fide* to rely on and comply with, say, the notice of 27 May 1970, or that of 21 December 1971, then this ought to make the Commission and the Court reluctant to fine, though of course, if it were proved that Article 85 had in fact been 'noticeably' infringed a revision of the agreement would be necessary.

When an agreement is notifiable and notified there are these five situations:

1. A negative clearance permits the contract to continue as drawn, for example in *S.A. des Fabricants de Conserve*, where an export agreement between six small French vegetable concerns was permitted; without such agreement they would not have been able to offer the vegetables outside France (fifth General Report on the Activities of the Committees, 1971, p. 97). For other clearances see the second General Report, 1968, p. 46 (*SOCEMAS*). In the third General Report, 1969, p. 64, it is stated that:

The exemptions granted on 22 July 1969 in the cases *Clima Chappée-Buderus* and *Jaz-Peter* concern two agreements to specialise in the manufacture of air-conditioning equipment and of clocks respectively, each concluded between one French and one German company. The two decisions confirm that the Commission takes a favourable view of co-operation agreements of this kind and that other specialisation agreements between firms from different Member States, offering comparable advantages, might be encouraged.

The negative clearance granted on 5 December 1969 in the case *Dunlop–Pirelli* concerns two reciprocal agreements on the manufacture of tyres and inner tubes by each of the two firms for the account of the subsidiary of the other party. The decision does not affect the Commission's future attitude to similar cases of reciprocal agreements on production for account of another firm, where such agreements are concluded in different economic circumstances.

2. In some cases the commission allows the agreement notified to continue as amended (e.g. *Ciment France*, fifth General Report, p. 96) because a notified agreement which is not acceptable to the Commission may be severable, and a new agreement of an acceptable character may be notified, as explained in *An Introduction to the Law of the E.E.C.*, p. 88, citing the *Consten–Grundig* case, [1966] C.M.L.R. 418 (European Court) and other cases there mentioned; see also the second General Report, 1968, p. 46 (*COBLAZ* and *C.F.A.*) and the fifth General Report on the Activities of the Committees, p. 97 (*Henkel–Colgate Palmolive*).

3. If the agreement is bad and is not amended, it should lapse (*Belgian Wall and Floor Tiles* case, in fifth General Report, p. 96).

4. If a void agreement is not allowed to lapse, but continues to be operated, the Commission may impose a heavy fine.

5. When there is wilful failure to notify a notifiable agreement, the agreement may then not be amendable; it will be void, and heavy penalties may be imposed. The highest penalty imposed by the Commission known at the time of writing (the end of 1972) is that of £4·2 million imposed on a group of fifteen E.E.C. sugar refining companies (see *The Times*, 14 and 19 December 1972).

In *An Introduction to the Law of the E.E.C.*, p. 82, reference is made to the *Dyestuffs* case, where there had been illegal price-fixing in relation to business in the Common Market by an unnotified agreement which *should have been notified*. Despite a Foreign Office memorandum protesting at the very heavy fine imposed by the Commission on I.C.I. by an overseas body (*ibid.*, p. 83) the Court of the European communities at Luxembourg upheld the Commission. (Of course, the Foreign Office objection to the fine *by a foreign body* could no longer apply now that, as members, Britain has accepted the Commission and the Court.) The long judgment of the Court in the I.C.I. case will repay attention.

In his submission before the Court the Advocate General observed:

Article 85 indisputably gives as the sole criterion the anti-competitive effect in the Common Market, without taking into account either nationality or the locality of the headquarters of the undertakings responsible for the breaches of competition. The same applies under Article 86 as regards abusive exploitation of a dominant position.[19]

At p. 627 the Court, in turning down the appeal by I.C.I., made it clear that:

The general and uniform increase, on these various markets, is only explicable by the convergent intention of these enterprises, on the one hand to redress the level of prices and the situation arising from competition under the form of discounts and, on the other hand, to avoid the risk, inherent in any price increase, of a change in the conditions of competition. The fact that for Italy the price increases announced were not applied, and that A.C.N.A. only partially followed the 1967 increase on the other markets, far from invalidating this conclusion, tends to confirm it. While it is permissible for each manufacturer to change his price freely and to take into account for this purpose the behaviour, present and foreseeable, of his competitors, it is on the other hand, contrary to the competition rules of the Treaty for a manufacturer to co-operate with his competitors, in whatever manner, to determine a co-ordinated course of action relating to an increase in prices, and to ensure its success by the prior elimination of all uncertainty as to mutual behaviour relating to the essential elements of this action, such as rates, subject matter, date and place of the increases.

It must not be forgotten too that an individual or firm may file a complaint against a firm operating in the Market, and the Commission and the Court do not need to be shown that there is a formal contract between the parties. Consideration for a contract, understanding or a gentlemen's agreement is not necessary to enable Article 85 to be applied.

Moreover, the Commission and the Court tend to look at the facts rather than legal forms when groups of companies are involved. In the *I.C.I.* case the Court seems to have confirmed the *Christiani* case, [1969] C.M.L.R. 36 (*An Introduction to the Law of the E.E.C.*, p. 92) but observed that a parent company could not shelter behind the separate personality of a subsidiary firm.

In these circumstances the formal separation between the companies, arising from their distinct legal personality, cannot, for the purpose of application of the competition rules, prevail against the unity of their behaviour on the market. Thus, it is indeed the applicant which carries out the concerted practice within the Common Market.[20]

19. *I.C.I. and Others* v. *E.E.C. Commission*, European Court of Justice, [1972] C.M.L.R. 557.
20. *I.C.I.* judgment, and see Mr Flanagan's appendix 'The concept of "enterprise" ', p. 124 below.

VIII. CONCLUSION

A penalty or fine imposed indicates that the E.E.C. Treaty resembles a penalty imposed by a trade association. It is not a fine imposed for a crime. Consequently, the assimilation of an infringement of an Article 85 fine to a crime seems somewhat misleading.[21]

If the Commission or the Court had to require proof of 'criminal intent', its job of protecting the consumer would be impossible. The Commission is, however, strict.

In the *Brasserie De Haecht* case, No. 2 [1973] C.M.L.R. 287, the Community Court held that no action could be brought for violating a 'tied house' agreement between Belgians, in respect of the sale of Danish beer, since the 'tied house' agreement was illegal and was not saved by Article 85(3) and Article 9(3) of Council Regulation No. 17 (Cawthra, p. 48), which leaves member States free to apply Articles 85 and 86 until the Council has indicated a procedure for negative clearance or to terminate an infringement.

The Court held that the mere acknowledgment of a model 'tied house' agreement by the Commission did not amount to the institution of proceedings under Regulation 17.

The Community Court had already said in December 1967 that tied houses were unlawful if they impeded the 'free flow of goods between Member States'. Nevertheless, Haecht merely filed the same type of 'tied house' agreement with the Commission. Thus the Court was not estopped from holding the agreement retroactively invalid.

Again, where an objectionable agreement between cement manufacturers was ended nineteen days before the decision of the Commission, without the Commission being informed, the Court held that the agreement was rightly held by the Commission to be invalid; *Vereeniging Van Cementhandelaren* v. *E.E.C. Commission*, 17 October 1972, [1973] C.M.L.R. 1.

Finally, whenever there is a new branch of international economic law such as the law of the E.E.C. we must be prepared for experiment and, if necessary, we, as lawyers, must increasingly call on the services of economists and accountants and on specialists in this new legal field.

21. See F. A. Mann, *I.C.L.Q.*, [1973], 35, at p. 38.

Chapter IX

INDUSTRIAL PROPERTY RIGHTS
IN THE E.E.C.

Maurice Kay

I. INTRODUCTION

Chapters VII and VIII on monopolies and restrictive practices have demonstrated the rigour of Community law in the promotion of competition. My concern here is with a closely related matter, namely the extent to which industrial and intellectual property rights (patents, trade marks, registered designs and copyright) existing under the laws of individual member States may be affected by Community law on such matters as competition and the free movement of goods.

Before embarking on an examination of the provisions of the Treaty of Rome and decisions of the Community Court of Justice which are relevant to this question, two introductory observations are necessary. The first is that the reconciliation of industrial property rights (which may be loosely described as statutory monopolies of a limited nature) with modern legislation aimed at curbing monopolies and restrictive business practices has proved to be difficult in all countries whose national law contains both elements.[1] Witness, for example, the recent movement of the American anti-trust authorities against the Xerox Corporation, which claims to be doing no more than exercising its patent rights,[2] and the reference to the Monopolies Commission in this country of Pilkington Bros.' dominant position as glass suppliers, which is also protected by patents.[3] That the analogous problem should arise in the context of Community law was only to be expected.

1. See the O.E.C.D. report *Market Power and the Law*, 1970, pp. 173–80; Gardiner, 'Industrial and intellectual property rights: their nature and the law of the European Communities', [1972] 88 *L.Q.R.* 507; Buxbaum, 'Restrictions inherent in the patent monopoly', [1965] 113 *U. Pennsylvania L.R.* 633. Cf. the little-used compulsory licence provisions of our Patent Act, 1949, ss. 37–40.

2. See *The Times*, 8 December 1972.

3. See *Report on the Supply of Flat Glass*, 1968, which was favourable to the company, and *Report on Chlordiezepocide*, 1973, the best example.

This leads me to the second introductory observation. There exists, as Professor Wortley has described, a body of purpose-built Community law aimed at curbing monopolies and restrictive business practices.[4] However, at present there is no *Community* law which confers industrial property rights. There are nine different national systems, which are competent to create and protect such rights on a territorial basis only. It is true that a manufacturer can protect himself by acquiring rights in a plurality of countries and that he is assisted in his task by international agreements,[5] but the rights he so acquires are essentially separate, national and territorial. Projects for a European system of granting patents and the provision of a single Community patent are being undertaken, as we shall see. However, it will be some time before these projects are turned into positive Community law, and, even when they are, the other types of industrial and intellectual property will still be the preserve of national law for a considerable time to come.[6] Thus concern here is not merely with the relationship between industrial property law and competition law, but also with that between nine national systems of industrial property law on the one hand and *Community* law relating to competition and the free movement of goods on the other.

II. THE TREATY PROVISIONS

The provisions of the Treaty of Rome which have fallen to be interpreted in this context are:

1. Article 222, which provides that the Treaty shall in no way prejudice the laws of member States governing forms of ownership.
2. Article 36, which provides that Articles 30–34 (which prescribe quantitative restrictions on imports and exports and abolish quotas).

   shall not preclude prohibitions or restrictions on imports, exports or goods in transit, justified on the grounds of public morality, public policy, public safety or security . . . or *the protection of industrial and commercial property*. Such prohibitions or restrictions shall not, however,

4. There is also, of course, national law of varying kinds dealing with these matters in all of the member States.
5. See especially the Paris Convention for the Protection of Industrial Property.
6. See Campbell, *Common Market Law*, vol. 1, pp. 295–6, for a description of early proposals for European conventions on trade marks and 'know-how'.

amount to a means of arbitrary discrimination or to a disguised restriction on trade between member States.

Needless to say, this somewhat ambivalent part of the Treaty has proved to be pregnant with interpretation potential.

3. Article 85, which, it will be recalled, prohibits restrictive business practices founded on agreements between enterprises, decisions of associations of enterprises and concerted practices which are likely to affect trade between member States. The significance of Article 85 in the context of industrial property rights is limited to those situations where such rights are exploited through 'agreements between enterprises', etc.

4. Article 86, which prohibits abuse of a dominant position by one or more enterprises. As there is no requirement of 'agreement' or 'concerted practice' here, there is considerable scope for application to the exploitation of national industrial property rights, but only where the enterprise can be said to occupy a 'dominant position within the Common Market or within a substantial part of it'.

III. INTERPRETATION OF THE TREATY PROVISIONS BY THE COURT OF JUSTICE

This brings me to my main task, that is, to assess the significance of the above provisions for the ownership and exploitation of industrial property rights. It would seem that the best way of approaching this task is by a chronological study of the four leading cases which have come before the Community Court.

1. *Consten and Grundig* v. *E.E.C. Commission.*[7] Grundig, a German manufacturer, marketed its products through German wholesalers for the German market and through a sole distributor in each of the other member States. Consten was the sole distributor in France under an agreement whereby it acquired *in France* one of Grundig's trade marks. At the same time Grundig dealers in the other countries had accepted an obligation not to export Grundig products. In spite of these protective arrangements, a number of French dealers succeeded in procuring Grundig products from German wholesalers. Consten therefore commenced proceedings in the French courts, but these proceedings were subsequently adjourned

7. [1966] C.M.L.R. 418.

when the Commission became seised of the issue of the propriety of Grundig's arrangements in the light of Article 85.

The Commission and the Community Court found that the Consten–Grundig agreement infringed Article 85. The important point is that although the *agreement* was nullified by this decision, the registration of the French trade mark was not. In attempting to delineate the relationship between national industrial property rights and Community competition law, the Court formulated two propositions. The first is that Community law

does not allow the *abusive use* of rights deriving from one or another national trade mark law in order to defeat the effectiveness of the Community Law on restrictive practices.[8]

'Abusive use' is a concept of great flexibility against which the Court will be free to test individual cases as they arise. In the present case the abuse arose from the fact that the trade mark rights were used in order to erect a barrier to parallel imports from other member States rather than to identify the origin of the goods. The Court therefore ordered the discontinuation of the agreement *and* of the use of the trade mark rights for purposes so inconsistent with Community law, but left the registration of the trade mark intact.

This leads us to the second proposition. Consten argued that their trade mark rights under French law were safeguarded by Article 222 of the Treaty of Rome, which, it will be recalled, provides that the Treaty shall in no way prejudice national laws governing forms of ownership. The Court's answer to this was that although Article 222 protected the *grant* or *existence* of national industrial property rights, it did not sanction any and every manner of *exercising* those rights under national law. It was therefore open to the Court to limit the exercise of the rights in order to sustain the spirit of Article 85(1). The Court's distinction between the existence and the exercise of industrial property rights was bound to attract criticism, and writers have been quick to point out that the distinction may be hard to draw, 'since the rights are only substantial if they can be exercised'[9] or, in the words of another writer, 'a right cannot consist of more than the various ways in which it can be exercised'.[10] But

8. [1966] C.M.L.R. 418, 476 (emphasis supplied).
9. Gardiner, *loc. cit.* note 1 above, p. 521.
10. Korah, 'Dividing the Common Market through national industrial property rights', (1972) 35 *M.L.R.* 634, 636. See also Alexander, 'Industrial property rights and the establishment of the European Common Market', [1972] 9

whatever may be its logical shortcomings, the distinction drawn by the Court in *Consten and Grundig* has dominated subsequent applications of the Treaty provisions to industrial property cases, to the extent that, in the *Deutsche Grammophon* case, the Advocate General said:[11]

According to these decisions, the principle is that although the Treaty leaves the *existence* and substance of industrial property rights untouched (the national legislature decides on these questions) their *exercise* is completely subject to Community law.

Thus, as Dr Valentine Korah admits, the distinction 'has proved a powerful and flexible weapon for accelerating the integration of the market'.[12] It is a theme which will recur as we consider the later cases.

2. *Parke Davis* v. *Probel*.[13] Parke Davis & Co., an American company, owned patents for a particular drug in all the member States, except Italy, where drugs are not patentable. In each of the five States where the drug was patented Parke Davis licensed a different manufacturer to produce the drug. Probel managed to import the drug into Holland from Italy, whereupon at the request of its Dutch licensee, Parke Davis brought proceedings against Probel in the Dutch courts, claiming infringement of the Dutch patent. The Dutch court then asked the Community Court for a preliminary ruling as to the application of Articles 85 and 86, 'perhaps considered with Articles 36 and 222'.

The Court held that, as far as article 85 is concerned, a patentee who seeks to exercise his industrial property rights does not contravene Community law unless he does so by way of 'agreements between enterprises, decisions by associations of enterprises and concerted practices'. And whereas in *Consten and Grundig* there had been an agreement prohibited by Article 85, in *Parke Davis*, it seems, there was not.[14] However, this must not be taken to establish that exclusive patent licence agreements *never* infringe Article 85. That they may involve such infringements is apparent from a series

---

C.M.L.Rev. 35, 39ff., where the writer states his preference for the 'abusive use' approach, unencumbered by the 'existence/exercise' distinction.

11. *Deutsche Grammophon G.m.b.H.* v. *Metro-SB-Grossmärkte G.m.b.H.*, [1971] C.M.L.R. 631, 647. This case is considered below.

12. *Loc. cit.* note 10 above, p. 636.

13. [1968] C.M.L.R. 47.

14. See [1968] C.M.L.R. 47, 52, *per* Advocate General.

of decisions of the Commission in 1972,[15] but time does not allow detailed consideration of these developments.

On the question of Article 86 (abuse of a dominant position) the Court held that a patentee is not, without more, in a dominant position and that, therefore, a patentee who uses his industrial property rights in the Parke Davis manner does not, without more, abuse a dominant position in the sense of Article 86. Nor was the fact that the patentee's prices were higher than those of importers who were infringing the patents taken to be evidence of abuse.

The most noticeable point about the *Parke Davis* case is the unusual situation resulting from the company having parallel patents in all but one of the member States. The question must be asked what would have been the position if parallel patents had existed in *all* member States (a far more usual situation) and if the action in the Dutch courts based on infringement of the Dutch patents had centred upon imports of goods in respect of which the patentee had already received licence fees from the licensee in the country of origin? Although the Community Court has not yet had to decide the question in a case involving patents,[16] it seems likely that it would give a different answer. As one writer has urged;[17] '. . . in the case of parallel patents, once the article has been sold by

15. *See Burroughs A.G. and Etablissements L. Delplanque et Fils' agreement*, [1972] C.M.L.R. D67, where the Commission decided that exclusive licence agreements could contravene Art. 85, but that there was no contravention in that case, mainly because the licensee controlled only a small share of the French market in the goods in question; *Burroughs A.G. and Geha-Werke G.m.b.H.'s agreement*, [1972] C.M.L.R. D72, where the same conclusion was reached; *Re Davidson Rubber Company's agreement*. [1972] C.M.L.R. D52, which involved a much more significant market share and was held to infringe article 85(1) but nevertheless to deserve exemption under article 85(3); and *Re agreement of A. Raymond & Co.*, [1972] C.M.L.R. D45, which, like the *Burroughs* agreements, was of insufficient significance in the Common Market to amount to an infringement. Together with the Commission's official notice of 24 December 1962 (*J.O.* 2922/62) itemising clauses found in patent licensing agreements but considered by the Commission to fall outside Art. 85(1), these cases contain essential advice to anybody concerned with the drafting of such agreements. They are considered by Korah, 'Patent licences under E.E.C. competition law', [1972] *J.B.L.* 324–6, and Drysdale and Stephens— Ofner, 'Patent licence agreements in the E.E.C.', [1972] 122 *N.L.J.* 1017. See the Commission's first *Report on Competition Policy*, 1972, para. 58 *et seq.*

16. But see *Re Voran Potatoes*, [1971] C.M.L.R. 592, a decision of the German Federal Supreme Court.

17. Gardiner, *loc. cit.* note 1 above p. 524. See also Korah, *loc. cit.* note 10 above, p. 637: '. . . a restriction on imports would not be justified by the protection of industrial property rights within Article 36, as the rewards for invention would already have been reaped in the . . . licence fee'. Note too, the approach of the Community Court in the *Deutsche Grammophon* case, considered below, which concerned copyright, and the text at note 31 below.

the patentee himself or his licensee, neither should retain control over further sales within the unified market'. We shall return to this point later, in the light of the *Deutsche Grammophon* case.

3. *Sirena* v. *Eda*.[18] In this third case an American company had assigned an Italian trade mark ('Prep Good Morning') to Sirena, an Italian company, as long ago as 1937. The American company later allowed a German company to use the identical German trade mark. Subsequent events are predictable. After the coming into force of the Treaty of Rome the German company sold goods, with the trade mark attached, in Italy, whereupon the Italian company commenced infringement proceedings in the Italian courts, which eventually referred the case to the Court of the European Communities. The judgment of the Communities Court may be summarised as follows:

(*a*) *Article 85*. The fact that an agreement dates from a time before the Treaty came into force does not prevent that agreement from being caught by Article 85, so long as it continues to produce proscribed effects.[19] On the main point, the Court said:[20]

> Article 85 of the Treaty applies where, by virtue of trade mark rights, imports of products originating in other member States bearing the same trade mark because their owners have acquired the trade mark itself or the right to use it through agreements with one another or with third parties, are prevented.

This brings us back to the distinctions between existence and 'exercise' of *Consten and Grundig*.

(*b*) *Article 86*. As regards article 86, the *Sirena* case does little more than extend to trade marks the *Parke Davis* reasoning on patents. Trade mark ownership by itself does not without more place the owner in a dominant position. Nor does the fact that his prices are higher than those of the 'infringer' necessarily mean that he is acting abusively. However, such

18. [1971] C.M.L.R. 260.

19. But see Alexander, *loc. cit.* note 10 above, who points out that after 1937 'no further tie, organizational, economic or legal, had existed between [the American company] and Sirena'. He suggests that Art. 85 should be applied to pre-Treaty trade mark arrangements only when organisational or contractual connections between different owners of the same trade mark continue to exist (pp. 43–4).

20. [1971] C.M.L.R. 260, 275.

higher prices may, on account of their size and the lack of objective justification, be indicative of abuse.[21]

(c) The Communities Court also took the opportunity to accept the Advocate General's submission that trade marks are less deserving of protection than other forms of industrial property and added that the exercise of trade marks is particularly liable to contribute to the division of markets and to prejudice the free movement of goods.[22]

4. *Deutsche Grammophon G.m.b.H.* v. *Metro-SB-Grossmärkte G.m.b.H.*[23]

The last of these four leading cases is the most complex, but also the most interesting. A German record company enjoyed under German law rights essentially the same as copyright. It licensed its French subsidiary, Polydor, to market its records in France. In Germany the company only supplied retailers who accepted a resale price maintenance arrangement, which was lawful under German law so long as it was universally applied. Metro, a German retail company, would not accept the r.p.m. arrangement and was therefore unable to obtain supplies of records from Deutsche Grammophon. However, it managed to obtain such records from a Swiss concern which had in turn obtained them from Polydor in France. When Metro sold these records in Germany below the maintained price, Deutsche Grammophon sought an injunction in the German courts, which then sought a preliminary ruling from the Community Court, the question being whether Deutsche Grammophon's copyright contravened Articles 5(2),[24] 85 or 86.

The Court's ruling seems to rest not on Articles 85 and 86[25] but

21. See Alexander, *loc. cit.* note 10 above, who points out that, according to the German company, it was able to undercut the Italian company by 50 per cent in Italy, notwithstanding additional transport costs (p. 44).

22. [1971] C.M.L.R. 260, 273. The Advocate General's tirade against trade marks is at p. 264. Another point arises in relation to trade marks. They are meant to guarantee origin, not form or quality. Therefore, as Dr Korah suggests, 'If the cheaper German product was different, one might argue that Sirena should have been allowed to repel imports on the ground that it was contrary to public morality or public policy within Article 36 for the German firm deliberately to deceive Italian [consumers] and take advantage of Sirena's advertising.' (*Loc. cit.* note 10 above, p. 638.)

23. [1971] C.M.L.R. 631.

24. Article 5(2) obliges member States to 'abstain from any measures which could jeopardise the attainment of the objectives of the Treaty'.

25. The Court's view of the scope of Art. 86 in this context reflects their previous approach in the *Sirena* case. See Alexander, *loc. cit.* note 10 above, pp. 44–5.

on article 36. This was approached by way of the general introductory article 5(2). Having stated the essential aim of the Treaty to be the integration of the national markets into one uniform market, the Court continued:[26]

This aim could not be achieved if by virtue of the various legal systems of the Member States, private persons were able to divide the market and cause arbitrary discrimination or disguised restrictions in trade between the Member States.[27]

Accordingly, it would conflict with the provisions regarding the free movement of goods in the Common Market if a Manufacturer of recordings exercised the exclusive right granted to him by the legislation of a Member State to market the protected articles in order to prohibit the marketing in that Member State of products that had been sold by him himself or with his consent in another Member State solely because this marketing had not occurred in the territory of the first Member State.

The judgment raises problems relating to the direct application of parts of the Treaty addressed to States in cases concerned with disputes between *private parties*,[28] but it has assumed enormous significance in the field of industrial property by shifting the emphasis away from Articles 85 and 86 and towards the part of the Treaty dealing with the free movement of goods, and by interpreting Article 36 in a way which places drastic limitations on the use of national industrial property rights. The Court said:[29]

Although Article 36 permits prohibitions on restrictions on the free movement of goods that are justified for the protection of industrial and commercial property, it only allows such restrictions on the freedom of trade to the extent that they are justified for the protection of the rights that form the specific object of this property.

This clearly suggests that each individual industrial property right (or, perhaps, the *subject* of each individual industrial property right?) must be separately assessed. However, given the somewhat limited view taken of trade marks, as distinct from patents, in the *Sirena* case[30] and the recent statement by the Commission[31] that it considers the *Deutsche Grammophon* reasoning to apply also to patents, the *Deutsche Grammophon* case must represent a general approach to the subject which is remarkable for its rigour. Consider, for example, a case of parallel patents—the sort of extension of the facts of *Parke*

26. [1971] C.M.L.R. 631, 658.
27. This, of course, is the language of the second part of Art. 36, quoted above.
28. See Korah, note 10 above, at p. 640.   29. [1971] C.M.L.R. 631, 657.
30. See [1971] C.M.L.R. 260, 264 (*per* Advocate General) and 273 (*per* the Court). See also *Béguelin* v. *G.L. Import–Export*, [1972] C.M.L.R. 81.
31. See *First Report on Competition Policy*, 1972, para 67.

Davis suggested earlier. The reasoning of *Deutsche Grammophon* surely cuts across the use of industrial property rights to separate national markets in that way. Similarly, parallel patent licensing agreements are now equally vulnerable under the *Deutsche Grammophon* decision.[32] Thus the tying of goods to national markets within the E.E.C. is broken down by Community law.

IV. CONCLUSION

What, then, can we make of all this? First, as was shown as early as *Consten and Grundig*, Article 85 constitutes one obstacle to the exercise of national industrial property rights, provided, of course, that there is an identifiable 'agreement, decision or concerted practice'.[33] We have also seen that Article 86 is another potential obstacle, but that it has not yet been shown to be clearly applicable in any of the decided cases. Its scope is therefore rather limited. Secondly (another point traceable to *Consten and Grundig*), an inelegant but decisive distinction has been made between, on the one hand, the *grant* or *existence* of national industrial property rights and, on the other, their *exercise*. This distinction, which has become extremely pervasive,[34] lurks behind all the cases, whether their rationale is based on the part of the Treaty dealing with competition (Articles 85 and 86) or the part dealing with the free movement of goods (Article 36).

Thirdly, as a result of the *Deutsche Grammophon* case, the emphasis has switched from the competition provisions to Article 36, which is drafted in general terms and which has been interpreted in a way which has wide but ill-defined potential for use against those who seek to compartmentalise the Common Market by reliance on national industrial property rights. As Alexander has written:[35]

The law of industrial property within the E.E.C. is definitely moving towards a position where products lawfully marketed in any part of the Common Market are entitled to free circulation in that market. Article 36 admits exceptions to this rule, *but their extent is narrowing continuously.*

32. In addition, that is, to the importance of Art. 85 for all patent licensing agreements. See note 15 above.

33. An example of the latter might be the concerted use of patent rights by distinct enterprises which had no identifiable agreement.

34. In addition, note Regulation 67/67, Art. 3(b) (1), now extended, Regulation 2591/72; *Re Transocean Marine Paints,* [1967] C.M.L.R. D9; *Re Remington Rand Italia,* [1968] C.M.L.R. 249. These and related matters are discussed by Alexander, *loc. cit.* note 10 above, pp. 40–2.

35. *Loc. cit.,* p. 51 (emphasis supplied).

The most noticeable consequence of the shift in emphasis towards Article 36 is that this article does not carry with it the sort of administrative machinery and provision for exemption and negative clearance which exist in respect of Article 85. It is questionable whether either the judicial system obtaining in national courts or the Community Court under the 'preliminary ruling' procedure is particularly suitable as a forum for the settlement of this sort of dispute.[36] This makes the use of industrial property rights even more perilous.

At the beginning of this chapter an inherent conflict between competition law (and the concept of free movement of goods) and industrial property law was indicated, and also the complicating factor of there being Community law in respect of the former but merely nine different systems of national law as regards the latter. The long-term answer to this additional complication can lie only in the development of *Community* industrial property rights. At the moment some progress is being made in relation to patents,[37] but little in relation to the other forms of industrial property.[38] Let us hope that purpose-built Community law will soon endeavour to reconcile the divergent policies referred to, for the present judicial approach seems excessively burdensome to patentees, and would be counter-productive if, as one writer suggests,[39] the result is a tendency to increased secrecy on the part of inventive companies, with a corresponding increase in industrial espionage.

36. These points are considered by Korah, *loc. cit.* note 10 above, pp. 642–3.

37. See *Patents in the Common Market*, H.M.S.O., 1970, which includes the text of a draft convention for the European patent. But even this must not be taken to be a panacea. See Empel, 'European patent conventions', [1972] 9 *C.M.L.Rev.* 13 and 456.

38. See note 6 above.   39. Korah, *loc. cit.* note 10 above, p. 643.

Chapter X

THE IMPACT ON ENGLISH COMPANY LAW

Terence Flanagan

British entry into the E.E.C. has made an immediate impact on English company law in the shape of section 9 of the European Communities Act, 1972, which came into effect on 1 January 1973. The provisions of section 9 fall into four general categories:

1. Those concerned with the *ultra vires* rule.
2. Those concerned with the rule in *Turquand's* case.[1]
3. Those concerned with pre-incorporation contracts.
4. Those concerned with the publication of information by companies.

This is the order in which these matters will be dealt with in this chapter.

Section 9 is designed to give effect in English law to the first directive of the Council of 9 March 1968[2] ('the directive'). Made under Article 54.3(g) of the E.E.C. Treaty, the directive aims to harmonise the safeguards given under the laws of the member States to members of, and third parties dealing with, companies and firms within the meaning of Article 58(2) of the E.E.C. Treaty. Because the directive was not originally drafted to apply to the United Kingdom, certain amendments have had to be made, and these were achieved in the Treaty concerning the accession of the new member States.[3] In particular, Article 1 of the directive now provides that its co-ordinating measures shall apply to the legal, statutory and administrative regulation of:

In the United Kingdom:
—companies incorporated with limited liability.[4]

1. *Royal British Bank* v. *Turquand* (1855) 5 E. & B. 248, (1856) 6 E. & B. 327.
2. 68/151/E.E.C. of 9 March 1968. *O.J.* No. L 65/8, 14 March 1968 (set out at pp. 110–17 of *An Introduction to the Law of the E.E.C.*, 1972, and see *ibid.*, chapter v by J. A. Emlyn Davies, p. 32.   3. Cmnd. 4862 I and II.
4. *Ibid.*, Art 29 and Annex I, III, H. See generally Sealy and Collier, [1973] *C.L.J.* 1, and Farrar and Powles, (1973) 36 *M.L.R.* 270. For the concept of 'enterprise' see appendix, p. 124 below.

Of course, the provisions of the directive are not directly applicable under Community law. Each member State has the choice of achieving the result required by the directive in its own way. The method chosen to bring English company law into line with the requirements of the directive was section 9 of the European Communities Act, 1972. Let us consider whether the section achieves this desired result.

1. ULTRA VIRES

Section 9, subsection (1), provides that:

In favour of a person dealing with a company in good faith, any transaction decided on by the directors shall be deemed to be one which it is within the capacity of the company to enter into, and the power of the directors to bind the company shall be deemed to be free of any limitation under the memorandum or articles of association; and a party to a transaction so decided on shall not be bound to enquire as to the capacity of the company to enter into it or as to any such limitation on the powers of the directors, and shall be presumed to have acted in good faith unless the contrary is proved.

The subsection is designed to bring about those changes in English company law required by Article 9 of the directive, relating principally to the *ultra vires* rule. Before the European Communities Act, the law was that any purported act by a company which went beyond the objects of the company as stated in its memorandum of association was a nullity. Moreover, as a result of the rule in *Ernest* v. *Nicholls*[5] a third party dealing with a company was deemed to have notice of the contents of its public documents, and so would be deemed to know that any *ultra vires* activity was in fact *ultra vires*. Although according to the logic of *Ashbury Carriage Co.* v. *Riche*[6] knowledge of the third party should be irrelevant, nevertheless it has been held that where a company has power to borrow money (which must be limited to a power to borrow money for the purposes of an *intra vires* activity)[7] and it borrows money for an *ultra vires* purpose, then the loan will be void only if the third party knew of the *ultra vires* application of the money.[8]

However, the imputed knowledge of the objects clause of the company will usually prevent the third party taking advantage of this inter. For example, in *Re Jon Beauforte (London) Ltd*[9] a company

5. (1857) 6 H.L. Cas. 401.　　　6. (1875) L.R. 7 H.L. 653.
7. *Introductions Ltd* v *National Provincial Bank Ltd*, [1970] Ch. 199.
8. *Re David Payne & Co.*, [1904] 2 Ch. 608.
9. [1953] Ch. 131.

was formed to carry on the business of costumier and gown maker. It decided to change its business to that of veneered panel maker, which was admitted to be *ultra vires*. In the course of its new business the company entered into various contracts, including one for the purchase of coke. The coke was ordered on notepaper headed 'Veneered Panel Manufacturers'. Although the coke might have been used for an *intra vires* activity, the coal merchant knew that it was required for the purpose of veneered panel making, which he was deemed to know was *ultra vires*. He therefore failed in his claim to prove in the liquidation.

It was to relieve the hardship in this type of case that the Jenkins committee[10] recommended the abrogation of the *ultra vires* rule in favour of a third party contracting with a company in good faith. Section 9 clearly overrules *Re Jon Beauforte (London) Ltd.*[11] Now, in favour of the coal merchant, the capacity of the company would have been deemed free from the limitations of the objects clause. To that extent the section achieves the recommendations of the Jenkins committee.

However, one problem that arises in connection with the interpretation of subsection (1) is the meaning of 'good faith'. This concept finds no place in Article 9 of the directive, the beneficiaries under that article being simply 'third parties' (*des tiers* in the French text). It is possible, therefore, that by restricting the class of third parties who benefit from the relaxation of the *ultra vires* rule, subsection (1) fails to comply with Article 9 of the directive. However, it is submitted that where possible subsection (1) should be interpreted so that it complies with the requirements of Article 9.[12] In this light it seems possible to give the words 'good faith' a definite and useful meaning.

Subsection (1) provides a rebuttable presumption of good faith on the part of the third party, and by relieving him of any obligation to enquire as to any limitation on the powers of the directors it shows that a third party who has not read the memorandum or articles may still be capable of dealing with the company in good faith. In both these matters the subsection follows the Jenkins committee recommendations. However, Jenkins also recommended that:

. . . the other party should not be deprived of his right to enforce the contract on the ground that he had actual knowledge of the contents of the

---

10. *Report of the Company Law Committee*, 1962, Cmnd. 1749, para. 42.
11. Above, p. 112, note 9.
12. *Corocraft Ltd.* v. *Pan American Airways Inc.*, [1969] 1 Q.B. 616.

memorandum and articles at the time of entering into the contract if he honestly and reasonably failed to appreciate that they had the effect of precluding the company (or any director or other person on its behalf) from entering into the contract in question.[13]

Subsection (1) makes no express provision for the situation where the third party has read the memorandum or articles. It seems clear though, that a third party who has actual knowledge (or even a strong suspicion) that the company is acting *ultra vires*, whether through reading the memorandum or otherwise, will not have good faith. This interpretation is compatible with Article 9(1) of the directive, which provides an escape clause for those member States which desire to limit the benefit of the generality of Article 9(1) to those third parties who knew, or could not be unaware in view of the circumstances, that a particular transaction was *ultra vires*.

This still leaves the problem of the third party who has read the objects clause in the memorandum but has honestly failed to appreciate its meaning. Since such a party would be acting in good faith, it is submitted that he would be within the protection of the subsection, even if his failure to understand the meaning of the objects clause was unreasonable. To that extent the subsection does not achieve the result recommended by the Jenkins committee.[14] It seems unfortunate that the opportunity of clearly implementing the Jenkins 'honestly and reasonably' formula was not taken when drafting section 9(1).

In any event, it might have been better not to have taken advantage of the loophole provided by Article 9(1) of the directive and to have enacted something along the lines of Article 67 of the proposed statute for the European company.[15] This article provides:

In its dealings with third parties, the company shall be bound by the acts of members of the Board of Management, notwithstanding that such acts are outside the object of the company, unless the same are *ultra vires* the Board of Management as provided by the Statute. Limitations placed on the Board's powers by the Statutes may not be relied on to defeat claims by third parties.

The explanatory note to this draft article points out that the formula avoids the opportunities for litigation inherent in the loophole to Article 9(1). The same argument applies to the Jenkins formula or

13. Cmnd. 1749, para. 42(c).
14. *Pace* the learned editor of *Charlesworth and Cain's 'Company Law'*, tenth edition, at p. ix.
15. Supplement to *Bulletin* No. 8, 1970, 24 June 1970.

section 9(1); in each case the company would have to show that the third party was aware of the *ultra vires* nature of the transaction in order to use this particular loophole. The shareholders of companies would not be unfairly prejudiced by an enactment in the form of Article 67. Indeed, it is doubtful whether the *ultra vires* doctrine in its present form gives them any real protection, and the company would in theory still have a right of action against the directors in respect of any loss occasioned by an *ultra vires* transaction.

As this last statement implies, the position of a company's directors under an *ultra vires* transaction is unchanged. Equally, the shareholder in the case of *Parke* v. *Daily News Ltd*[16] would still be able to restrain the company from acting *ultra vires*. Because the subsection is silent on the matter, it would seem that the other party to an *ultra vires* contract could raise the company's lack of capacity as a defence to any action on the contract,[17] unless, perhaps, the company had already performed its part of the bargain.[18] A third party could not sue a company on an *ultra vires* transaction whilst at the same time refusing to perform his part of the contract. He would not then be dealing with the company in good faith and would be outside the scope of section 9(1).

Further problems of interpreting section 9(1) arise in connection with the words '. . . any transaction decided upon by the directors'.[19] For example, what is the position of a third party dealing with a single director, or with a committee of directors, and not with the whole board? It is arguable that unless the particular transaction has been decided upon by *all* the directors, then the third party is not within the protection of the subsection. In practice, of course, the day-to-day business of a company is delegated by the board to a single managing director or a committee of directors, so it would be unfortunate if this were the case.[20] The decision of those generally authorised by the board to run the business of the company might, however, be treated as the decision of the directors. This does, however, rather stretch the language of the section. An alternative would be to argue that 'transaction' included any broad

16. [1962] Ch. 927.
17. *Bell Houses Ltd* v. *City Wall Properties Ltd*, [1966] 1 Q.B. 207.
18. *Bell Houses Ltd* v. *City Wall Properties Ltd*, [1966] 2 Q.B. 656, at p. 694, *per* Salmon L.J.
19. 'Director', by virtue of the European Communities Act, 1972, s. 9(2), and the Companies Act, 1948, s. 455, includes any person occupying the position of director by whatever name called.
20. See, for example, table A, Arts 102 and 109.

area of policy decided on by the board, so that lower officials who implemented the policy would be carrying out a 'transaction decided on by the directors'. The simplest expedient would be to invoke section 1 of the Interpretation Act, 1889: '. . . in every Act . . . unless the contrary intention appears . . . words, in the plural shall include the singular'. However, the fact that 'the directors' is the expression generally used in the Companies Act, 1948,[21] to denote 'the board' may show sufficient contrary intention. Section 9 of the European Communities Act must, of course, be construed as one with the 1948 Act.[22]

Difficulty arises from the use of the word 'directors' in the sub-section. This may be contrasted with the terms of Article 9(1) of the directive, which refers to the company's being bound *vis-à-vis* third parties,'. . . par les actes accomplis par ses organes . . .' It appears that the Continental concept of 'organe' can include a single director. In any event, we are not driven by the directive to interpret 'the directors' as 'the board'. The opposite is true: if a third party is protected only when he deals with the whole board, the subsection might not comply with Article 9 of the directive. The uncertainty is to be regretted, but if it is resolved in favour of the third party dealing with a single director, then it is clear that section 9(1) implements to a large extent the recommendations of the Jenkins committee on the reform of the *ultra vires* rule.

II. TURQUAND'S CASE

It was pointed out by the Jenkins committee[23] that it would be no use abrogating the *ultra vires* rule (discussed in section 1 above) in favour of a third party if, at the same time, the company could wriggle out of a contract by raising the lack of authority of its directors. Although the well known case of *Royal British Bank* v. *Turquand*[24] established that a third party was not concerned to see that the internal regulations of the company were complied with as regards the authority of its agents, this was limited by the rule that anybody dealing with a company was deemed to have notice of its public documents.[25] Hence, if the articles of association made it clear that a particular transaction exceeded the authority of the

21. See, for example, table A, Arts. 102 and 109.
22. Section 9 (8), European Communities Act, 1972.
23. Cmnd. 1749, Para. 42.
24. (1855) 5 E. & B. 248, (1856) 6 E. & B. 327.
25. *Ernest* v. *Nicholls*, (1857) 6 H.L. Cas. 401.

agent with whom the third party was dealing, then a third party could not rely on *Turquand's* case, even though he was not actually aware of the contents of the articles.

The Jenkins committee recommended[26] the abrogation of constructive notice so that a third party dealing with a company should not be deemed to have notice of any limitation on the powers of the company's agents imposed by the memorandum or articles. Section 9(1) deals with this problem when it provides that in favour of a person dealing with a company in good faith '. . . the powers of the directors to bind the company shall be deemed to be free of any limitations under the memorandum or articles of association . . .'

The problems concerned with the meaning of 'good faith' discussed above[27] would apply here as well. Although the subsection does not provide that '. . . the power of the directors to bind the company *in connection with a transaction decided on by the directors* shall be deemed to be free of any limitation under the memorandum or articles of association . . .' this is clearly the meaning of the subsection, so problems concerned with what is a 'transaction decided on by the directors' occur again.[28] However, the subsection does alter the rule in *Turquand's* case[29] to some extent.

Firstly, if a particular transaction decided on by the directors is *ultra vires* the company (and so necessarily beyond the authority of the directors), the company will not escape liability to a third party dealing in good faith merely because the articles and memorandum show that the directors were not authorised to carry out that transaction. Questions of the capacity of the company to contract will not 'creep in again, as it were on a lower level', the level of agency. Secondly, even if the transaction were not *ultra vires* the company, but was shown by the articles to be beyond the competence of the directors, then the third party dealing with the company in good faith will be similarly protected. Fortunately, this type of case will now be even more rare than the former, since it is the modern practice to draft articles in a permissive form. An example of a case where the subsection might have to be involved is where the articles contain a provision that limits the borrowing powers of the directors to a certain sum. If a third party loaned the company an amount in excess of this limit, the debt would at first sight appear unenforceable against the company to the amount of the excess. However, even before the 1972 Act the third party in

26. Cmnd. 1749, paras. 41 and 42.
28. See pp. 115, 116 above.
27. Pages 113, 114.
29. See p. 116 above.

this situation might have remedies in quasi-contract, by tracing, or for breach of warranty of authority. Section 9(1) gives him a little bit more protection.

Even after the 1972 Act, the position of a third party dealing with a single director of a company is not without difficulty. In the first place, it might be held that such a party is not dealing with the company in a transaction decided on by the directors and is therefore not within the protection of section 9(1). The old rules of constructive notice of the public documents would therefore continue to apply. Secondly, assuming that the section applies and the powers of the directors to bind the company are deemed free of any limitation under the memorandum or articles of association, then the third party will be left without any action against the company if the director with whom he deals has not been authorised to act for the company, although there is no prohibition in the articles against such authorisation being given. The cases show that the company will not be bound where a single director, acting outside his actual authority, enters on behalf of the company into a transaction which a single director would not usually have authority to enter into.[30] These cases remain important after the Act: it cannot be argued that because the power of the directors to bind the company is deemed to be free of any limitations under the memorandum or articles, then the power of a single director to bind the company is deemed free of any lack of authorisation. In most cases, however, the third party will be able to rely on the apparent authority of a director[31] or other officer[32] of the company.

Article 2(1)(d) of the directive (which deals with the publication of the names of directors) adds that 'such publication must clearly state whether the persons authorised to act for and on behalf of the company may do so alone or must act jointly'. No provision is made in the 1972 Act for the publication of this information. This raises the question of whether the Act complies with the requirements of the directive, and whether a third party dealing with an English company is as well protected as he should be. Section 9(1) cannot be taken as solving all the difficulties faced by a third party when he deals with a company which then, for some reason or another, attempts to avoid liability.

30. *Houghton & Co.* v. *Nothard, Lowe & Wills Ltd*, [1927] 1 K.B. 246. *Rama Corporation Ltd* v. *Proved Tin & General Investments Ltd*, [1952] 2 Q.B. 147.
31. *Freeman & Lockyer* v. *Buckhurst Park Properties (Mangal) Ltd*, [1964] 2 Q.B. 480.
32. *Panorama Developments (Guildford) Ltd* v. *Fidelis Furnishing Fabrics Ltd*, [1971] 2 Q.B. 711.

III. PRE-INCORPORATION CONTRACTS

Section 9(2) provides that

> Where a contract purports to be made by a company, or by a person as agent for a company, at a time when the company has not been formed, then subject to any agreement to the contrary the contract shall have effect as a contract entered into by the person purporting to act for the company or as agent for it, and he shall be personally liable on the contract accordingly.

This is designed to implement Article 7 of the directive and restates the *ratio* of *Kelner* v. *Baxter*[33] to the extent that the case relates to the liability of those who act as agents for a non-existent company. There the promoters entered into a contract 'on behalf of' the unformed company. It was held that those who sign 'as agent' for a non-existent principal are liable to third parties. But *Kelner* v. *Baxter* was distinguished in *Newborne* v. *Sensolid (Great Britain) Ltd*,[34] where Newborne, the promoter, purported to enter into a contract on behalf of the non-existent company. The contract was signed 'Leopold Newborne (London) Ltd. Leopold Newborne'. This showed that Newborne was not acting as agent for the company, but that the contract purported to be made by the company itself: Newborne's signature was merely added to authenticate the contract of the company. It was accordingly held that the contract was a complete nullity and Newborne could not enforce the contract personally, as he had not signed 'as agent'. The results of the application of the organic theory of corporations in this case were described by the Jenkins committee as 'anomalous'.[35] The committee recommended that persons who purport to contract for a non-existent company should be entitled to sue and be liable to be sued on the contract. Section 9(2) gives effect to this recommendation 'subject to any agreement to the contrary' and thereby overrules *Newborne's* case.

The Jenkins committee's recommendation[36] that a company should be able to ratify a pre-incorporation contract does not appear to have been implemented. Article 7 of the directive does not require such a change to be made.

---

33. (1866) L.R. 2 C.P. 174.
34. [1954] 1 Q.B. 45.
35. Cmnd. 1749, para. 44.
36. *Ibid.*

IV. PUBLICITY

Although, taken collectively, the provisions of English company law relating to disclosure by companies are in advance of those required by the E.E.C. directive, in certain matters of detail adjustments have had to be made. Articles 2–6 of the directive deal with the requirements as to publicity, and the necessary adjustments to English law are accomplished by section 9, subsections (3)–(8), of the 1972 Act.[37]

Section 9, subsections (3) and (4), of the 1972 Act introduce the new concept of 'official notification' into English company law. This means the publication in the *Gazette* by the Registrar of Companies of notice of the issue or receipt by him of certain documents. These documents are:

(a) Any certificate of incorporation of a company.
(b) Any document making or evidencing an alteration in the memorandum or articles of association of a company.
(c) Any return relating to a company's register of directors, or notification of a change among its directors.
(d) A company's annual return.
(e) Any notice of the situation of a company's registered office, or of any change therein.
(f) Any copy of a winding-up order in respect of a company.
(g) Any order for the dissolution of a company on a winding up.
(h) Any return by a liquidator of the final meeting of a company on a winding up.

In addition, the publication in the *Gazette* by a liquidator in a voluntary winding-up of a notice of his appointment under section 305 of the Companies Act, 1948, amounts to an official notification. It is worth pointing out that the duty on the Registrar by section 9(3) of the 1972 E.C. Act and on the liquidator by section 305 of the Companies Act is not to publish the document itself but merely a notice of the document in prescribed form.

Subsection (4) of section 9 of the 1972 Act deals with the effects of a failure to officially notify in four particular cases:

(a) the making of a winding-up order in respect of the company, or the appointment of a liquidator in a voluntary winding up of the company; or
(b) any alteration of the company's memorandum or articles of association; or

37. Subject to what is said above, p. 118 about Art. 2(1)(d).

(c) any change among the company's directors; or

(d) (as regards service of any document on the company), any change in the situation of the company's registered office.

Rather confusingly, subsection (4) refers to 'the event' being officially notified, whereas subsection (3) makes it clear that in relation to the documents (a) to (h) mentioned in that subsection it is the document that is officially notified. However, where there is no official notification in the cases (a) to (d) of subsection (4) it is provided that the company cannot rely on the happening of those events as against a third party unless the company can show that the event was known to the third party at the material time.

This imposes a heavy burden on the company, as actual knowledge is always difficult to prove. But even after official notification, the company is not completely safe. The subsection provides that the company cannot rely on the happening of the event if the material time fell on or before the fifteenth day after the date of the official notification and the third party can prove that he was 'unavoidably prevented' from knowing of the event at that time. Where the fifteenth day falls on a 'non-business day' (as defined) the period of grace is extended to the next day that is not a 'non-business day'. It is not certain what 'unavoidably prevented' means, but if the words are given their natural meaning, then the period of grace will be of little use to a third party, since it will rarely be impossible for him to read the *Gazette*.

Subsection (4) marks a departure from the usual practice of the Companies Act on the punishment of offenders against the publicity provisions. Instead of suffering a default fine, the offending company under subsection (4) suffers by not being able to rely on the matters not officially notified when it deals with third parties. It should be noted that the protection given to third parties by subsection (4) is in addition to that given by subsection (1). So, for example, an alteration in the company's memorandum which has been officially notified might still be ineffective against a third party dealing with the company in good faith.

Subsections (5) and (6) are designed to ensure that an up-to-date copy of a company's memorandum and articles of association appears on the register. By subsection (6) companies are obliged to send to the Registrar before 1 February 1973 a printed copy of the memorandum and articles, with any alterations made before 1 January 1973, unless this has already been sent. In addition, where an alteration has been made by any statutory provision, thcn a printed copy of the relevant Act or instrument must be sent on or before the same date. Similar provision is made by subsection (5) for statutory alterations to the memorandum or articles made on or after 1 January 1973, except that the time limit for sending the copy of the Act or instrument and the altered copy of the memorandum or articles is fifteen days after the Act or instrument comes into force. This subsection also provides that where, after 1 January 1973,

a company is required by this section or otherwise to send to the Registrar any document making or evidencing an alteration in the company's memorandum or articles of association (other than a special resolution under section 5 of the Companies Act, 1948), the company shall send with it a printed copy of the memorandum or articles as altered.

This means that where the articles or memorandum are altered by special resolution, then at the same time as a printed copy of the resolution is sent to the Registrar (which it must be, within fifteen days of the passing of the resolution)[38] a printed copy of the memorandum or articles, as altered, must also be sent to him. The same procedure would have to be followed where the memorandum was altered by ordinary resolution under section 61 of the 1948 Act, because section 63 of the Act requires notice of such a resolution to be given to the Registrar, again within fifteen days of the passing of the resolution.

Although the two subsections refer to 'printed' copies, it is the practice of the Registrar to accept photocopies, or even typed copies. Both subsections provide for default fines.[39]

Subsection (7) provides that certain particulars must be mentioned in legible characters in all business letters and order forms of every company. These particulars need not be printed: it is sufficient if they appear in legible characters. Nor need they appear at the top of the particular document. The particulars to be mentioned are:

(a) the place of registration of the company, [i.e. England, Scotland] and the number with which it is registered;
(b) the address of its registered office; and
(c) in the case of a limited company exempt from the obligation to use the word 'limited' as part of its name, the fact that it is a limited company.

38. Companies Act, 1948, s. 143.
39. As to which, see Companies Act, 1948, s. 440.

In addition, any reference to the amount of share capital (in a business letter or order form) must be to paid-up share capital. The reference in (c) above is to charitable and similar companies which are exempt from the obligation to use the word 'limited' as part of their name under section 19 of the Companies Act, 1948. Since such companies will not be able to distribute any dividends to their members, it may be thought that section 9 need not have applied to them. This is because the directive applies only to companies and firms within Article 58 of the E.E.C. Treaty. That article excludes from the definition of companies and firms 'non-profit-making companies or firms'.

However, as Mr Emlyn Davies has pointed out,[40] 'profit-making' appears in the French text as pursuit of 'un but lucratif', and a better translation of this would be 'having for their object the acquisition of gain by the company or by the members thereof'.[41] This makes it clear that a prohibition on the payment of dividends does not make a company 'non-profit-making'.

The provisions of subsection (7) apply in addition to those of sections 108 and 201 of the Companies Act, 1948. As with those sections, failure to comply is punishable by fine.

Subsection (8) provides that section 9 (1972 Act) shall be construed as one with the Companies Act, 1948. It also makes provision for the application, by statutory instrument, of section 9 and sections 107 and 437 of the Companies Act, 1948, to certain unregistered companies. No regulations have yet been made under the subsection.

V. CONCLUSIONS

The European Communities Act, 1972, can be seen as an attempt to alter English company law to the minimum extent necessary to comply with the requirements of the directive. The opportunity to implement some of the Jenkins committee[42] recommendations was not fully grasped, apparently on the grounds that anything not required by the directive should be shunned. The most glaring example of this appears to be the failure to reverse *Kelner* v. *Baxter*[43] on the point that ratification of a pre-incorporation contract is impossible.

The Act, however, is significant in showing the effect in England

40. *An Introduction to the Law of the E.E.C.*, pp. 41–2.
41. Cf. s.435(2)(b) of the Companies Act, 1948.
42. Cmnd. 1749.   43. (1866) L.R. 2 C.P. 174.

of the first tentative steps towards harmonisation of European company laws. This enormous task is being tackled on several fronts; the directive and the further proposed directives under Article 54(3)(g) of the E.E.C. Treaty are part of far-reaching proposals which include the statute for a European company. Undoubtedly, any future English company law reform will have to take into account the reforms proposed at Community level. It can only be hoped that when further Community reform of company law takes place it will be consolidated so that we shall not be faced with a series of piecemeal reforms.

APPENDIX

THE CONCEPT OF 'ENTERPRISE' ('UNDERTAKING')

IN THE E.E.C.

To what extent do the concepts of corporate personality and of enterprise coincide? An examination of the jurisprudence of the Commission and Court of Justice of the E.E.C. on this question may give an indication of the way English courts could re-examine their treatment of the problem commonly referred to as 'lifting the veil'.

A question that has frequently arisen is whether an agreement between two associated companies whereby they agree not to compete with each other is prohibited by Article 85.[44] For example, in *Re Christiani & Nielsen N. V.*[45] the company in question was the wholly owned Dutch subsidiary of Christiani & Nielsen A/S of Denmark. The Dutch company agreed with its parent not to operate outside Dutch territory without the parent's consent, to inform the parent in detail of its works, projects and staffing arrangements, to carry out the directives of the parent company and to pay the parent company royalties on work carried out. In return, the parent company agreed not to operate in Dutch territory and to put its patents, inventions and know-how at the disposal of the subsidiary, the board of which it could nominate. Similar agreements were entered into between the parent company and its wholly owned subsidiaries in France and Germany. Christiani & Nielsen N.V. applied for negative clearance of the agreement under Article 2 of Council Regulation 17, i.e. for a statement that the agreement did not offend the rules on free competition in the E.E.C.

The Commission granted negative clearance on the grounds that Article 85(1) applied only where there was competition between enterprises that was capable of being restricted. Here, irrespective of the agreement, there could be no such competition, since the parent company had the power to determine the behaviour of the subsidiary.

This requirement [i.e. of competition] is not necessarily fulfilled, in relations between two undertakings which carry on their activities in the same sector, by

---

44. See pp. 87–8 above.   45. 69/195/E.E.C., [1969] C.M.L.R. D36.

the mere fact of the existence of a separate legal personality for each of the undertakings. In that respect, it is imperative to know whether, on the factual level, autonomous activity of the subsidiary with regard to the parent company is possible on the economic plane.[46]

In other words, 'enterprise' is an economic concept transcending legal personality. The subsidiary company here was not an enterprise but merely '. . . an integral part of the economic whole making up the Christiani & Nielsen group'.[47]

Similar reasoning was employed by the Commission in allowing negative clearance in *Re Kodak*.[48] There negative clearance had been requested on behalf of all Kodak's wholly owned subsidiaries in the E.E.C. in respect of the arrangement whereby all the subsidiaries imposed identical conditions of sale on their products. Negative clearance was granted, since it was established that in fixing the conditions of sale the subsidiaries were acting on the precise instructions of the parent company, to which they were in fact subservient.

Both those decisions were relied on by the Advocate General (Karl Roemer) in his submissions in the case *Deutsche Grammophon G.m.b.H.* v. *Metro-SB-Grossmärkte G.m.b.H.*[49] (which is dealt with more fully by Dr Kay in chapter IX). The Advocate General agreed that the marketing agreement between Deutsche Grammophon and its 99·5 per cent-owned French subsidiary was not capable of infringing Article 85. It was

. . . an agreement between two market participants who probably do not compete with one another since the subsidiary does not act independently but is subject to the instructions and control of the parent company . . . [I]f there is merely a distribution of tasks within a uniform economic complex, it does not constitute an impairment of competition and Article 85 does not apply . . . [50]

The Court did not give a ruling on this matter, since it was able to dispose of the case under Article 36 of the E.E.C. Treaty.

However, the Court has approved this line of reasoning, and extended it, in *I.C.I. et al.* v. *E.C. Commission*.[51] There I.C.I. appealed against the decision of the Commission whereby the company had been fined for agreeing with other dyestuffs producers to raise the prices of certain dyes. I.C.I. operated in the E.E.C. territories through subsidiary companies, and one of the arguments on appeal was that the Commission had no jurisdiction to fine I.C.I., a company registered outside the territory of the Community, merely by reason of the effects produced inside the Community by acts done outside. The Court dismissed this argument on the grounds that the acts of I.C.I.'s subsidiaries in raising prices could be attributed to the parent company, whence the instructions to make the increases came.

When the subsidiary does not enjoy any real autonomy in the determination of its course of action on the market, the prohibitions of Article 85(1) may be considered

46. [1969] C.M.L.R. D36, at pp. D38–D39.   47. *Ibid.*, at p. D39.
48. 70/332/E.E.C. [1970] C.M.L.R. D19.
49. 78/70 [1971] C.M.L.R. 631.
50. [1971] C.M.L.R. 631, at pp. 650–1.
51. 48/69 [1972] C.M.L.R. 556, mentioned by Professor Wortley in chapter 8.

inapplicable in the relations between the subsidiary and the parent company with which it then forms one economic unit. In view of the unity of the group thus formed. the activities of the subsidiaries may, in certain circumstances, be imputed to the parent company.[52]

This is a direct application of what A. A. Berle, Jr., described as 'the theory of enterprise entity'.[53] In Berle's view '. . . the entity commonly known as "corporate entity" takes its being from the reality of the underlying enterprise . . .'[54] Therefore, where the corporate entity is challenged in some way, '. . . its existence, extent and consequences may be determined by the actual existence and extent and operations of the underlying enterprise, which, by these very qualities, acquires an entity of its own, recognised by law'.[55]

At one time the legal person, corporate or otherwise, coincided with the economic unit of the single-purpose company or individual capitalist. Now corporate forms of business organisation have diverged from this simple pattern, with consequent difficulties for both legislature and courts. These difficulties relate particularly to the treatment of a group of companies where the legally separate corporations have become 'as a business matter, more or less indistinguishable parts of a larger enterprise'.[56] Berle showed how the *ad hoc* attempts of the American courts to make the enterprise as a whole liable for the acts of one of its parts could be rationalised by an application of the theory of enterprise entity. Professor Wortley has shown that legal development in this country has tended towards this concept.[57]

Although restricted by *Salomon* v. *Salomon & Co. Ltd*,[58] English courts have on occasion held that a parent and subsidiary can be treated as one entity. Unfortunately, such decisions are usually based on findings that the subsidiary is '. . . . the creature, the puppet . . .',[59] '. . . the agent or employee or tool or simulacrum . . .'[60] of the parent company. These terms of course, have no meaning in the context in which they are used; any attempt to reconcile the cases on 'lifting the veil' on the basis that they have a meaning is doomed to failure.[61] Yet there persists the feeling that there must be some connection between the cases where 'the corporate entity is disregarded' and that this connection must lie in the organisation of the particular company whose 'entity' has been 'disregarded'. There is a groping towards the enterprise theory, i.e. an attempt to apply a factual economic test to determine the scope of the entity to be dealt with.[62]

---

52. [1972] C.M.L.R. 556, at p. 628.
54. *Ibid.*, at p. 344.
56. *Ibid.*, at p. 348.
58. [1897] A.C. 22.

53. 47 *Col. L. Rev.* (1947) 343.
55. *Ibid.*
57 *Jurisprudence*, chapter 18.

59. *Littlewoods Mail Order Stores Ltd* v. *I.R.C.*, [1969] 3 All E.R., at p. 860, *per* Lord Denning M. R.

60. *Smith Stone & Knight Ltd* v. *Birmingham Corporation*, [1939] 4 All E.R. 116, at p. 121, *per* Atkinson J.

61. See, for example, Gower, *Modern Company Law*, third edition, p. 217: development has been '. . . essentially haphazard and irrational'.

62. See, for example, the six matters deemed relevant by Atkinson J. in *Smith Stone & Knight* v. *Birmingham Corporation*, note 16 above, for determining whether a subsidiary company was the 'agent' or 'tool' of its parent company: (1) Were the

But even supposing that it is established that two or more companies form, together, one economic enterprise, are they to be regarded by the law as one for all purposes? The answer to this question is not to be found in applying tests of puppetry or agency but is implicit in the theory of enterprise entity and is demonstrated by the reasoning of the E.E.C. Commission and the Court.

The enterprise theory serves only to resolve the problem of which unit the law deals with when the economic unit and the legal unit diverge. But the economic unit is relevant to the law only when the law is designed to regulate the behaviour of the economic unit. So, for example, in *Re Christiani & Nielsen N.V.*:[63] the Commission made it clear that the economic criterion of enterprise was to be used because what was relevant as far as the competition rules were concerned was the results of the economic behaviour of the companies on the market. If the Commission had instead applied a criterion of legal personality to identify an 'enterprise', the result would not have furthered the object of the competition rules. It would have ignored the policy behind the rules and would have interpreted the rules in an 'essentially haphazard' and 'irrational' manner, by making them strike down a harmless agreement. So in each case it must be a question of balancing policy factors to determine whether an application of the concept of legal personality is to be preferred to an application of the concept of economic enterprise.

The Court and Commission, with only the very general guidelines of Article 85 on which to work, have managed to build up a meaningful definition of 'enterprise' whereby businessmen may predict the relevance of corporate personality in the application of the Community competition rules. One can only hope that English courts follow their example in the manifold areas of law where the corporate personality of associated companies is relevant. As Lord Denning has said, 'The legislature has shown the way with group accounts and the rest. And the courts should follow suit.'[64]

---

profits treated as the profits of the present company? (2) Were the persons conducting the business appointed by the parent company? (3) Was the parent company the head and the brain of the trading venture? (4) Did the parent company govern the adventure, decide what should be done and what capital should be embarked on the venture? (5) Did the parent company make the profits by its skill and direction? (6) Was the parent company in effectual and constant control?

63. Above, note 45.

64. *Littlewoods Mail Order Stores Ltd* v. *I.R.C.*, note 59 above.

Chapter XI

THE VALUE ADDED TAX

Martin Davey

I. THE TREATY REQUIREMENTS ON FISCAL MATTERS

The Treaty of Rome specifically states that the task of the European Economic Community is 'to promote throughout the Community a harmonious development of economic activities . . .'[1] This is to be achieved by the establishment of a common market and the progressive approximation of economic policies of member States.[2] To enable these policies to be implemented the Treaty sets out a number of 'activities' of the Community, the first one being the removal of internal tariffs and quotas and 'all other measures of equivalent effect'.[3] This activity is dealt with in detail in Articles 9–37. Article 9(1) provides that the Community is to be based upon a customs union which shall involve the prohibition between member States of customs duties on imports and exports and of all charges having equivalent effect, and the adoption of a common customs tariff in their relations with third countries. A time schedule was prepared, and the aims of Article 9 were realised in the E.E.C. of the Six by 1 July 1968, some eighteen months ahead of schedule.

A similar elimination of the duties and restrictions referred to in Article 9 will take place between the original member States and the new member States and between the latter among themselves, extending over a period from 1 April 1973 to 1 July 1977.[4] Article 12, which will also apply to new member States, provides that the member States shall refrain from introducing between themselves any new customs duties on imports or exports or any charges having equivalent effect, and from increasing those which they already apply in their trade with each other. This rule has been declared to be self-executing.[5] We have seen that Article 9 provides that the Community is to be based on a customs union, but this is

---

1. Article 2. 2. *Ibid.*
3. Article 3(a). 4. Treaty of Accession, Article 32.
5. *N.V. Algemene Transport en Expeditie Onderneming Van Gend en Loos* v. *Nederlandse Tariefcommissie*, [1963] C.M.L.R. 105.

not the end. It is only one of the aims provided for in the Treaty, which also calls for the free movement of factors of production, common policies for agriculture, social affairs and transport, the harmonisation of fiscal and monetary policies and the approximation of the laws of member States to the extent required to ensure the proper functioning of the Common Market.[6] Thus the initial establishment of a customs union is but the first stage of achieving the longer-term objective of creating an economic and tax union.

Once customs barriers have been eliminated in the E.E.C., attention will be drawn to the distortive effects caused to intra-Community trade by the dissimilarities in internal taxation, particularly in indirect taxation. To discover how the Treaty of Rome provides for the elimination of some important distortive elements, we must turn to the taxation provisions[7] of the Treaty and the related provisions[8] concerned with the approximation of laws in general. Since this paper is concerned with the value added tax we shall deal now with the provisions directly concerned with the harmonisation of indirect taxation. They have been rightly described by one study as the most important aspect of the fiscal provisions of the Treaty of Rome.[9]

II. HARMONISATION OF TAX LAWS

Article 99 of the Treaty provides that the Commission shall consider how the interests of the Common Market might be furthered by the harmonisation of the legislation of the various member States concerning turnover taxes, excise duties and other forms of indirect taxation, including countervailing measures applicable to trade between member States. This provision should be read along with Article 100, which is not confined to matters of taxation, and provides that the Council shall, *acting unanimously* on a proposal from the Commission, issue directives for the approximation of such legislative, regulative and administrative provisions of member States as directly affect the establishment or functioning of the Common Market. Articles 101[10] and 102 contain provisions for dealing with either existing or proposed distortive legislative, regulative, or administrative provisions in the laws of member States.

6. Article 3.   7. Articles 95–9.   8. Articles 100–2.
    9. The C.B.I. Europe Steering Committee, in their study *Britain and Europe*, 1966, vol. 1, p. 20.
    10. Article 101 does not require unanimity after 'the first stage'.

Member States are free to maintain different tax systems, provided that there is no distortion of competition between themselves as a consequence.

Harmonisation does not mean the tax systems must be made uniform, but only that they must be mutually adapted to the extent that this is necessary to make them neutral from the point of view of competition and thus bring them into line with the competition system of the Community . . .[11]

Learned writers[12] seem to agree that fiscal harmonisation in the context of the Treaty of Rome does not require unification of national tax systems, but only their modification to eliminate harmful effects on free trade between members of the Community.[13]

Once turnover taxes or their equivalent have been harmonised, this will highlight other areas of taxation, e.g. direct taxation, which are in need of harmonisation. The ultimate extent to which national tax systems will be modified will depend upon a variety of factors relative to the economy of the member State, which must administer its economy in the light of Community policy. Even the harmonisation of rates of taxes common to member States will make major inroads upon their fiscal autonomy, bearing in mind the differing social objectives furthered by national tax systems. This problem has led one writer to conclude that, in regard to fiscal harmonisation, the only duty within the Treaty, incumbent upon member States is to realise as neutral a system of turnover taxes as possible.[14]

11. Hans von der Groeben, member of the E.E.C. Commission, in 'Policy on competition in the European Economic Community', supplement to *Bulletin* of the E.E.C., July–August, 1961, p. 15.

12. K. V. Antel, 'Harmonisation of turnover taxes in the Common Market', 1 *C.M.L.Rev.* 41; T. W. Vogelaar, 'Tax harmonisation in the European Community', 7 *C.M.L.Rev.* [1970] 323; A. J. Easson, 'The British tax reforms—a step towards harmonisation', 8 *C.M.L.Rev.* [1970] 326.

13. 'Harmonisation should be understood as the partial modification of the national legal system with the aim of eliminating permanent institutional sources which distort the action of free competitive forces and to facilitate trade across the frontiers' (Radler, *Direct Taxation of Commercial Companies and the Problem of Co-ordinating Taxation in the Six Countries of the E.E.C.*, Amsterdam, 1960, p. 220). 'It is not essential for the success of the E.E.C. to unify or standardise the various fiscal systems in respect of rates, but merely to achieve a certain uniformity in their structure' (Van Houtte, *Fiscal Problems in the Common Market*, 1960). 'To achieve a measure of agreement between the various systems of improving taxes in force in the six member countries which would allow the best possible realisation of the aims of the Treaty of Rome, namely the creation of a joint common market where freely competitive conditions will prevail' (Antel, *loc. cit.*, p. 42).

14. Antel, *loc. cit.*, p. 51.

III. WHY HARMONISE INDIRECT TAX SYSTEMS ?[15]

At the time of the Treaty of Rome all member States, with the exception of France, operated a 'cascade system' of turnover tax. This was a tax, at a relatively low rate, which was imposed on a wide range of products in such a way that each time a commodity was passed forward by a 'taxpayer' in business, in a finished or semi-finished condition, it bore tax at the rate in force. It was a tax with multiple application; each time the commodity was passed along the chain of production it bore tax and the tax entered into the price and was taxed again at the next stage. Hence the tax had a cumulative effect. One consequence was that it tended to encourage vertical integration of businesses, thus hindering the division of labour and specialisation.[16]

Thus where an integrated and non-integrated firm are working in the same industry, the former will have a competitive

15. Tax Foundation, *Tax Harmonisation in Europe and U.S. Business*, New York, 1968, p.8; Douglas Dosser and S. S. Han, *Taxes in the E.E.C. and Britain: the problem of harmonisation*, P.E.P. Papers, European Series, No. 8, 1967; *Journal of World Trade Law* (1968), vol. 2, No. 1; D. Swann, *The Economics of the Common Market*, second edition, Harmondsworth, 1973.

16. The following example illustrates the point.

EXAMPLE. The working of the cascade system in a series of transactions between separate companies as compared with similar transactions inside a single group of companies is as follows.

A. One company with the equivalent of three in production process		B. Three separate companies in production process	
1. Raw material transfer	No tax	1. Raw material sale Add tax at 4%	£100 4
			£104
2. Partly manufactured parts transferred to fabricating division	No tax	2. Sale of partly manufactured parts Add tax at 4%	£200 8
			£208
3. Sale of assembled article to public for Add tax at 4%	£300 12	3. Sale of assembled article Add tax at 4%	£300 12
	£312		£312
Total tax paid at one point in production process is £12.		Total tax at 4% cumulatively is 4 + 8 + 12 = £24.	

(From *Taxes for Britain: the Impact of the Common Market*, *Economist* Intelligence Unit and National Association of British Manufacturers, 1962, p. 13.)

advantage.[17] There is no doubt that the tax leads to firms integrating to obtain the benefits of the tax and this has created an undesirable balance between large and small firms, particularly in Germany. There are other disadvantages of the 'cascade' tax in relation to international trade, because turnover taxes qualify as rebatable indirect taxes according to the rules of G.A.T.T. (the General Agreement on Tariffs and Trade).[18]

IV. VALUE ADDED TAX—THE INVOICE SYSTEM[19]

What is value added tax? It is a form of turnover or sales tax. In theory, it is a tax imposed at each stage of the production of goods

17. In the case of example A the tax payable was £12, whilst in example B it was £24. The reason is that in the first example the article passed through one taxable stage only, while in the second it passed through three stages because it was manufactured by three different companies. Thus the cost of producing the given product (exclusive of tax) may be the same whether the production is by a vertically integrated company (as in the first example) or by a vertical series of independent enterprises (as in the second example), but as we have seen, the tax paid by the former will be less than that paid by the latter. It can be appreciated therefore that the tax induces vertical integration, that is to say, producers can avoid the tax to some degree by combining, with the consequence that products no longer move from hand to hand, and the non-integrated producer is thereby left with a higher tax burden than the bigger and integrated producer.

18. At this point it is necessary to mention two fundamental rules relating to the treatment of indirect taxes in international trade. They are the 'country of destination' and the 'country of origin' rules. Generally speaking, under the 'destination principle', when a product is exported from its country of origin any indirect tax levied on the product is reimbursed. When it arrives at the country of destination a countervailing duty equal to the indirect tax in that country of destination is imposed. This should be contrasted with the 'origin principle', under which a product bears the indirect tax levied in the country of origin, and, if exported, continues to bear it. Thus no rebate is made. On the other hand, under such a system, because there is no need to reimburse taxes on export, there is no need to impose countervailing duties when the product arrives at the country of destination. The system at present in operation is the destination principle. This is because the rates of tax are different in each country, and for our particular purposes, in the member States. With this distinction between the 'destination' and 'origin' principles in mind, it should be noted that one feature of the cascade tax is that because of its nature exporters have difficulty in discovering what taxes have been paid before the final stage. Thus when this system of taxation is combined with the destination principle, it can be seen that exporters in a country operating such a system can be refunded only an average rate of tax paid. Thus the refund given on exportation may be too high, in which case there is a hidden export subsidy, or too low, in which case a penalty is imposed on the exporter. It can be seen that in this way the cascade system leads to distortions in intra-community trade. Consequently, a substitute had to be found, and the one chosen was the value added tax of the invoice type.

19. *Value Added Tax—a Report by the National Economic Development Office*, second edition, 1971, H.M.S.O. (the 'N.E.D.O.' report).

or the supply of services, on the value added by the person concerned. In reality the tax is levied on the sale price even if no value has actually been added. Value added tax is a tax which falls on consumer spending in the domestic economy, but one which is collected in instalments in the course of production and distribution in proportion to the value added at each stage in the process. Any tax paid by the producer (in the tax-inclusive price of his purchases) may be offset as a claim by him against the tax liability on his sales. Thus when the manufacturer of a component pays to the government the tax due on his sale, he will recover it by passing it on in the price to his customer, who in turn can then count it as a credit against any subsequent tax liability on his sales. Thus as the goods pass through the distribution and production process the government receives the ultimate tax in instalments, each seller paying the tax and crediting it to his purchaser until the process ends with the eventual consumer, who bears the full brunt of the tax in his purchase price.[20]

20. The following simple example (adapted from the Green Paper on value added tax, Cmnd. 4621, p. 7) illustrates the basic working of the tax.

EXAMPLE. *Value added tax—invoice system, assuming a 10% rate of tax.*

	Tax-exclusive price (£)	Tax on transaction (£)	Tax paid to authorities (£)	
1. Producer of intermediate product imports raw materials, for	50	5	5	Producer pays £5 tax at importation.
2. Producer makes intermediate product and sells to manufacturer for	100	10	5	Producer accountable for £10 tax but takes credit for £5 tax paid and invoices £10 tax to customer.
3. Manufacturer makes final article and sells to retailer for	250	25	15	Manufacturer accountable for £25 tax but takes credit for £10 tax invoiced to him by producer. He invoices £25 tax to retailer.
4. Retailer sells article to consumer for	400	40	15	Retailer accountable for £40 tax but takes credit for £25 invoiced to him by manufacturer.
Total paid by final consumer	400	plus 40		

Each time a person pays a tax element in his purchase price he receives an invoice from the seller stating the tax paid. However, this does not apply when the retailer sells to the final consumer. The final consumer is not entitled to a V.A.T. invoice because he is not allowed any credit for the tax paid.

When a 'taxpayer' accounts to the tax authorities there are prescribed accounting periods and at the end of each accounting period each 'taxpayer' totals (a) all the tax invoiced to him, or, in the case of imports, paid by him on importation (in the latter case there is no U.K. supplier, so he pays tax direct to the tax authorities); and (b) all the tax arising on taxable transactions which he himself carries out, i.e. his sales. He then remits to the tax authorities the amount by which the latter (known as outputs) exceed the former (inputs). If the input tax is greater than the output tax (meaning that he has paid out more tax than he has charged) he will make a claim on the tax authorities for repayment of the excess.[21]

Value added tax of the invoice type is a tax on consumer spending in the home economy.[22]

Each transaction in the example attracts tax at the rate in force. Thus when the producer imports into the U.K. the raw materials at the price of £50, he must pay £55, of which £5 goes as V.A.T. to the tax authorities. [There is no U.K. supplier.] When he sells his intermediate product (i.e. partly manufactured product) to the manufacturer for £100 he must pay tax of £10, which he obtains by charging it to his purchaser in the selling price. Thus he charges £10 tax in the price and sells the product for £110. The £10 is for the Revenue, but he only pays over £10 less £5 tax already paid by him on importation with which he is credited. Thus he pays £5 to the Revenue and keeps the £5 balance, which is equal to the tax he paid on importation, so he is no better or worse off at the end of the day. The manufacturer is now £10 out of pocket. When the manufacturer sells the final article to the retailer, the former is liable for tax on the price, so he charges it to the retailer in the selling price, £250. Thus £250 + 10 per cent tax (amounting to £25) = £275. The manufacturer now hands over the tax received by him, i.e. £25, less the tax he has already paid, i.e. £10, with which he is credited. So he pays over to the Revenue £25 less £10 = £15. The retailer is now £25 out of pocket. When he sells the final product for £400 he adds tax at 10 per cent (amounting to £40) = £440. The retailer credits himself with the £25 which he has already paid to the manufacturer and hands over the balance (£40 − £25 = £15) to the tax authorities. Thus the only person out of pocket is the final purchaser, the real, in fact the only, taxpayer—or, better, to distinguish him from the taxpayer, the tax *bearer*. He cannot pass the tax on to anybody. Thus the Revenue has received the tax on the final selling price (£40) but in instalments over a period of time.

21. This could occur when a person registered for V.A.T. has not disposed of goods on which he has paid tax.

22. That the full German title of the tax is more accurate—*Nettoumsatzsteuer mit Vorsteuerabzug*, 'net turnover tax with prior tax deduction'—has been observed

It might well be asked, why is the tax not levied in conformity with its reality and collected at the final link in the chain, i.e. on the consumer transaction? To do this would be to make a retail sales tax and it would involve a very considerable burden of taxation at the final stage when the goods (or services) pass to the final consumer. It would be impracticable because of collection difficulties and the possibility of evasion. On the other hand, the invoice system of value added tax ensures that each 'taxpayer' has a direct interest in completing his returns regularly and correctly in order to obtain the credits due to him.

A value added tax which has been paid on goods about to be exported makes it easy to produce to the tax authorities of the exporting country documents showing the precise tax paid to enable an accurate reimbursement to be made or a countervailing levy to be made in the case of imports. Once the rates of V.A.T. are harmonised, member States can between themselves automatically switch to the 'country of origin' principle, since every State will then charge the same rate of V.A.T., goods can continue to bear the tax on exportation and need not be charged tax when they reach the country of destination. There will then also be a common rate applicable to goods from States who are not members of the Community, similar to the common tariff barrier which we discussed earlier.

V. THE COMMON VALUE ADDED TAX SYSTEM

Having regard to the provision of Articles 99 and 100 and the report of the Neumark committee of 1962,[23] the Council of Ministers of the European Economic Community adopted two directives, dated 11 April 1967, on the harmonisation of turnover taxes in the member States.[24] These directives are very important because any new

elsewhere: by David Stout in his paper read at a business economists' group conference sponsored by United Dominions Trust Ltd and published under the title *The Value Added Tax—the U.K. Position and the European Experience*. Another more accurate description of the invoice system is that adopted in France: 'fractional payments'.

23. *Report of the Fiscal and Financial Committee of the E.E.C.* (the Neumark report), Brussels.

24. Directives of the Council dated 11 April 1967 (67/227/E.E.C. and 67/228/E.E.C., *J.O.*, p. 1301). For English translation see *European Communities Secondary Legislation*, Part 11, *Taxation*, H.M.S.O., reproduced at p. 8011 of *Encyclopedia of Value Added Tax*, ed. G. S. A. Wheatcroft and J. F. Avery Jones. An English translation and a discussion of the directives is also to be found in 7 *European Taxation* (1967) 148, published by the International Bureau for Fiscal Documentation (Amsterdam), based on the French and Dutch texts.

member State will be required to implement them promptly.[25] The first directive provides for the removal of the cascade type of turnover tax and the adoption of a common value added tax system. The directive also goes on to define the essential principles on which the new value added tax is to be based, whilst the second directive makes detailed arrangements for the application of the common system. The first directive set a time limit[26] of 1 January 1970 for member States to comply with the directives, although this was extended by a third directive[27] to 1 January 1972, which extended the deadline for the benefit of Belgium and Italy.[28]

Member States have now all adopted the value added tax.[29] So too did Denmark from 3 July 1967[30], Eire from 1 November 1972[31] and the United Kingdom from 1 April 1973.[32] Non-member States who have also introduced the tax are Sweden (1 January 1969)[33]

25. See also European Communities Act, 1972, s. 2.

26. Article 1.

27. 69/463/E.E.C.; published in *O.J.*, No. L 320, of 20 December 1969, p. 34.

28. These States had difficulty in meeting the original time limit, and on 14 July 1969 and 12 September 1969 respectively the governments of Italy and Belgium informed the Commission that they would be unable to comply with the time limit of 1 January 1970. The Commission in the third draft directive very reluctantly granted an extension to 1 January 1971 (Italy had requested a two-year extension and finally adopted a value added tax to come into operation on 1 January 1973. The Council of Ministers gave their approval to this final extension after a previous extension to 1 July 1972. See *O.J.*, 18 July 1972, and *O.J.*, 24 December 1971), changed to 1 January 1972 by the directive. At the same time the Commission proposed the complete abolition of fiscal frontiers among member States by 1 January 1974 and a reduction of the average rates applied by Belgium and Italy at 1 October 1969. This latter point was contained in the directive but no final directive has yet been issued on the eventual abolition of fiscal frontiers, which the Commission had envisaged would take place by 1 January 1974 by way of a prior reduction of rates to two and an extension of the value added tax to the retail stage. The E.E.C. Commission prepared a draft directive for a uniform assessment of value added tax in member States for the Council of Ministers on 29 June 1973; *O.J.* No. C 80, 5 October 1973.

29. The five original member States who were operating a cascade system of turnover tax changed over to a form of value added tax which complied with the directives. France had carried out a series of tax reforms in 1954–55 and as a result had adopted a value added tax up to the wholesale stage. In 1968 it was extended to the retail stage and to services in order to comply with the directives. Germany changed over to a value added tax system on the lines indicated in the directives by a law which came into force on the same day as the French reforms—1 January 1968. The Netherlands changed over on 1 January 1969, Luxembourg on 1 January 1970, Belgium on 1 January 1971, Italy on 1 January 1973. See N.E.D.O. report, p. 31.

30 N.E.D.O. report, *ibid.*   31. Value Added Tax Act, 1972.

32. Finance Act, 1972, Part I.   33. N.E.D.O. report, p. 31.

Norway (1 January 1970)[34] and Austria (1 January 1973).[35] Switzerland is in the final stage of preparation for the introduction of a value added tax for 1975.[36] It has also been reported that Greece proposes to introduce such a tax.[37]

Let us consider the type of value added tax provided for by the directives.

First directive. The preamble to the first directive states expressly that the cascade systems of turnover taxation are undesirable in that they distort conditions of competition and are to be replaced by the adoption by all member States of a common system of V.A.T.[38] ranging over goods and services and extending to the retail trade. However, in view of the difficulties, both practical and political, which may be caused by such an extension, the directive states that member States should have the option, subject to prior consultation, to apply the system only up to and including the wholesale stage and to apply a separate tax to the retail stage or at the stage prior thereto.[39] The directive recognises the need to proceed slowly and that the first stage would at least remove the evils of the cascade tax by ensuring that within each member State similar goods will suffer the same tax burden irrespective of the number of stages in the production and distribution process, and that in international trade the amount of the tax borne by the goods will be known, so that exact compensation for the tax can be effected.[40]

The second directive

1. Conformity with the first directive involves at least a partial surrender of fiscal autonomy by member States in order to achieve the maximum benefit of the new system for the Community as a whole. The following is an outline of the salient features of the system prescribed by the second directive.

2. The tax is to be levied on all goods and services supplied within the country and on the import of goods.[41] As we have seen, member States may limit the tax to the wholesale stage, with a supplementary tax applicable at the retail stage.

3. Taxation of services is compulsory only where they have a

---

34. *Ibid.*
35. *Tax News Service*, 30 June 1972.
36. *Ibid.*, 31 May 1972.
37. *Ibid.*, 15 April 1972.
38. V.A.T. is usually called T.V.A. in Europe, a term first used in France (*taxe sur la valeur ajoutée*).
39. Articles 2 and 5.
40. First directive, preamble.
41. Articles 2 and 3.

markcd direct effect on the price of goods. A list of these services includes:[42]

(a) Transfers of patents, trade marks and other similar rights, as well as the granting of licences with regard to these rights.

(b) Activities, other than those included under Article 5(2)(d) which deals with the manufacture of goods for a taxable principal), relating to tangible movable property which are executed on behalf of a taxable person.

(c) Services directed to preparing or co-ordinating the execution of construction projects, as for example, services provided by architects and firms supervising such works.

(d) Commercial publicity services.

(e) The transport of goods and the storage of goods, as well as accessory services.

(f) The rental of tangible movable goods to a taxable person.

(g) The providing of personnel to a taxable person.

(h) Services provided by consultants, engineers, planning offices and similar services, in the technical, economic or scientific fields.

(i) The discharge of an obligation not to practise, in whole or in part, a professional activity or exercise a right specified in the present list.

(j) Services of forwarding agents, brokers, commercial agents and other independent intermediaries, in so far as they relate to deliveries or importations of goods or the rendering of services enumerated in the present list.

It is left to member States to impose such taxes as they deem appropriate in respect of the large group of services not included in the list.

4. A 'taxable person' is to be understood as meaning any person who independently and regularly engages in transactions within the scope of the activities of a manufacturer, trader or a person who renders services, whether or not for profit.[43]

5. Generally speaking, the taxable base is to constitute, in the case of deliveries and services rendered, everything which constitutes the consideration for the delivery of the goods or the rendering of the services, including all costs and taxes, with the exception of the tax on value added itself. Thus it is a tax-exclusive base.[44]

42. Annex B to Second Directive. 43. Article 4.
44. Article 8; see also Alan A. Tait, *Value Added Tax*, 1972, p. 11.

6. Certain deliveries of goods and the rendering of certain services may be subjected to increased rates or to reduced rates, and when the special rate applies, the system should provide for the deduction of the entire tax paid at the earlier stage.[45] Article 11 also provides that where a transaction is exempt or non-taxable the tax paid at the previous stage is not deductible. Exceptions are exports of goods or the rendering of services in relation thereto and the rendering of services relating to importation of goods where the State concerned has had prior consultation with the Commission, which has approved.[46] Provision is made for the situation where goods and services are used to effect both transactions carrying the right to a deduction and those which do not carry such a right, by permitting a proportional deduction.[47]

7. Every taxable person must maintain a sufficiently detailed book-keeping system so as to permit the application of the tax on value added and the control thereof by the tax administration. Every taxable person must deliver an invoice in respect of the deliveries of goods to and the rendering of services for another taxable person. Every taxable person must also send a monthly return showing all the information necessary for the computation of the tax, and at the same time he must pay the tax which is then due.[48] Variations in collection methods are allowed for limited purposes, e.g. the simplification of collection or the prevention of frauds.[49]

8. Each member State, subject to consultation,[50] is permitted to make its own provisions for the application of the tax to 'small enterprises' (not defined).[51]

9. Article 15 provides that the Commission is to submit to the Council, as soon as possible, proposals for directives concerning the common methods for the application of the tax on value added to transactions relating to agricultural products.[52] Until fiscal frontiers are abolished, member States are given freedom, subject to consultation, to apply to those engaged in agricultural activities the system which it considers best adapted to its national requirements and possibilities.

Article 17 provides, *inter alia*, that until the abolition of fiscal

45. Articles 8 and 11.   46. *Ibid.*   47. *Ibid.*
48. Article 12.   49. *Ibid.*   50. See Art. 16.   51. Article 14.
52. 28 February 1968 draft directive submitted by the Commission, concerning the harmonisation of the legislation of member States with respect to the turnover taxation of agricultural products, Doc. Com. (68) 89 (*Tax News Service*, 15 March 1968).

frontiers member States are free to provide reduced rates and/or exemptions or use 'zero rating'[53] for well defined reasons of social interest and for the benefit of the ultimate consumers.

VI. THE EUROPEAN EXPERIENCE[54]

We mentioned earlier that as far as many European States are concerned value added tax is an evolutionary step from the imperfect cascade systems. The French system was the easiest to adapt because it involved a modification of the existing indirect tax system rather than a more radical restructure, which the change involved for other States. We have already seen that Belgium and Italy failed to meet the deadline for the adoption of a value added tax, the former because of an unhealthy economic climate, with rapidly rising prices, and the latter because of the same problem coupled with fundamental objections to the concept of the tax and difficulty with relation to the removal of export advantages (through drawbacks) and to the administration of the tax. The other member States changed to value added tax within the time limits, but not without problems, although Germany seemed to encounter relatively fewer problems.[55]

The general consensus in Europe is that a single rate is preferable to a multi-rate system.[56] This is mainly because it is easier to administer and is also considered to be the most neutral from an economic point of view. It is worth considering that the reason for a multi-rate system was the fact that all the countries which have adopted the value added tax have changed over from another system of broadly based turnover taxation and therefore it was found necessary to adopt differing rates in order to pursue secondary objectives considered desirable in that particular country. There is no doubt, though, that a single-rate system reduces a considerable proportion of the administrative burden of the tax.

VII. RELIEFS[57]

Reliefs from the general scope of the tax can take several forms. One method is by exemption, which can be either for transactions

53. *Post.*
54. Tait, *op. cit.*, p. 144; N.E.D.O. report, p. 31; 8 *European Taxation* (1968) 240.
55. See appendices 1 and 2 to this chapter.
56. See the paper by Mme Georges Egret of the Conseil national du patronat français in the publication referred to in note 22 above.
57. See N.E.D.O. report.

involving a particular class of goods or for transactions for a particular class of business.

Exemption for a transaction means that no liability to account for tax to the tax authorities arises when the transaction is performed. On the other hand, the trader undertaking the exempt transaction is given no credit for tax invoiced to him by his suppliers in respect of the goods or services which he uses in the exempt transaction. He can, of course, recoup the tax which he had paid to his suppliers be reflecting it in his selling price, but since he is not accountable to the tax authorities he is not permitted to issue a tax invoice to his purchaser. Thus a 'hidden tax' element has entered into the price of the goods. If they are sold to a taxable person the latter will be unable to obtain any credit for the hidden tax. Thus exemption is by no means as advantageous as it sounds. For these reasons its usefulness lies in relieving transactions at the end of the chain (i.e. the retail stage) to which it is deemed desirable to extend a measure of relief.

An administrative advantage of exemption is that a trader whose only business consists of carrying out exempt transactions will not need to be registered by the tax authorities. This reduces costs on both sides. If, however, a trader deals in both exempt and taxable goods, he may be enabled to take credits for tax falling on to the goods which he has received to his taxable sales but not to his exempt sales. Of course, it may not be possible for a taxpayer to designate particular inputs as relating to particular outputs, and in this case the second directive provides for the adoption of the '*pro rata* rule'. This means that credit for tax on inputs would be allowed in the ratio of taxable outputs to total outputs. The ratio would provide the percentage of the total tax on the trader's inputs for which he could claim credit.[58] The second directive provides that any such assessment should be made on a provisional basis to be adjusted at the end of the year.[59] Article 11 also contains complex arrangements which are designed to prevent a trader dealing in taxable and non-taxable transactions from purchasing expensive capital equipment in a year when he dealt only in taxable transactions and then claiming credit for the tax on the whole of those assets.

Zero rating is another important form of relief which may be granted in the appropriate situation. This means that where a transaction is zero rated it is brought within the scope of the tax

58. Article 11.   59. *Ibid.*

but is subject to a rate of o per cent on outputs. If the person carrying out the taxable transaction is a taxable person he is accountable in the usual way; but the result is that his outputs carry no tax because a zero rate is applied to them, whilst he is allowed credit for the tax on his inputs. It can be seen that this form of relief differs sharply from that of exemption and is justified only in rare circumstances. It is a suitable form of relief for exports (cf. the G.A.T.T. rules discussed earlier).

We saw above that a multi-rate system involves administrative inconvenience and expense (apart from the E.E.C. requirements). In the same way large numbers of exemptions and zero-rated transactions cause a similar problem. Consequently the ideal value added tax system, whilst being single-rate, will reduce reliefs to the minimum necessary. The main broad sector relieved from the tax in all countries is banking and financial services, in which there are institutions where a value added cannot readily be ascribed to the transaction. In several countries the liberal professions are relieved or partially relieved through the application of lower rates. For example, in Germany and Denmark provisions are made for certain professional persons to choose whether to join or not, the advantage of joining being that they will be permitted to obtain a credit on purchases. It is impossible to give a comprehensive list of reliefs granted by the States operating a value added tax, but the N.E.D.O. report gives a list of the items which have commended themselves for relief in most States. They include: sea-going vessels, certain aircraft and their parts, the services of these ships and aircraft, medicines (prescribed and used in hospitals), broadcasting and television, newspapers, works of art when sold and/or exported by the artist, medical services, certain educational services, non-trading services by certain charities.

We have seen that a large number of registrable taxpayers means an increase in the cost of administering the tax and a considerable upheaval, in the way of keeping special accounts and registration with the tax authorities, for small businesses. This is mitigated in several States (e.g. Germany, Denmark, the United Kingdom) by exempting small enterprises from the law. However, in the case of the two former examples the exempt business is able to claim a credit for its input tax, whereas in the U.K. small businesses are not compelled to register but they are permitted to register if they wish. (Note the advantage of registration in regard to credit for input tax paid.)

VIII. VALUE ADDED TAX IN THE UNITED KINGDOM[60]

A value added tax came into force in the United Kingdom on 1 April 1973.[61] The British value added tax has been drafted to conform closely to the requirements of the relevant Council directives.[62] Not only does it conform in considerable detail but it is also an attempt to introduce a value added tax with optimum benefits which will readily lend itself to the later stages of fiscal harmonisation in the Community. This has been achieved by examining the operation of the tax in States which have had experience in its application. Thus it has adopted a single-rate system, which, as we have seen, is of considerable advantage from an economic, administrative and Community outlook point of view. Small traders are exempt but can opt in, and accounting is to be on a three-month basis. The tax will replace selective employment tax and purchase tax, both of which had been reduced to some extent in anticipation of the introduction of value added tax. The actual rate adopted is 10 per cent,[63] which, along with that in force in Luxembourg, is the lowest rate of value added tax in the Community. Some of the administrative difficulties caused by adopting a multi-rate system can be imagined by comparing the two returns required by the French and Danish tax authorities, which States operate a multi-rate and single-rate system respectively. (See N.E.D.O. report, pp. 47–9.)

Before leaving the British system it is to be noted that the zero-rated[64] items include food (with a list of exceptions and exceptions thereto!), water, books, newspapers, periodicals, etc., newspaper advertisements, fuel and power, the construction of buildings and ancillary matters, services to overseas traders or for overseas purposes, transport, certain caravans, gold, banknotes, drugs, medicines and appliances supplied on prescription. Exports are also zero-rated, of course.[65] The zero rating of food is unique amongst member States of the Community.

60. White Paper *Value Added Tax*, Cmnd. 4929; see also *Report of the Committee on Turnover Taxation*, Cmnd. 2300, 1964, and D. Dosser, *British Taxation and the Common Market*, London, 1973.

61. Finance Act, 1972, and Orders made thereunder.

62. Although the government has justified the tax on economic grounds.

63. *Ibid.*, s. 9. This could have been altered before 1 April 1973 by the Treasury, to a rate between $7\frac{1}{2}$ and $12\frac{1}{2}$ per cent and thereafter it can be altered by 20 per cent of the rate. In his budget speech of 6 March 1973 the Chancellor of the Exchequer announced that the rate would be 10 per cent.

64. For details see Finance Act, 1972.

65. Finance Act, 1972, s. 12.

IX. THE TREATY OF ROME—ARTICLES 92 AND 95-8

Article 92 declares that aids which distort or threaten to distort competition, by favouring certain undertakings or the production of certain goods, are incompatible with the Common Market. It also provides for certain other categories of aids which either are or may be considered by the Commission to be compatible with the Common Market.[66]

Article 95 specifically prohibits the imposition on products imported from other member States of any internal taxation of any kind in excess of that imposed directly or indirectly on similar domestic products. The article also prohibits the imposition on the products of other member States of any internal taxation of such a nature as to afford indirect protection.

It has now been held that a particular levy cannot be both a tax with equivalent effect to a customs duty in the sense of that phrase in Articles 9 and 12 of the E.E.C. Treaty (which prohibit increases in existing customs duties and the imposition of new customs duties on imports or exports, or any charges having equivalent effect) and an internal tax to which Article 95 applies. In *Deutschmann* v. *Aussenhandelsstelle für Erzeugnisse der Ernährung und Landwirtschaft*[67] the Community Court of Justice was asked for a preliminary ruling by the Verwalterungsgericht of Frankfurt-am-Main as to whether administrative charges made when import licences for food and other agricultural products were issued, and without payment of which the licences would not be issued, were within Article 95. The Court was of the opinion that they would not be within the scope of Article 95. It was argued that the charges were within the scope of Article 95 because they did not apply to similar national products and they indirectly burdened the imported product itself. However, the Federal Republic of Germany successfully argued that because of the context of Article 95 in the Treaty it must apply only to taxes in the strict sense of the word. Clearly, a single charge of tax cannot be within the scope of both Article 95 and Articles 9 and 12 (because the Treaty provides a different phasing out procedure for the different types of obstacle to free movement of goods with which those articles are concerned). Thus it would appear that Article 95(1) applies only to internal taxes which affect both imports

66. Articles 93 and 94.
67. 9 *Recueil* 607-8, 8 July 1965 (case 10/65), [1965] C.M.L.R. 265.

and national products, but the former more harshly than the latter.[68]

There is no doubt, of course, that a value added tax is within the scope of the article. It is also important to note that the Court of Justice has also held that as Article 95 is a provision of the Treaty which imposes clear and unqualified obligations upon member States and which requires no further action for its implementation, it is directly effective and can be relied upon by individuals before their national courts.[69]

Article 95 states that 'No Member States shall impose, directly or indirectly, any internal taxation . . . in excess of that imposed . . . on similar domestic products.' Consequently it has been held in Germany by the Bundesfinanzhof that where the tax does burden products, only the excess by which it does so is invalid. The rest of the charge is valid.[70]

Article 96 provides that 'where products are exported to the territory of any Member State any repayment of internal taxation shall not exceed the internal taxation imposed on them, whether directly or indirectly'.

Any rebate which exceeds the actual tax paid puts the goods at a competitive advantage and thus distorts intra-Community trade where an excess repayment is directly made to an exporter.[71]

The effect of Article 97 is now spent.[72]

68. See the submission of the Advocate General and also *Re import duties on gingerbread: E.E.C. Commission v. Luxembourg and Belgium*, 8 *Recueil* 813, 14 December 1962 (cases 2–3/67), [1963] C.M.L.R. 199, 217.

69. *Molkorei-Zentrale Westfälen/Lippe G.m.b.H.* v. *Hauptzollamt Paderborn*, 14 *Recueil* 212 ff., 3 April 1968 (case 28/67), [1968] C.M.L.R. 187. The above also contains a ruling on the meaning of 'a tax equivalent to that charged on domestic products'.

70. *Firma Alfons Lütticke G.m.b.H.* v. *Hauptzollamt Sarrelouis*, [1969] C.M.L.R. 221, 232–3.

71. It is none the less the case where the rebate was too high because it had to be estimated in the case of indirect taxes which entered into export costs in such a way that their true level was impossible to detect. We saw earlier that this was a great problem in relation to States operating a cascade system of tax. To date Italy has been brought before the Court on several occasions for breach of Arts. 95 and 96: *Re drawback on Italian machine parts, E.E.C. Commission v. Italy*, 11 *Recueil* 1057 (case 45/64, [1966] C.M.L.R. 97; *Re export tax on art treasures*, 10 December 1969 (case 7/68), [1969] C.M.L.R. 11.

72. It provides that any member States operating a cascade system of turnover tax may establish 'average rates' for specific products or groups of products when imposing tax on imports or granting a rebate on exports, provided that there is no infringement of the principles of the foregoing two articles. The Council has adopted a directive which introduces a common method of calculating the average rates referred to in Art. 97 (30 April 1968, 68/221/E.E.C.). The scope of this

Article 98 is a 'sweeping up' provision which stipulates that in the case of charges other than turnover taxes, excise duties and other forms of indirect taxation remissions and repayments in respect of exports to other member States may not be granted and counter-availing duties in respect of imports from member States may not be imposed unless the Council have given their approval for a limited period.

X. EFFECT OF VALUE ADDED TAX ON OTHER TAXES IN MEMBER STATES[73]

Article 98 has proved important for certain excise duties in member States.

Excise duties[74] are relatively less important in the Community than in the United Kingdom. They create a problem no less than other indirect taxes because the practice of member States is not uniform in respect of either the goods upon which the duties are levied or the rates at which they are levied.

If the common aim is to optimise both production and trade, then what is required is a harmonisation of the duties and the adoption of the 'origin principle'[75] in the same way as that envisaged for value added tax.

Consequently the E.E.C. Commission submitted a draft directive[76] to the Council of Ministers aimed at harmonising the specific taxes on mineral oils within the member States. It provided for the taxes to be harmonised by 1 January 1976. The objective is the creation of a common energy policy, the removal of distortions in the competitive conditions in the various member States which have arisen as a result of the considerable differences in the amount of this tax and the promotion of E.E.C. trade in mineral oil products. A similar draft directive[77] was submitted relating to the harmonisation of taxes on fuel oils. Also six directives have now been published concerning the harmonisation of excise duties on alcohol, wine,

---

article has been reduced gradually, as all the member States have now introduced a common system of value added tax. The Court of Justice has held that, in contrast to Art. 95, Art. 97 does not create individual rights against the member States (*Molkerei-Zentrale,* above, note 67). This is because of the discretion afforded by the article to member States, and its provision that where member States do not comply with its terms the Commission shall address appropriate directives or decisions to the States concerned.

73. See A. J. Easson, *C.M.L.Rev.* 326, 332.
74. See note 77 below.   75. Below.
76. Approved by the Council on 3 August 1973: *Tax News Service,* 1973, 1–37.
77. *Tax News Service,* 1971 1–13, 1–51.

beer and mixed beverages.[78] A draft regulation has also been submitted to the Council on the harmonisation of excise duties on tobacco.[79]

XI. DIRECT TAXATION[80]

The Treaty of Rome is specific[81] only on the harmonisation of indirect taxes, and it might be expected that harmonisation of direct taxes affecting individuals and companies in member States will present greater problems and take considerably longer than the harmonisation of indirect taxes. However, it is a fact that just as the removal of tariff barriers sheds light on the problems created by other indirect fiscal barriers, in the same way the removal of those barriers will undoubtedly lead to the revelation of distortions caused by different patterns or incidence of direct taxation.[82]

XII. CONCLUSIONS

This paper has tried to examine the taxation provisions of the Treaty of Rome in context, and particularly steps towards the adoption of a common system of value added tax. Once one particular area of taxation has been harmonised, other inequitable situations are exposed as being in need of elimination. Progress in the field of taxation reform generally has been marked and has led the Community closer to a situation where the fundamental objectives of the Treaty will be realised, providing truly equitable competitive conditions which can be utilised for the optimum benefit of all member States and their peoples.

APPENDIX I
EFFECT ON PRICES[83]

In France and Germany the introduction of the tax did not seem to have any significant effect on prices, although in the case of the latter it was introduced at the time of a minor recession when prices were unlikely to be

78. *Official Gazette*, 29 April 1972. 79. *Bulletin* 36.
80. The Commission's programme for the harmonisation of direct taxes— *Bulletin* of the E.E.C., August 1967 (supplement).
81. But see Arts. 100 and 101 of the Treaty of Rome for powers implicitly covering harmonisation of direct taxes.
82. For harmonisation of company taxation see the sources referred to in 3 *C.M.L.Rev.* 334, appendices.
83. Tait, *op. cit.*, and N.E.D.O. report, p. 43.

raised by firms and prices and costs were rising irrespective of the introduction of the tax.[84] On the other hand, in Denmark the cost of living rose by 7·9 per cent in the first six months after the introduction of value added tax, owing mainly to the tax being levied on food and also for the first time on services. However, the situation was alleviated by some very substantial wage increases shortly before the introduction of the value added tax, and it was also accompanied by tax concessions for lower incomes and increased allowances for persons not liable to tax. The sharp price increase which followed the introduction of value added tax in the Netherlands was met with a price freeze, as was the case in Norway, Sweden and Luxembourg.

APPENDIX 2
RATES[85]

The table below sets out the rates which were in force in European States which have adopted a value added tax at the beginning of 1974.

	Standard rate	Reduced rate	Intermediate rate	Sumptuary rate
Austria	16	8	–	–
Belgium	18	6	14	25
Denmark	15	–	–	–
Eire	16·37	5·26	–	30·26
France	20	7	17·60	33·33
Germany	11	5·5	–	–
Italy	12	6	–	18
Luxembourg	10	2	–	–
Netherlands	16	4	–	–
Norway	20	–	–	–
Sweden	17·65	–	–	–
United Kingdom	10	–	–	–

84. Note the current anti-inflationary measures being taken by the U.K. government.

85. Second Directive, Arts. 9 and 17.

Chapter XII

THE LAW OF THE COMMON AGRICULTURAL POLICY

Joseph Jaconelli

I. THE BACKGROUND

It is hardly necessary to emphasise the difficulties to which agriculture has given rise, both in negotiations between the original six members of the E.E.C. and in the accession of Britain to the Community. In attaining the status of the most highly integrated area of Community activity the agricultural sector has thrown up numerous interesting problems for students of various disciplines. To the economist it has demonstrated all the difficulties involved in the choice of a suitable system of agricultural price support. To the political scientist it has demonstrated the difficulties of reaching compromises between bitterly opposing national interests. It is no surprise that some of the worst crises in the evolution of the E.E.C. have been encountered in the discussion of agricultural questions, and have been resolved only at the end of very long sessions which have come to be known as 'les marathons agricoles.' And to the lawyer agriculture represents the area of economic law in which supranational control by regulation has reached its most advanced stage.

One should begin by posing the most basic of questions—why is it necessary to have regulations to support agricultural prices at all? Indeed, *prima facie*, any form of subsidy to farmers would seem to conflict with the essentially *laissez-faire* spirit of the Treaty of Rome. Yet virtually all industrialised countries operate some form of price support system for their agricultural sectors. The reasons can be found by applying to the problem the economist's analytical tools of supply and demand.[1]

One traditional reason for high maintained prices is to stimulate increased production. This is hardly a compelling motive in the

1. Further reading on the economics of agricultural price support should include Samuelson's *Economics*, eighth edition, chapter 21, pp. 385-98, and D. Metcalf, *The Economics of Agriculture*, chapter 7.

Common Market, plagued as it is by such phenomena as 'butter mountains'. The emergence of such huge food surpluses is often a by-product of support schemes based on high guaranteed prices. On the other hand, at lower guaranteed price levels farmers may find it very difficult to acquire capital.

A second reason is to protect the farmer against volatile agricultural price movements. Weather conditions, in particular, will affect the level of supply unpredictably from year to year. In addition, the long period of production involved in most agricultural products makes it impossible for the sector to react quickly to changes in consumer demand and to adjust the supply accordingly. This inflexibility may result in windfall profits as well as in losses, but small farms in particular will be especially vulnerable to any lengthy period of low prices.

The third reason is undoubtedly the most important of all: to reduce the disparity between agricultural and urban incomes. For the agricultural sectors in industrialised countries today are characterised by several features which make for relatively low returns. Technical innovation leads to an expanded output per unit of input, but as *per capita* incomes rise generally, and people become more affluent, they spend a proportionately smaller part of their incomes on basic foodstuffs. Therefore the supply of food increases considerably, while demand remains static. The net result is to depress agricultural prices and hence agricultural incomes too. This reduction in agricultural incomes should lead to an exodus from that sector into industry. Certainly this has been a marked trend in the economies of Western Europe ever since their respective industrial revolutions, but the speed of exit from agriculture has never been great enough to produce anything near parity between incomes in the agricultural and the industrial sectors. The trend has reached a very high level in the U.K., where only 2·8 per cent of the working population is employed in agriculture. In the Community, by contrast, farming was the principal occupation of no less than 25 per cent of the working population in the mid-1950's, when the Common Market was conceived, and even now the figures are as high as 14 per cent for France and 19 per cent for Italy. In economists' jargon, the productive factors in agriculture, especially labour, are relatively immobile. In one respect the U.K. has had a distinct advantage: it contains a large percentage of farm workers who are readier to move off the land than the peasant proprietors of family holdings.

The stark difference between the state of the agricultural sectors in Britain and most of Western Europe has resulted in very contrasting legal methods of agricultural price support. With a highly industrialised economy and barely 3 per cent of the working population employed in agriculture, British post-war policy has traditionally been to allow a free market for food. There has been virtually unrestricted entry of food into Britain at relatively low world market prices. Until 1973 Britain had been able to obtain most of its food requirements from the cheapest sources and at the lowest cost in foreign-exchange reserves. In order to retain such benefits while shielding British agriculture from severe price competition, the British farmer has been guaranteed certain prices in the 'annual review' of farm prices. The difference between the average market price for a given product and the guaranteed price has been made up by a *deficiency payment*. For example, the guaranteed price of wheat might be £45 per ton, and the average market price £40, so that a deficiency payment of £5 per ton would be paid to all sellers. One farmer might have sold his wheat for £40 per ton. Another, less fortunate or less efficient, might have obtained only £38. But both would receive the same deficiency payment of £5 per ton.

Thus the British farmer has gained his livelihood partly from the market in the form of the relatively low prices that he has obtained there (his prices being forced down by world prices), and partly from the taxpayer in the form of deficiency payments from the Exchequer. The burden on the Exchequer would be at its least in the U.K., since only 3 per cent of the working population is employed in agriculture and the sector accounts for only 3·2 per cent of the gross domestic product. Another virtue of this system of agricultural support is that it clearly enhances the importance of the farmer's efficiency. Nevertheless, opinion has for some time been moving away from the attractions of deficiency payments and towards the adoption of a different system of price support. The main drawback of the traditional British scheme has been that the financial liability of the Exchequer has been unlimited. A drop in the price of imports will have the effect of widening the gap between the market and guaranteed prices, so increasing the subsidy bill. Fluctuations in the domestic supply of a product may have equal results. A clear example of this unexpected rise in the subsidy bill payable by the Exchequer was the rise in the fatstock subsidy from £46·2 millions in 1960–61 to £113·3 millions in 1961–62. Such divergences are clearly embarrassing, both financially and politically.

Mention has already been made of the excessive amount of labour still committed to agriculture in the Community. Moreover, the average farm size today in the original Six is thirty acres, as compared with seventy-five acres in the U.K. Much of the problem can be attributed to the European laws of inheritance, which had for long demanded the equal division of a farmer's land among all his heirs. It was therefore obvious that any common agricultural policy adopted by the Six would have to be guided by very different considerations from those governing the British situation.

That part of the Treaty of Rome which deals with agriculture, Articles 38–47, merely laid down that a common agricultural policy should be established. This was the result of a conflict between two opposing factions in the very drafting of the Treaty. Two delegations, the French and Italian, wished to see written into the Treaty not only the objectives to be attained in the common agricultural policy but also the very means of achieving them. The prevailing faction, with a more empirical approach, wished to deal with agricultural questions as and when they arose after the Treaty had been signed. Article 39 stipulated the objectives to be attained, namely to increase agricultural productivity by technical progress and rationalisation; to ensure a fair standard of living for the agricultural community; to stabilise markets; to provide certainty of supplies; and to ensure supplies to consumers at reasonable prices. All this amounted to little more than an agreement to agree, with only the most general guidelines. Little progress was made in the stages immediately following the entry into force of the Treaty, commencing with the essentially stocktaking conference held at Stresa on 3–12 July 1958.

Now it is generally true that agricultural questions are among the most complicated in any international negotiations, so wide are the differences of principle and self-interest at stake. Before 1964 agriculture was totally excluded from G.A.T.T. agreements, and, according to one distinguished economist, Professor H. G. Johnson,[2]

The Kennedy round achieved virtually nothing in the important area of trade in agricultural products, where the protection of domestic producers by tariffs and especially by import quotas, subsidies and other governmental assistance is rampant and has been increasing perceptibly over the post-war period.

2. In Institute of Economic Affairs Occasional Paper No. 27, 1969, p. 15.

It is necessary to realise that the British system of deficiency payments, despite some of its attractive economic qualities, could hardly be applied in the E.E.C. There would have been enormous administrative difficulties in computing and distributing the deficiency payments claimable by each of innumerable small farms— difficulties which would be multiplied in the case of commodities such as barley and corn which are used by the producer himself to feed livestock. In addition, the sheer weight of deficiency payments from the various budgets would have been intolerable. The position was quite simply that neither national parliaments nor the institutions of the E.E.C. would appropriate sufficiently large deficiency payments to meet what was taken to be an adequate standard of living for farmers.

The solution adopted in the Common Market was to have a guaranteed price for each product. The Continental farmer obtains his living in the market place, by the actual price which he receives for his products, the market price being set and maintained by the E.E.C. authorities. This stands in marked contrast to the British farmer, who has gained his living partly from the market and partly from the taxpayer, in the form of deficiency payments.

The goals of the agricultural programme were to be achieved by establishing a Community market organisation for each sector of agricultural activity. This Community organisation was to be brought about in two stages. Preliminary regulations were to be introduced to establish a transitional period, during which experience would be gained, and at the end of the transitional period the original regulations would be amended or superseded accordingly and final measures of a more lasting nature would be introduced. Naturally, this gradual and piecemeal cession of sovereignty to international agencies required considerable bargaining between the parties involved. Four and a half years were required before the transitional agricultural provisions could be shaped and implemented for grains alone by the publication of Regulation 19 in 1962.

Indeed, the example of grain best illustrates the mechanics of the Common Agricultural Policy. Grain is by far the most important single farm commodity[3] and requires the most sophisticated system of market management. It had been subject to a common organisation since 1962. The next move, the agreement on uniform grain prices, was reached in 1964, but these were not implemented until

3. The prices of pig meat, eggs and poultry depend largely on the price of feed grains.

1 July 1967,[4] when the original Regulation 19 was superseded by Regulation 120/67.

A basic *target price* (*prix indicatif*) is fixed within the Common Market area for each kind of grain; this is fixed at a level which is deemed to provide a reasonable return for most farmers. Now if there were free trade, cheap imports would undercut the prices thus set. The Commission, therefore, imposes a uniform, but variable, *import levy* (*prélèvement*), which ensures that food imports from the outside world are not offered on the internal managed market at less than the target price. The import levy is varied as often and as much as necessary to make up the difference between the lowest price on the world market and the target price. Any change in the world price is therefore reflected immediately in the amount of the levy. Although the size of the levy may change from day to day, the size of the levy at any one point of time is uniform at every point of the Community border. As long as the local market price is below the target price the levy excludes all imports, because purchasers will not find it profitable to buy imported products. Therefore, under this system, non-E.E.C. countries are relegated to the status of residual suppliers.

If prices should fall inside the E.E.C. market (for example, because of an excessive supply of grain), there is a *support price* or *intervention price* (*prix d'intervention*) which is about 8 per cent below the target price. If the market price falls to this level it will be held there by support buying on the part of the Commission itself. This is achieved through a special body, the European Agricultural Guidance and Guarantee Fund (F.E.O.G.A., as it is better known from its French initials), which has officers stationed at each of the main marketing centres in the Community. If the price falls to this support level, these officers are obliged to buy everything offered to them at that price. Thus support prices are the effectively guaranteed prices for producers. They result in a complete removal from the internal market of that portion of the supply which cannot be sold at or above the support price.

The above model is, however, rather simplified. There are three important refinements to the support system relating to time, space, and the diversity of the products involved.[5]

---

4. For an account of the bargaining which led to uniform grain prices see *La Décision dans les Communautés européennes*, ed. Gerbet and Pepy, pp. 269–96, 'L'Adoption du prix unique des céréales'.

5. A detailed analysis of these three refinements is contained in Kenneth W. Dam, 67 *Columbia L.R.* (1967) 209, at pp. 222ff.

Firstly, time is a complicating factor. Grains are normally produced once a year but are required for consumption, and hence are purchased, throughout the whole year. Therefore the grain price is seasonally stepped up in the course of the year following the harvest; target and support prices are increased during the marketing year to reflect such factors as storage and interest costs, the state of grain stocks, etc. Farmers are thus induced to hold harvested stocks until they are needed instead of selling them immediately.

The second refinement is caused by the diversity of products and qualities all caught by the title of 'grains'. The analysis so far has treated grains as a unitary product. However, the fact is that each major grain is a substitute, to a greater or lesser extent, for every other grain. Therefore target and support prices for one type of grain cannot be set without taking account of the prices for other grains. When the final uses are alike in the eyes of the consumer, then rather small relative changes in price may sharply affect the pattern of consumption (and indeed production also), especially if these changes are considered likely to last for any considerable length of time.

If the difference in quality between domestic and imported grains were left out of account in calculating the levy, then the levy would be unable to carry out its function of protecting the internal market. If it be assumed that the domestic E.E.C. price for wheat is £40 per ton, and the world market price for higher quality wheat of the same type is £35, a levy of the difference, (£5 per ton), would not keep out the higher quality foreign wheat. With both domestic and foreign wheat selling for £40 per ton, consumers would prefer the foreign, higher-quality wheat. Therefore the levy must exceed £5 by the value of the quality difference.

The third and most important refinement is that of space. Transport costs for agricultural commodities are so important that no marketing system can ignore them. It is because of these transport costs that it is impossible to have unitary target and support prices, identical for any one commodity at all points of the Community. Obviously, some areas within the Community are deficit areas, while others are ample grain-producing areas, always eager to gain new markets for their produce.[6] At present the area of greatest grain scarcity in the Common Market is considered to be the Ruhr, in which the main marketing centre is Duisburg. In order to attract

6. France, in particular, was most eager to promote a common organisation in grains so that she could sell her considerable surpluses in the rest of the Six.

grain to Duisburg, this was made the highest-priced point. Thus wheat would be attracted there both from France and from outside countries (through the port of Rotterdam). The price differential has to be large enough to persuade, for example, French grain dealers to transport their grain to Duisburg and sell it there, rather than to sell it nearer home. The price fixed for Duisburg, being the area of greatest scarcity, is the basic (and the highest) target price for the whole Community, and from it are calculated regional target prices, which have to be adjusted so as to encourage a flow of stable inter-regional trade.

The port of Rotterdam is the main entry for imported grains supplying the Ruhr. There, as at other Community ports, is a minimum import price at which non-E.E.C. supplies of grain can be delivered; this is called the *threshold price (prix de seuil)*. Grain shipped to the E.E.C. which is below the threshold price is brought up to this level by the variable import levy. The threshold price set at Rotterdam must be lower than the Duisburg price in order to allow for transport costs to the Ruhr. Thus the levy for any particular day is calculated by taking the target price at Duisburg, deducting the cost of transport from Rotterdam to Duisburg, and then deducting the world market price. The result is that by the time the wheat reaches Duisburg, where it is particularly needed, it will be on sale at the target price set for Duisburg, regardless of its origin.

Target price set for Duisburg	£44 –
Cost of transport–Rotterdam–Duisburg	2
	42 –
World price	34
Levy for that day	£8

The Common Agricultural Policy, as outlined above in regard to grains,[7] has certain advantages for the farmer. His subsidy is contained in the food prices themselves, and like any subsidy recipient he prefers to keep the subsidy free from review in a budget. From the consumer's point of view, his food prices will be higher, but less money needs to be raised from him in taxation, since the Exchequer no longer gives out deficiency payments. Therefore the E.E.C.

---

7. Obviously, since some products are perishable, they cannot be subjected to such a sophisticated system as is employed in regard to grain. There are thus many variations on the basic model of grain marketing, the variation employing such differentiated terminology as 'sluice-gate price' (*prix d' écluse*), 'basic price' (*prix de base*), and 'guide price' (*prix d'orientation*).

system affects the individual *qua* consumer rather than the individual *qua* taxpayer.

The discussion so far has taken grains by way of example only. Other types of agricultural produce have been assimilated into the common organisation in successive stages, so that by the end of 1968 common price and marketing arrangements were largely in operation for all the main temperate agricultural products, accounting for more than 90 per cent of agricultural production in the E.E.C. It is necessary to qualify this success by pointing out that trade in most products is still subject to technical restrictions (e.g. as to grade, purity regulations, and permissible additives) and that progress in the removal of such non-tariff barriers by means of harmonisation of the relevant laws has so far not been as rapid.

During 1962–63 and 1963–64 grains, grain product, pig meat, poultry and eggs were the main products which became subject to the common organisation and eligible for price support from F.E.O.G.A. Milk, milk products, and fruit and vegetables were added subsequently. Beef and veal, sugar, certain processed agricultural products and grape seed oil were added in 1967–68.

In view of this gradual assimilation of agricultural produce into Community control, it is important to realise that member States do retain their original jurisdiction over matters which have not yet been subjected to Community legislation. In these matters at least the member States retain an unfettered hand. This point was clearly demonstrated in *Re import licence for oats.*[8] The background to this case was that a bond had to be deposited with the relevant authorities in order to obtain an import certificate under Regulation 19 of the E.E.C. council (the original grain regulation.) The actual amount of such bonds had been left to be fixed by the member States themselves, who had fixed differing amounts for them. It was complained to the Community Court that this arrangement conflicted with the ideal of a common price policy for agricultural products, and moreover was economically discriminatory.

In rejecting these arguments the Court held that member States had an original jurisdiction in these matters and did not require delegated authority from the E.E.C. to regulate matters which were not, as yet, the subject of Community legislation. The Court observed (at p. 114).

Provision has not yet been made for the amount of the bond under the cumbersome procedure of Article 26 of Regulation 19 . . . Article 39(2) of

8. [1968] C.M.L.R. 103.

thc Treaty states that the appropriate adjustments need to be made gradually. By Article 40(1) [of the Treaty of Rome], 'the Member States shall *gradually* develop the common agricultural policy during the transitional period'. Again, the reference in Article 40(3) of the Treaty to a 'common price policy, *if any*, implies that a common agricultural market can only be developed step by step . . . and Article 26 of Regulation 19 envisages a cautious process of harmonisation for specific difficult points, which include particular problems about the system of bonds, through the intervention of the Management Committee for Cereals, consisting of representatives of the Member States.

. . . The aim of the E.E.C. Treaty and Regulation 19 in all respects is not to bring about a precipitate assimilation of the agricultural policies of the Member States, which have agricultural structures differing widely in many respects. It is clear that, with so many measures of integration needing to be effected, those which will enable the agricultural market to get started must be taken first.

Thus if a particular sphere of agricultural activity has not yet been subjected to Community control, the individual member States retain their full original jurisdiction on the matter. The opposite side of this coin is demonstrated by the case of *Hauptzollamt Bremen-Freihafen* v. *Bremer Handelsgesellschaft*,[9] where a national authority illegally ruled on a matter which was in fact encompassed by Community law. The question in issue was essentially one of interpretation, whether the agricultural commodity in issue was 'manioc flour' under Article 1(d) of Regulation 19 (and so subject to the Community levy) or whether it fell within a certain tariff heading which had remained outside the scope of Regulation 19 (and so was free from customs duties and levies).

Article 23(1) of Regulation 19 forbids member States to issue internal provisions affecting the scope of the Regulation on the definition of the product to which it refers, even where there is *no relevant Community interpretation*. The Court ruled that its interpretation of Regulation 19 must prevail.

At p. 486 of the judgment it was said.

Since, by virtue of Article 189(2) of the Treaty, Regulation 19 is directly applicable in all the Member States, in the absence of provisions to the contrary, the Member States are prohibited from adopting measures for the implementation of the regulation intended to modify its scope or add to its provisions. To the extent that the Member States have assigned legislative powers in tariff matters to the Community in order to ensure the proper operation of the common agricultural market, they no longer have the power to make autonomous provisions in this field.

And at p. 487, 'Common organisations of agricultural markets such

9. [1970] C.M.L.R. 466.

as that which is to be established by Regulation 19 can only fulfil their purpose if the provisions made for their realisation are uniformly applied in all the Member States . . .'

Finally, in dealing with the mechanics of the Common Agricultural Policy, it is necessary to discuss the mode of its financing[10] through F.E.O.G.A. The establishment of such a fund was envisaged in Article 40(4)[11] of the Treaty of Rome and implemented by the controversial Regulation 25 of 4 April 1962, supplemented by Regulation 17/64 (concerning the conditions for obtaining aid from F.E.O.G.A.). Articles 2 and 3(1) of Regulation 25 stipulate the expenses to be covered by the fund; they are in respect of:—

(a) 'Measures adopted with a view to stabilising markets.' This function has already been amply covered in the discussion of support buying of grains.

(b) 'Joint action decided on in order to achieve the objectives defined in Article 39(1)(a) of the Treaty, including structural alterations required for the smooth working of the Common Market . . .' The main effort in this direction has been the Mansholt plan (*Agriculture 1980*), published in 1968 and discussed later in this chapter.

(c) 'Refunds on exports to third countries.' The essence of the Common Agricultural Policy for most products is the ideal of 'Community preference'. It has already been pointed out that third countries are relegated, through the operation of the import levies, to the status of residual suppliers; they are regarded, in addition, as a residual market. Under normal circumstances, the high level of administered Community prices would render it impossible for E.E.C. food exporters to compete on world markets.

Therefore, export subsidies, financed by F.E.O.G.A.,[12] are payable in respect of most products of which there is a surplus within the E.E.C. market. The main implementation of this scheme of export refunds is to be found in Regulation 1041/67. It has been held in *Re rotten sausages*[13] that where food intended for human consumption

10. For the development of the method of financing the Common Agricultural Policy, refer to Gerbet and Pepy, *loc. cit.*, pp. 297–321, 'Le Financement de la politique agricole commune'.

11. Article 40(4) reads: 'In order to enable the common organisation referred to in paragraph 2 to attain its objectives, one or more agricultural guidance and guarantee funds may be set up.'

12. For an account of the collection of revenue by the Community the reader is referred to Dr White's chapter III, pp. 29–32.   13. [1972] C.M.L.R. 488.

is exported, the exporter can claim an export subsidy under Regulation 1041/67 only if it is in fact fit for human consumption; as the Court said at p. 489, 'If the products are intended for human consumption their use for this purpose must not be excluded or substantially restricted as a result of their qualities or their condition. This provision is binding and applies directly in every Member State.'

II. PROBLEMS RESULTING FROM U.K. ACCESSION

It is now possible to examine some of the agricultural problems involved in the accession of the U.K. to the Community. The sharp contrasts between the British and Community methods of price support, as outlined earlier in this chapter, should give some idea of the problems of bringing the British system into line. A transitional period, fixed at five years by the Treaty of Accession, was necessary to allow the relatively low food prices of the U.K. to rise gradually to Community levels. The British price will be brought into line with the common price in six stages (Article 52(1) of the Treaty of Accession). These progressive alignments will take place each year at the beginning of the marketing year for each product in question, and the time limit has been set at 1 January 1978 for the application of the common prices in the new member States.

The essence of the transitional system is that, while food prices rise, deficiency payments to British farmers should be gradually eliminated. Therefore, whereas now the British farmer gains his income partly from the market and partly from deficiency payments, at the end of the transitional period he will gain his income entirely from the market. The U.K. has been authorised to maintain deficiency payments until 31 December 1977. A danger was thus created that the British farmer would gain an excessive income during the transitional period by virtue of his gains from higher prices and the retention of deficiency payments. Hence Article 54(3) of the Treaty of Accession was introduced to curb any excessively generous deficiency payments:

These subsidies may not have the effect of raising the returns of producers above the level which would have resulted from the application to these returns of the rules for the alignment of prices laid down in Article 52.

A further complication is that during the transitional period there will be four separate price levels—that of the original Six plus those of the three new member States. In order to maintain fair competition as between low-price and high-price countries, a tax is imposed on agricultural goods when they move from a market with a low price level to a market with a higher price level. When goods move in the opposite direction they are to receive a subsidy. Article 55(2) of the Treaty of Accession provides that these 'compensatory amounts' (i.e. both the tax and the subsidy) 'shall be equal to the difference between the prices fixed for the new Member State concerned and the common prices'. It is the difference between the intervention prices of the produce in question which determines the size of the compensatory amounts applicable in trade between the original Six and the new member States.

Already the British annual review of farm prices has been arranged a month earlier in order to fit in with the E.E.C. schedule. With the obligation in the Treaty of Accession to raise average market prices by six equal steps from 1 April 1973, the prices fixed in the annual review are bound to be determined to a large extent by the target prices decided in Brussels. Moreover, in order to fit in with the Common Agricultural Policy the British annual review will have to assimilate such produce as fruit and vegetables, eggs, etc., which have hitherto been outside its scope. The review will have to encompass not only the products which are listed in the schedules to the Agriculture Acts but also those products which are subject to Community regimes.

Therefore the British deficiency payment will be phased out gradually. This is fully in accordance with Articles 43 and 45 of the E.E.C. Treaty, which envisage the continuation in being of national marketing organisations until such time as the Common Agricultural Policy is fully implemented. However, during the transitional period Britain will not be able to impose any additional import duties on agricultural produce in contravention of Article 12, even though such import duties may be an integral part of an agricultural marketing scheme and *prima facie* have the protection of Articles 43 and 45. This emerged clearly from *Re import of milk products: E.E.C. Commission* v. *Luxembourg and Belgium.*[14] The defendants unsuccessfully argued

. . . that the right recognised in the Member States to maintain the said organisations would imply freedom to have recourse not only to the methods used at the date of the Treaty entered into force, but also to all those necessary for the conservation of their efficacy and the adaptation to a change in circumstances.

14. [1965] C.M.L.R. 58.

The Court of Justice, in rejecting this argument, declared:

Article 12 forbids the introduction of new customs obstacles so as to facilitate the fusion of the national markets and the establishment of a common market. Without itself constituting a measure of economic disarmament the said prohibition of any new customs weapons constitutes an indispensable condition for the substitution both of a common market for the different national markets, and of a common agricultural organisation for the national organisations. Thus Article 12 constitutes an essential rule and any possible exception, besides being of strict interpretation, should be clearly provided . . .

The statutory authority for the implementation of the Common Agricultural Policy in Britain is section 6[15] of the European Communities Act, 1972. This envisages the setting up of an 'Intervention Board for Agricultural Produce',[16] which 'shall be charged, subject to the direction and control of the Ministers, with such functions as they may from time to time determine in connection with the carrying out of the obligations of the United Kingdom under the common agricultural policy of the Economic Community'. It is anticipated that the Board will play an increasing role in extending the Common Agricultural Policy to Britain, but one area in which difficulty can be expected lies in the division of responsibility between the British Ministry of Agriculture and the E.E.C. authorities for the actions of the Intervention Board.

Agriculture, with its hundreds of detailed regulations, represents the economic sector where supranational control has reached its most developed point. It indicates the way ahead in other sectors, especially transport. Indeed, the Treaty of Rome places the achievement of a common transport policy on a level with the Common Agricultural Policy. Agriculture occupies title II and transport title IV of the second part ('Foundations of the Community') of the Treaty.

The evolution of the Common Agricultural Policy is reflected in the annual regulations statistics. If one looks at the figures, one sees that the big increase in the annual number of regulations issued stems from 1962; before that year only a handful of regulations had been published annually. For it was 1962 which marked the begin-

15. For the debate on clause 6 of the European Communities Bill, see Hansard (H.C.), vol. 839, Thursday 22 June 1972, cols. 735–850, and Friday 23 June 1972, cols. 851–62.

16. The Board was set up by S.I. 1972 No. 1578. It has been announced in the House of Commons that the powers of the Parliamentary Commissioner for Administration will be extended to cover the Board.

ning of the transitional measures of the Common Agricultural Policy. The Council agreed upon the first measures, the most important of which was concerned with grain (Regulation 19); this included both wheat and animal feeding stuffs. Thus grain was the key commodity which closely affected the prices of certain other agricultural products and their transitional regulations, such as pig meat (Regulation 20), eggs (Regulation 21) and poultry meat (Regulation 22.) In the case of fruit and vegetables (Regulation 23) a less sophisticated form of organisation was established.

On looking at the statistics after 1962 it will be seen that the greatest increase in the number of regulations occurred in 1967, when 1,085 regulations were issued, as opposed to 228 in the previous year. For 1967 was the year in which, *inter alia*, four final regulations came into operation— for grains (Regulation 120/67), pig meat (Regulation 121/67), eggs (Regulation 122/67) and poultry meat (Regulation 123/67). From 1 July 1967 there was free circulation of these commodities among the Six; the size of import levies, export refunds, etc., was the same through the Six and regulated by the Commission.

It is now necessary to examine some of the case law on agriculture. Despite the scope of the post-war Agriculture Acts and the statutory instruments made thereunder, agricultural matters have very seldom been the direct subject matter of litigation in the English courts, though three recent cases on administrative law provide rare illustrations.[17] The Community case law on agriculture is more

17. *Agricultural Training Board* v. *Aylesbury Mushrooms*, [1972] 1 All E.R. 280, incidentally reflects the lobbying power of farmers' organisations. The Minister of Labour, acting under the provisions of the Industrial Training Act, 1964, made an order setting up a training board for the agricultural industry. Before doing so he was statutorily bound to 'consult any organisation or association of organisations appearing to him to be representative of substantial numbers of employers, engaging in the activities concerned . . .' It subsequently emerged that the Mushroom Growers' Association had never received a copy of the draft order and had no knowledge of the consultations between the Minister and the National Farmers' Union. It was held that, in view of the importance attached to consultation in the scheme of the Act, there had been no real consultation but merely an attempt to consult, and accordingly the order did not apply to the Association.

In *Agricultural Training Board* v. *Kent*, [1970] 2 Q.B. 19, it was held that an assessment notice of the levy to be paid under the Industrial Training Act, 1964, must clearly state the training board's address for the purpose of service of a notice of appeal against the levy. The right to appeal against the notice was of fundamental importance, and failure to comply with this provision in the Act rendered the whole notice invalid.

In *Padfield* v. *Minister of Agriculture*, [1968] A.C. 997, the Milk Marketing Board, acting under a statutory marketing scheme, fixed prices to be paid to producers. A group of producers wanted an increase in the basic price paid to them by the Board,

ample than the British. Perhaps the first case provides the best illustration because, in resolving the conflict, the Court had recourse to the underlying rationale of the Common Agricultural Policy. In *Deutsche Getreide und Futtermittel Handelsgesellschaft* v. *Hauptzollamt Hamburg Altona*[18] the question was whether a consignment of maize which had been damaged by moisture in transit and so had its value reduced by 25 per cent should have to pay the same levy at the Community border as undamaged maize. The Court held that the company involved had to pay the same levy regardless of questions of value. It held that the import levies imposed on agricultural products are flat charges, which do not depend on the particular features of the products imported. The case clearly involved some consideration of Regulation 19 (on the subject of grain). The Court, at p. 216, summarised the two issues involved.

In the first question the Court is asked to decide whether Regulation 19 must be interpreted to the effect that the same levy must be imposed on maize, which has been reduced in value by moisture seepage in transit before importation, as that on undamaged maize. If this question is answered in the affirmative, the Court is asked to decide whether the Regulation is valid in this respect.

After pointing out that there was no specific provision in Regulation 19 to cover the exact facts of the case, the Court said that recourse must be had to the rationale of the Common Agricultural Policy. Arguing from this basis, the essence of the company's case was (in the words of the Advocate General) that

The purpose of the market system for cereals is to ensure a reasonable standard of living for the agricultural population and to stabilise the markets by means of price controls. A price adjustment is carried out to protect prices within the Community. The prices of imported products are raised to the level prevailing in the Community. However, as the plaintiff company rightly stresses, this purpose does not extend to the imposition of rates of levy on cereals damaged in transit that are merely required to achieve the price level prevailing for sound cereals. To this extent, therefore, one might in fact speak of a misuse of power. . . .

However, the Court rejected this argument as insufficiently precise.

---

and they complained to the Minister. The Act provided that, 'if the Minister so directs', a committee was to be appointed to investigate such a complaint. The House of Lords ordered him to set up such a committee because his refusal to do so was frustrating the policy of the Agricultural Marketing Act.

18. [1971] C.M.L.R. 205.

. . . products which have been damaged before the import and thereby reduced in value, may, despite this loss, affect the agricultural market just as much as any other products, the quality of which was lower than the standard quality right from the start and which are nevertheless subject to the general levy.

Thus the application of a little economic logic resolved a legal problem.

Another instructive case is *Re import duties on sweet oranges*: *Germany v. E.E.C. Commission.*[19] When the Common Market authorities took the first steps towards the introduction of a common external tariff on 1 January 1962, Germany found that the price of oranges would increase considerably, as nine-tenths of the demand for oranges had been satisfied by countries outside the Common Market. The German government therefore asked the Commission for permission to suspend partially the import duties on sweet oranges. The Commission refused, for two reasons. It intended to develop the Community's own orange-producing areas in the underdeveloped regions of southern Italy, and a grant of the German government's request would hinder the execution of these plans. In addition, it was argued by the Commission that the position of oranges should be considered in the context of the general sweet-fruit market; to import cheap oranges would upset the markets in apples, pears and peaches.

Germany appealed to the Community Court, arguing its case on three of the four grounds that exist for the annulment of Community decisions—violation of basis procedural rules, breaches of the Treaty, and *détournement de pouvoir*. A close examination of these arguments is outside the scope of this chapter, but two points are of particular interest. Under the heading of 'breach of the Treaty' the German government invoked Article 39(1)(e). Article 39 sets out the objectives of the Common Agricultural Policy, one of which is 'to ensure supplies to consumers at reasonable prices'. The Court held that the fact that the Commission's ruling would lead to an increase in the price of oranges did not mean that the price would not be 'reasonable' within the terms of Article 39(1)(e). As the Court said at p. 392:

It follows, once the Commission admits the existence of a direct competition between oranges and apples, pears and peaches, that a stabilisation of the market in these latter products would be thwarted by the import of oranges at a low price. If, then, the refusal to make a grant leads to an increase in

19. [1963] C.M.L.R. 369.

the price of oranges, this fact alone does not imply that, from that time, these prices were no longer 'reasonable' in the sense of Article 39(1)(e).

The German government also argued, *inter alia*, that the Commission had been influenced by irrelevant considerations, namely the interests of German apples, pears and peach producers. The Court held, however, that the Commission may consider the effects of a reduced rate of duty on other products, and not merely the product under consideration. As the Court said at p. 391,

It is legitimate for the Commission, in estimating the expediency of making a grant, to consider the effect of it, not only on the products mentioned in the request but also on other competing products. To restrict the notion of a market in the way argued by the applicant would lead to an artificial isolation of markets in different products. Such a conception would over-look the interdependence of differing markets and give the lie to the realities of economic life.

No exposition of the legal status of agriculture in the E.E.C. would be complete without some discussion of the position of State aids to agriculture under Article 92 of the Treaty of Rome. This article has already been discussed by Professor Wortley in its industrial context (see chapter VII). He indicated, in particular, how national governments could easily distort competitive conditions in favour of their own producers by such devices as direct grants, low rates of interest, guarantees of credit, etc. The prohibition of State aids is not absolute. Article 92(3) provides certain exceptions which may be considered 'compatible with the common market', for example 'aid to promote the economic development of areas where the standard of living is abnormally low or where there is serious underemployment'. Moreover, Article 42[20] makes it clear that the general prohibitions contained in Article 92 are to apply to agriculture only in so far as is determined by the Council:

The provisions of the chapter relating to rules on competition shall apply to production of and trade in agricultural products only to the extent determined by the Council . . .

20. The British government has been providing numerous grants to agriculture, some of which can be found set out in the Agriculture (Miscellaneous Provisions) Act, 1963—for example, aids to promote efficient marketing (s. 9) for winter keep on livestock-rearing land (s. 10), and for grassland renovation (s. 11). Even if the Commission wished to prohibit such subsidies, it would find it difficult to establish that they had affected or distorted competition between member States in any way within the terms of Article 92. Indeed, some subsidies given to farms in hilly localities (e.g. for the maintenance of regular breeding herds in such places) seem ideally qualified to satisfy the requirements of Article 42(a) (. . . 'for the protection of enterprises handicapped by structural or natural conditions').

The Council may, in particular, authorise the granting of aid:

(a) for the protection of enterprises handicapped by structural or natural conditions:

(b) within the framework of economic development programmes.

Certainly in the enforcement of Article 92 the E.E.C. authorities have been more active on the industrial than the agricultural front. As regards Article 42, and the future control of agricultural aids, the Council received its first major recommendations from the Commission as early as 1966. However, little progress seems to have been made. The current position[21] is that the Commission was to make decisions in stages by 1 July 1973 on all types of agricultural aid and was to draw up general guidelines for agricultural aid in the light of the evolution of the Common Agricultural Policy. One writer[22] has detected a certain ambivalence in the attitude of the E.E.C. authorities towards agricultural aids in view of the fact that the Guidance Section of F.E.O.G.A. has been known to make grants for such projects as irrigation and site construction:

On a purely formal legal level, it suggests the anomaly that the Guidance Section will be empowered to finance certain projects that the Commission considers incompatible with the common market. More to the substance, it will be interesting to see whether the member States will permit the Commission to retain this residual power to disapprove projects falling within the Fund's Community Programs.

Mention has already been made of the problem of agricultural surpluses, both caused and exacerbated by the deliberate maintenance of high Community prices. Indeed, it can be stated that the prices of agricultural produce in the E.E.C. have been regarded not as a means of matching supply with demand but rather as a means of maintaining peasant farmers' incomes, which are governed very largely by social and political considerations. Such surpluses are not only wasteful but they also increase the expenditure[23] necessary to support prices in the internal market and to finance export subsidies. Therefore, the feeling has been growing that the

21. See the fifth *General Report on the activities of the Communities*, 1971, pp. 205–6.
22. Dam, *loc. cit.*, p. 245.
23. The funds provided by the guarantee section of F.E.O.G.A. have increased considerably since it first began in 1962–3. For example, grain:

	U.S. $ (millions)		
	1962–63	*1965–66*	*1968–69*
Total	28·0	120·4	666·0
Comprising *Market Intervention*	6·5	16·3	212·0
and *Export Subsidies*	21·5	104·0	454·0

E.E.C. farm problem is to be solved ultimately not through price support policies but by means of radical structural reform.[24]

This feeling achieved its clearest expression in the publication of the Mansholt plan (*Agriculture 1980*)[25] in November 1968. The plan anticipated measures aimed to help both the five million people who were expected to leave agriculture over the following ten years and those who would remain in agriculture. For the former, it proposed job retraining schemes and (for those aged over 55 years, and who wished to give up farming) annual income equalisation payments. For the latter, it recommended the formation of farms which would be efficient economic units; minimum figures quoted, for example, were forty to sixty cows for milk, and 150 to 200 cattle for beef. These modernised farms, it was anticipated, would be formed either by amalgamating several farms of approximately the same size, or by taking a moderately sized farm as a nucleus and adding the surrounding areas of land.

Obviously, such schemes have economic and social ramifications extending far beyond the scope of this chapter, but it will be useful to mention three legal–political aspects of the Mansholt plan. Firstly, in order to facilitate the creation of commercially viable farms by amalgamating several small estates, it may well be necessary for the member States to amend their property law both to facilitate the creation of larger farms and to define the previous owners' legal interests in the new estate. Secondly, will the Community or the member States themselves bear the brunt of implementing the structural reforms? Two factors point to the burden being placed on member States. Community expenditure on structural reform, from the Guidance Section of F.E.O.G.A., has had to be decreased because of the very considerable increases in the liabilities of the Guarantee Section. Moreover, there would be considerable fear that to allow Community institutions direct control over the reorganisation of farming units would lead to a totally unwarranted and undesirable concentration of power within the Community's administrative machinery. Thirdly, the urgency of evolving a strong regional policy, within the context of Article 92, will be increased considerably if the Mansholt plan is to be fully implemented. Depopulation of agricultural areas will create or aggravate problems

24. See generally Rickard, 'Structural policies for agriculture in the E.E.C.', 21 *Journal of Agricultural Economics* (1970) 407.

25. A full account of this 'Memorandum on the Reform of Agriculture in the European Economic Community' is contained in the second *General Report on the Activities of the Communities*, 1968, pp. 135 ff.

which have already been caused in Britain by the decline of the staple industries of the industrial revolution.

In considering the options[26] for the future development of the Common Agricultural Policy, it is worth recalling the events of 1969, when the devaluation of the French franc and the revaluation of the German Deutschmark disrupted the delicate pricing mechanism of the Community. Indeed changes in exchange rates will make the continuation of a single integrated market very difficult as long as income support is tied to the price level of agricultural produce. Whether this problem will ultimately be solved by monetary union remains to be seen. In a wider context, the full execution of the Mansholt plan may well, in time, lead to a fundamental reappraisal of the Community's system of agricultural price support.

26. For a succinct analysis of the various possible developments in the more fundamental aspects of the Common Agricultural Policy, see Marsh and Ritson, *Agricultural Policy and the Common Market*, P.E.P. European series, No. 16, pp. 56–93.

Chapter XIII

THE FREE MOVEMENT
OF WORKERS

Ken Foster

The Treaty of Rome, in establishing the European Economic Community, recognised that it was fundamental to the nature of such an economic institution that certain matters should be entirely free from regulation. Therefore it embodied four basic economic freedoms, viz. the freedom of movement of goods, of capital, of labour and of services. The principle of unrestricted movement of labour, with which this chapter is concerned, is a cornerstone of any common market.[1]

In the Treaty of Rome the basic principle of free movement of labour is enshrined in Article 48, whilst Article 49 describes the procedure for achieving this aim. These articles involve the removal of all restrictions based on nationality which prevent a person from one member State moving to another member State to take up employment in the private sector.[2] In order to take advantage of these articles, a person must enjoy the status of a Community worker,[3] which is defined as a person employed, or seeking employment, under a contract of employment[4] and who is a national of an E.E.C. State.[5]

The principle of free movement of workers has three main aspects which required implementation in order to realise the desired objective:

1. Cf. the Nordic economic grouping, which established free movement of labour as one of its first objectives.
2. Article 48 does not apply to employment in the public service.
3. The status of 'Community worker' derives from Community Law, not internal national law; see *Unger*, [1964] C.M.L.R. 319.
4. See *Vaasen–Göbbels*, [1964] C.M.L.R. 508, 521. Persons rendering services, and persons wishing to establish themselves in business, are entitled to free movement by virtue of Arts. 59–66 and Arts. 52–8 respectively. This distinction between freedom of establishment and freedom to supply services is rare in international practice.
5. For this purpose the Treaty of Accession, 1972, has a special definition of British nationals. This is discussed below.

1. The removal by each member State of all immigration restrictions on the entry of Community workers.

2. Ensuring non-discrimination in the treatment of Community workers while resident in another member State, both in relation to employment and other matters such as housing.

3. Protecting the social security rights of Community workers while resident in another member State so that they are not penalised by migration, either in their native country or in their adopted country.

I. THE REMOVAL OF ENTRY RESTRICTIONS

This has been achieved within the Community by a gradual transition. The first stage[6] allowed Community workers to enter another member State and fill an employment vacancy if no suitable national applicant had applied within three weeks.

The second stage[7] provided for equal treatment between nationals and Community workers, subject to certain restrictions relating to the requirement of prior notification to a local employment exchange before a vacancy could be filled by a Community worker and allowing a member State unilaterally to suspend these provisions and thereby restore preference for their own nationals.[8] The final stage,[9] which was introduced on 1 July 1968, removed these restrictions of notification and suspension, and allowed full freedom of movement, subject only to the limitations of the Treaty itself.[10] These are:

1. *Article 48(3)*, which allows restrictions to be placed upon the entry of individuals if they can be justified on the grounds of public policy, public security or public health. Such restrictions must only be in relation to an individual and cannot be used to justify general immigration controls.[11] Additionally, such reasons cannot be invoked for economic purposes[12] in order to control the entry of Community workers.

6. Regulation No. 15/61 (15 August 1961), *J.O.*, 1961, p. 1073.
7. Regulation No. 38/64 (23 March 1964), *J.O.*, 1964, p. 965.
8. Articles 1 and 2 of Regulation No. 38/64. The right of suspension, which merely involved notification to the Commission, was limited to specified regions or industries.
9. Regulation No. 1612/68 (1 July 1968), *J.O.*, 1968, L 295/12.
10. For a more detailed account of the transitional arrangements, see K. Lewin, 'The free movement of workers', 2 *C.M.L.Rev.* (1964) 300, and H. ter Heide, 'The free movement of workers in the final phase', 6 *C.M.L.Rev.* (1970) 466.
11. By virtue of Art. 3(1).   12. By virtue of Art. 2(2).

2. *Article 48(4)*, which excludes employment in the public service from the scope of free movement. The term 'public service' is not defined, but, as an exception to a fundamental Community principle, it should be interpreted restrictively. It would seem therefore not to include nationalised or State-controlled industries, and to be limited to the civil service.

3. *Article 49(d)* allows a member State to restore priority for its own nationals if the equilibrium of the labour market is upset by an influx of Community workers to such an extent that the standards of living in a particular region or industry are seriously threatened. This exception now requires a formal Community procedure to be implemented and the Council's permission obtained, as opposed to the previous right of unilateral suspension.

The E.E.C. therefore now allows a Community worker free access to any member State to accept employment. But in order to ensure that this basic right is made more realistic several other rights have been granted to migrant workers:

1. Community workers are also given the right to enter another member State freely in order to seek employment if they have not pre-arranged employment.

2. An initial right of residence in the host State should be granted for a minimum of three months so long as the worker can provide for his own maintenance, whether or not employment is found.

3. Once a Community worker has commenced work, he is to be entitled to a residence permit valid for five years, which cannot be withdrawn if he loses his initial employment. This permit is automatically renewable every five years if the worker is in employment at the time of its renewal. These provisions give an indefinite right of residence in the host country so long as the worker is not unemployed when applying for the renewal of his residence permit.[13]

4. The family of a Community worker are given the same rights of unrestricted entry and permanent residence as the worker himself. The existence of this socially necessary principle has never been questioned, although it is not directly specified in the Treaty, and the only difficulty has been the exact definition of

13. Regulation No. 1251/70 (29 June 1970). *J.O.*, 1970, L 142, deals with the right of residence of Community workers within the host State after their employment has ceased and if they are unemployed when applying for renewal of a permit.

'family'. The current definition[14] obliges member States to grant the right of unrestricted entry to the spouse[15] of any Community worker, any children under 21, and any other dependent relative.

II. NON-DISCRIMINATION

This is the second main aspect of free movement of workers and includes the principle that member States must treat Community workers on an equal basis with their own nationals in relation to employment.[16] The present regulation[17] prohibits all statutory or administrative provisions regulating employment opportunities which are not equally applicable to the State's own nationals, and also states that all discriminatory provisions in collective agreements or individual employment contracts are to be treated as null and void. It should be emphasised that this regulation only prevents discrimination between nationals and Community workers, and that it does not afford protection to non-Community foreign labour.

In addition, there are several other important obligations upon member States in relation to the general principle of non-discrimination:

1. A Community worker must have an equal right to join a trade union on the same conditions as national workers.[18]
2. A Community worker must receive the same income tax treatment in relation to his earnings as a national worker.
3. Community workers should have equal access to housing with nationals.[19]

III. SOCIAL SECURITY BENEFITS

This third aspect of free movement of labour is imperative to fully implement its operation so that Community workers and their dependants are not penalised as a result of migration. The basic difficulty arises because the host State does not usually give foreign workers any entitlement to benefits until they have contributed for a sufficient period under that particular State's social security system. The main problems to be overcome are the question of

14. Regulation No. 1612/68, Art. 10.
15. See Mrs Kloss, chapter XIV below.   16. Article 48(2).
17. Regulation No. 1612/68, Art. 3.   18. Regulation No. 1612/68, Art. 8.
19. Regulation No. 1612/68, Art. 10.

counting different periods of employment in different countries as continuous and the question of entitlement to benefits when the Community worker is incapacitated while working abroad. These problems were faced at a very early stage and are governed by regulations dating from 1958.[20] These assign to the Council the task of adopting such measures as are necessary for the establishment of free movement of workers. A detailed consideration of these highly technical regulations, their subsequent amendment and their interpretation in over twenty major decisions of the Court of Justice is beyond the scope of this chapter, but their basic purpose was well expressed in the *Unger* case,[21] where the Court said that 'in cases of doubt the said Articles and measures adopted to implement them must be interpreted in such a way that they tend to prevent the legal position of the migrant workers, notably in the matter of social security, being prejudiced'.[22] However, the problem of aggregation of contributions has been met by allowing migrant Community workers to accumulate different periods of employment in any E.E.C. country so that all will count towards their entitlement to benefit. This gives an effective continuity of insurance cover. The other problem of entitlement to benefits has been solved by all E.E.C. countries agreeing to the compulsory application of their own national social security legislation to all Community workers employed with their country. It has been decided by the Court of Justice[23] that this provision does not prevent a migrant worker from also claiming benefits under his own national social security legislation as well, so long as such legislation does not penalise him by compelling him to pay contributions to his national scheme without receiving any additional protection.

IV. THE UNITED KINGDOM'S ENTRY

The United Kingdom on entry into the E.E.C. accepted the established rules relating to free movement of workers, with two qualifications. The first[24] allows member States to complain to the institutions of the Community of social difficulties arising from the free movement of workers. This provision differs from the exception in Article 49(d)

20. Regulation Nos. 3/58 and 4/58, *J.O.*, 1958, p. 561. These in turn are based on Art. 51.
21. [1964] C.M.L.R. 319; see also *Torrebens*, [1969] C.M.L.R. 377.
22. [1964] C.M.L.R. 319, 334.
23. *Moebo*, [1964] C.M.L.R. 338.
24. Treaty of Accession, 1972 (Cmnd. 4862), declaration 1.

in that it is based on social, and not economic, criteria. Its insertion was inspired by fears from the existing members, especially Holland, of the possible effect on race relations of the influx of large numbers of coloured United Kingdom citizens.[25] The second qualification[26] agreed is that the whole of Ireland, both north and south, should be permitted exemption from the Community's rules for a five-year period from 1 January 1973. This means that Community workers will continue to be subject to the existing controls in attempting to enter these two territories. The official reason is said to be the present high level of unemployment in these areas, which requires that domestic workers be protected from foreign competition for jobs.[27]

A further limitation upon total free movement of workers within the E.E.C. has been achieved by the restricted definition of 'nationals' which the British government has accepted for the purpose of Article 48. This accords the privilege of free movement principally to 'Persons who are citizens of the United Kingdom and Colonies . . . who . . . have the right of abode in the United Kingdom and are therefore exempt from United Kingdom immigration control.'[28] This means that United Kingdom citizenship is a necessary, but not a sufficient, qualification for free movement. In addition, the United Kingdom citizen must possess a right of abode.[29] Other categories, in particular Commonwealth citizens, gain no right of freedom of movement under the Treaty of Rome.

V. THE UNITED KINGDOM'S CHANGES

The obligation to implement unrestricted entry of Community workers into this country necessitated some amendments to the

25. The Dutch Foreign Minister has stated that 'the measures were directed against the possibility of an uncontrollable flood of labour from Britain'. (*The Times*, 11 August 1972.)

26. See Cmnd. 4715, para. 144.

27. The fact that free movement would have allowed southern Irish workers unrestricted entry into Northern Ireland might suggest that the present political situation in Ulster partly inspired this qualification.

28. Cmnd. 4862, 1, p. 118. The only other group included in the definition of 'nationals' are British subjects not possessing United Kingdom citizenship nor the citizenship of any other Commonwealth country who have the right of abode in the United Kingdom. This category are numerically very small. There are also special provisions for Gibraltarians. See generally K. R. Simmonds, 'Immigration control and the free movement of labour', 21 *I.C.L.Q.* (1972) 307.

29. By virtue of the Immigration Act, 1971, s. 2(1)(a)–(c).

United Kingdom immigration law and practice. As regards entry to the United Kingdom, the present position[30] is thus:

1. An E.E.C. national[31] is entitled to unconditional entry on production of a valid national passport or identity card, and no longer requires a work permit.
2. Entry can be refused only on medical grounds,[32] or that the exclusion is conducive to the public good.[33]
3. No condition imposing any restriction on his employment is to be imposed upon an E.E.C. national.[34]
4. Initial admission should normally be for six months.
5. Where an E.E.C. national enters to take or seek employment, members of the family should also be admitted without restriction.[35]

These provisions on the right of entry go further than our E.E.C. obligations in that they apply to all E.E.C. nationals entering for whatever purpose, rather than (with the exception of the family's right of entry) being limited to those taking or seeking employment. An additional concession is the admission for six months initially, rather than the three months required by E.E.C. regulations.

In relation to controls after entry has been granted, the present position[36] is as follows:

1. An E.E.C. national who takes up employment within six months of entry is effectively granted the right of permanent residence in this country, subject to minimum limitations.[37]

30. See 'Statement of immigration rules for control on entry: E.E.C. and other non-Commonwealth nationals' (H.C. 81).
31. This status is defined (*ibid.*, para. 50) as a national of any E.E.C. country other than the Irish Republic (whose citizens have unrestricted entry anyway) but not including French and Dutch citizens from their overseas territories, e.g. Surinam. These groups have free movement of labour within the rest of the E.E.C. and our unilateral restriction seems unjustified.
32. *Ibid.*, para. 61. 33. *Ibid.*, para 65. 34. *Ibid.*, para. 51.
35. *Ibid.*, para. 53. 'Family' is defined in accordance with Regulation No. 1612/68, Art. 10, see above.
36. See 'Statement of immigration rules for control after Entry: E.E.C. and other non-Commonwealth nationals' (H.C. 82).
37. *Ibid.*, para. 34. Initially such a person is issued with a residence permit for five years on finding employment, unless he has been a charge on public funds (e.g. through claiming supplementary benefit) while in the country. If the employment is expected to be less than twelve months the residence permit should be limited to the duration of the employment. A residence permit should be curtailed at any time if the holder is living on public funds although capable of maintaining himself (para. 36). The initial time limit of five years should be removed after he has remained here for four years in employment, subject to general considerations in para. 4 of the rules (e.g. danger to national security).

2. Members of an E.E.C. country nationals' family are allowed to remain on the same conditions.[38]

3. The right of permanent residence given to an E.E.C. worker and his family continues even if he retires on a pension, or becomes permanently incapable of work as a result of an industrial accident or disease.[39]

4. An E.E.C. national is liable to deportation on the same conditions as other non-patrials.[40]

However, apart from these changes in immigration law, the British Government has done very little to bring law and practice into line with the obligations accepted under Articles 48 and 49, and the directives thereunder. For example, the requirement that admission to employment should not discriminate between domestic nationals and E.E.C. nationals[41] may need legislative amendment, as the Race Relations Act, 1968, appears inadequate to deal with discrimination by employers which is based on nationality. The recent House of Lords decision in *Ealing L.B.C.* v. *Race Relations Board*[42] indicates that such discrimination is lawful under the Act so long as it can be clearly distinguished from discrimination on the prohibited ground of 'national origins'.

At present, certain occupations are statutorily closed to non-British nationals; the major examples—the civil service without a certificate, and the armed forces—are permissible under Article 48(4) as being employment in the public service. There is also at least one private occupation—that of river pilot—which is still statutorily closed to aliens.[43]

Some other occupations are limited to non-nationals possessing a residential qualification. The Football League, for example, prohibits non-British nationals from playing professional football unless they have resided in this country for two years.[44] This rule is

38. Paragraph 38.

39. Paragraph 39. The family retains the right of permanent settlement even if the E.E.C. worker dies as a result of an industrial accident or disease.

40. Sections 3(5)–(6) and 5(1)–(4) of the Immigration Act, 1971; paras. 40–63 of the immigration rules (H.C. 82).

41. Regulation No. 1612/68, Art. 3. See above.

42. [1972] A.C. 342.

43. Aliens Restrictions (Amendment) Act, 1919, s. 4. The similar provision which limited certain merchant shipping posts to British nationals has been repealed: Merchant Shipping Act, 1970.

44. A similar rule applies to professional cricket, although this is of less practical importance in the foreseeable future. We are unlikely to have an influx of French cricketers.

clearly contrary to the Treaty of Rome, and any attempt to enforce it could be declared null and void.[45]

Similarly, there appear to be a few collective agreements restricting foreign labour still in existence. The National Union of Hosiery and Knitwear Workers, for example, are party to an agreement which provides for a 10 per cent quota of foreign labour in their industry. If such an agreement were implemented to exclude Community workers, this too would be null and void.

A further aspect of the Community's rules on free movement of labour is the requirement that Community workers must have an equal right to become a member of a trade union on the same conditions as national workers.[46] In the United Kingdom the rules of some trade unions do prohibit non-nationals from membership,[47] while others provide for entry on different conditions.[48] Such rules will be invalid under the E.E.C. regulations, but could be effectively governed by section 65(2) of the Industrial Relations Act, 1971, which provides that applicants for membership of any trade union (registered or unregistered) shall not be excluded 'by way of any arbitrary or unreasonable discrimination'.

VI. CONCLUSIONS

It is important to emphasise that the free movement of workers which has been achieved in the E.E.C. does not mean that it can be accurately described as a common labour market. It is possible to distinguish three theoretical situations in relation to employment opportunities for non-nationals:

1. A national labour market—whereby priority in relation to employment vacancies is given to nationals of one's own country, usually by controlling the entry of aliens.

2. Free movement of labour—whereby a State retains its discretion to admit immigrant workers as it wishes, but accepts a duty to allow unrestricted entry to workers from certain States (e.g. the E.E.C.).

45. The difficulty of removing such rules when unchallenged because of passive acquiescence by all employers concerned is illustrated by the fact that the Italian F.A. retains a similar rule five years after the full implementation of free movement of labour.

46. Regulation No. 1612/68, Art. 8.

47. E.g. membership of the British Airline Pilots' Association is limited to British subjects.

48. E.g. the Musicians' Union requires foreign applicants for membership to have had twelve months' residence in the United Kingdom.

3. A common labour market—whereby preference is given to workers from certain States (e.g. the E.E.C.) over all other workers from any other State. The requirement of priority to certain workers necessarily prohibits equality of treatment by the host State to all foreign workers.

The E.E.C. is currently at the second stage, i.e. free movement of labour. This means that so long as a member State allows other E.E.C. nationals free entry for work, it can treat non-E.E.C. workers as it wishes; it could therefore allow equal, unrestricted access to both Community workers and other groups of foreign workers. The establishment of a common labour market would entail priority in employment (e.g. when a vacancy arose) being given to E.E.C. workers. In effect, the Community would become a supranational labour market. The Community is now actively considering the feasibility of establishing a common labour market, and the 1968 regulations provided that 'The Member States shall examine together with the Commission all the possibilities of having vacancies filled in priority by subjects of the Member States'.[49] The same regulations provide that Community workers should enjoy the same priority in filling employment vacancies as nationals;[50] but this provision only prevents discrimination between nationals and Community workers; it does not provide (as a common labour market would) that these two groups should be given preference over all other foreign labour.

In discussing the social and economic effects of the immigration of foreign workers, it is necessary to distinguish between Community immigrants (e.g. Italians) and non-Community immigrants (e.g. Turks and Spaniards). There has not been any large-scale migration of Community workers; although there was some initial interchange, even this has decreased recently. The removal of all formal restrictions within the Community created a *laissez-faire* situation, and the labour market has operated upon classic economic principles, with labour moving from areas of high unemployment, such as southern Italy, to areas of low unemployment, such as West Germany. But, apart from the Italians, the average Community worker has shown very little willingness to move elsewhere.

It has been the immigration of non-Community labour which has been quantitatively much greater to the E.E.C., especially from Spain, Portugal, Yugoslavia, Turkey and Algeria. Within the

49. Regulation No. 1612/68, Art. 19.   50. *Ibid.*, Art. 1(2).

original six countries it has been non-Community labour which has accounted for the major part of all immigrant labour.[51] These non-Community immigrants from less developed countries are overwhelmingly manual, unskilled workers who concentrate in certain occupations, usually those with low wages and/or bad working conditions, which neither the national nor the Community workers want or are available to do. The social and political problems involved in this widespread immigration are immense.[52]

The E.E.C. has supported the policy of free movement of workers by provisions for occupational retraining, administrative co-operation between employment exchanges and the creation of the European Social Fund, which is designed to increase the geographical and occupational mobility of Community workers by financial payments for resettlement or retraining on redundancy.[53] However, the Commission is now attempting to minimise permanent labour migration by pursuing the general policy of encouraging enterprises to take jobs to people (especially through their regional policy) rather than encouraging people to move elsewhere to find jobs.

51. In France, for example, 86 per cent of all foreign workers are from non-E.E.C. countries.

52. Some of the political and social problems are discussed by S. Castles and G. Kosack, 'Immigrants', 22 *New Society* (1972) 505.

53. See Arts. 123–8.

Chapter XIV

SOME PROBLEMS OF PRIVATE INTERNATIONAL LAW

Diana Kloss

I. MATTERS DECIDED BY NATIONAL LAWS

Much Common Market literature uses the expression 'conflict of laws' to cover cases where there is a clash between the law of the Community and national law. This chapter is concerned with cases involving the private rights of an individual where a conflict arises between one system of law and another. The term 'private international law' will be used for the avoidance of confusion.

The Rome Treaty leaves most questions of private law to be determined by the laws of the member States. Just as the English rules of contract and tort will not be substantially altered by our joining the Community, so the ordinary rules of private international law will not be fundamentally changed, at least at first. However, as trade with the Market countries increases, a greater number of cases involving an issue of private international law is likely to arise, particularly in the commercial field.

The Treaty expressly leaves certain matters to be decided by the national laws of the member States, which may well include their private international law. For example, Article 215 states that the contractual liability of the Community itself shall be governed by the law applying to the contract in question. An English court would therefore apply the 'proper law' of the contract to such a case, that is, either (a) the law which the parties have expressly agreed shall govern the contract, or (b) in the absence of express agreement, the law with which the contract is most closely connected on the facts. If the parties agree in the contract that any disputes arising shall be dealt with by arbitration in a particular country, this is usually taken by English courts to imply a submission to the law of that country. However, in a recent House of Lords case, *Compagnie d'Armement Maritime S.A.* v. *Compagnie Tunisienne de Navigation S.A.*,[1]

1. [1971] A.C. 572, H.L.

it was held that this conclusion does not necessarily follow in every case. The House of Lords has also held, in *James Miller* v. *Whitworth Estates*,[2] that the parent contract and the arbitration proceedings thereunder can be governed by different proper laws if this is clearly the intention of the parties.

There is still doubt in English law whether the parties are free to choose any law as the proper law, though totally unconnected with the contract. It seems that such a choice may be upheld by an English court unless there is an intention to evade a provision of the objective proper law which would render the contract void or illegal.[3] There is also authority for the rule that 'a contract (whether lawful by its proper law or not) is, in general, invalid in so far as the performance of it is unlawful by the law of the country where the contract is to be performed'.[4] In *Regazzoni* v. *Sethia*[5] it was held by the House of Lords that an English court will not enforce a contract or award damages for its breach if its performance would involve doing an act in a foreign and friendly State which violates the law of that State. This would include refusing to enforce contracts contrary to the law of a State embodying Community law, e.g. Articles 85 and 86.

Of course, the rules of private international law of other countries may differ from our own. A recent example is a case before a Belgian court, *S.A. Willems* v. *S.A. Dopff*,[6] where the Belgian court was faced with a contract between a Belgian national and a French national. It was held that the law by which the contract was to be governed was Belgian, because their private international law rules direct the judge to the law of the forum in cases where it is impossible to find agreement between the parties.

Article 181 of the E.E.C. Treaty provides that:

2. [1970] A.C. 583, H.L.

3. *Vita Food Products* v. *Unus Shipping Co.*, [1939] A.C. 277; *Golden Acres* v. *Queensland Estates Ltd* [1970], 19 *I.C.L.Q.* 701.

4. Dicey and Morris, eighth edition, rule 132; *Ralli Bros.* v. *Compania Naviera Sota y Aznar*, [1920] 2 K.B. 287, C.A.

5. [1958] A.C. 301, H.L. It is interesting to note that Professor Jennings in his opinion on the *Dyestuffs* case, No. 48/69, [1972] 9 *C.M.L.Rev.* 494, gave as one of the reasons for rejecting the competence of the E.E.C. Commission in respect of acts committed by I.C.I., then a company registered in a non-member State, that the contracts whereby I.C.I. sold dyestuffs to its E.E.C subsidiaries were governed by English law and hence constituted an activity carried on by I.C.I. in Great Britain, i.e. outside the Community at the relevant date. The European Court, however, looked at the *effects of* I.C.I.'s transactions and upheld the Commission's decision.

6. [1971] C.M.L.R. 75.

The Court of Justice shall have jurisdiction to give judgment pursuant to any arbitration clause contained in a contract concluded by or on behalf of the Community, whether that contract be governed by public or private law.

Where an arbitration clause is incorporated into a Community contract the European Court will have to develop its own rules of private international law. Will it feel bound by Article 215 to determine the issue by the 'proper law' of the contract, or will it create its own principles, based perhaps on the majority view among the courts of the member States? The latter solution would, of course, lead to greater uniformity than the former. This problem might also arise from a disputed contract of employment between the Community and an employee, despite the existence of detailed service regulations and conditions of employment.[7] Article 179 provides that the Court of Justice shall have jurisdiction in any dispute between the Community and its servants within the limits and under the conditions laid down in the staff regulations or the conditions of employment. However, the European Court has in practice developed its own law in this area, based on the regulations and general principles of law taken from national legal systems.[8]

For example, in *Alvis* v. *Council of the E.E.C.*[9] Alvis, who worked as a translator, was dismissed without a hearing. The Court held that the institutions of the Community must allow their employees a hearing before dismissal, as this is a generally recognised rule of administrative law among the member States.[10]

Articles 210 and 211 provide that the Community shall have legal personality and in each of the member States shall enjoy the most extensive legal capacity accorded to legal persons under their laws; it may, in particular, acquire or dispose of movable and immovable property and may be a party to legal proceedings. Again, therefore, the Treaty refers to the rules of national law, though these are qualified—the national law must accord to the Community the most extensive legal capacity available under its provisions, and a minimum capacity is specified. (It is likely that 'laws' in Article 211 refers to internal law rather than rules of private international law, otherwise difficult questions of renvoi might arise.)

Another matter which is left to be decided by national law flows

7. See now Art. 24(1) of the Merger Treaty, 1965.
8. See Akehurst, *The Law Governing Employment in International Organisations*, 1967.
9. No. 32/62, [1963] C.M.L.R. 463.
10. A similar rule has only recently been incorporated into English statute law; see Industrial Relations Act, 1971, and Code of Practice.

from Article 85 (restrictive agreements). Article 85(2) provides that 'Any agreements or decisions prohibited pursuant to this Article shall be automatically void.' It is clear that they are also illegal, since they are 'prohibited', and penalties may eventually be imposed unless exemption is given. Although the Treaty defines those agreements which contravene Article 85 (which Article has been held in several cases to be directly applicable)[11] and also directs that such agreements are automatically void,[12] it leaves the *consequences* of nullity to be determined by national law, for example the question of whether money or property transferred in pursuance of a void contract can be recovered. It might have been argued that such an issue should be a matter for Community law in order to promote uniformity. However, in the *Ulm* case[13] the Court held that 'the automatic nullity provided for in Article 85(2) applies to all contractual provisions which are incompatible with Article 85(1). The consequences of that nullity for all other elements in the agreement are not the concern of Community law.' The submission of Advocate General Roemer contained these sentences:

. . . the law of the Treaty on competition only touches with nullity those parts of an agreement which have a bearing from the point of view of competition law. For the rest, it is not necessary, in our opinion, to settle on the level of Community law, i.e. uniformly for all the member States, the question of the effects of the partial nullity of an agreement on the whole of the undertakings included in the contract. For that question it is the applicable national law which can claim precedence (it should be determined according to the rules of private international law) . . .[14]

This decision was followed by the Kartellsenat of the West German Bundesgerichtshof in *Re Yoga Fruit Juices*,[15] where it was held that it was for German law to determine the enforceability of an arbitration award made under an agreement in breach of Article 85 between an Italian and a German company. It was not a question of Community law but 'a question of the scope of the right and the duty

11. See, for example, *Wilhelm* v. *Bundeskartellamt*, [1969] C.M.L.R. 100.
12. The interpretation put on Art. 85 by the Court of Justice was that agreements could not be 'automatically void' as long as there existed a possibility of obtaining an exemption under Art. 85(3)—*Bosch* case, No. 13/61, [1962] C.M.L.R. 1, but see now the important decision in the *Brasserie de Haecht* case (No. 2), No. 48/72, [1973] C.M.L.R. 287; *Esso* v. *Kingswood*, [1973] 3 All E.R. 1057.
13. No. 56/65, [1966] C.M.L.R. 357.
14. [1966] C.M.L.R. 372. In the *Béguelin* case, No. 22/71, [1972] C.M.L.R. 81, the Court held that since the nullity imposed by Art. 85(2) is absolute, the agreement has no effect on the relationship between the contracting parties and cannot be set up against third parties.
15. [1969] C.M.L.R. 123.

to review arbitration awards which the individual State has assigned to its national courts'. It was held that the award was unenforceable because it gave damages for breach of an agreement in conflict with Article 85 and was therefore contrary to German public policy.

It should be noted that the European Court has held that it is possible to sever the 'void' parts of an agreement from the rest, which will then be valid,[16] and, as Professor Wortley has shown, the Commission regularly does this.

An English court faced with a contract affecting trade between member States and offending against Article 85 would *prima facie* refer it to the 'proper law' of the agreement. Two difficulties might arise:

1. If the agreement is void there is arguably no proper law. This could be solved by applying the 'putative' proper law, i.e. that law which would have governed had there been a contract.

2. If the 'putative' proper law were the law of a country *outside the Market*, would the English court uphold the agreement? It is submitted that English courts would be bound now, after British entry into the E.E.C., to strike down a restrictive practice in breach of Article 85 as contrary to public policy, whatever the proper law of the agreement. If the contracting parties attempted to avoid Article 85 by stipulating in the contract that the proper law should be that of a country outside the Community, this would be struck down as an attempt to evade an overriding provision of the Treaty. Even before British entry, an English court would have been likely to refuse to enforce an agreement which contravened Article 85 on the ground of illegality by the law of the place of performance.[17]

Another question arising from Article 85 is this: 'Would an action lie in an English court for breach of statutory duty if damage were caused to a third party by an agreement in violation of Article 85?' There are two ways of approaching this question in English internal law: through breach of statutory duty or through intentional interference with the interests of the plaintiff by unlawful means. The first tort is, of course, better established than the second.[18] In order

16. *Grundig–Consten* case, [1966] C.M.L.R. 418.
17. It is submitted that even before U.K. entry into the E.E.C. the English courts would not have classified Art. 85 as penal, so as to refuse to give any effect to it: *Foster* v. *Driscoll*, [1929] 1 K.B. 470, C.A.
18. See Clerk and Lindsell, *Torts*, thirteenth edition, 1969, pp. 804, 805.

to bring an action for breach of statutory duty the plaintiff would have to show that the purpose of Article 85 was to give compensation to persons injured as well as to punish and prevent certain restrictive practices.[19] But English courts have been prepared in the past to grant civil remedies to plaintiffs injured by an agreement contrary to the 1956 Restrictive Trade Practices Act even before it had been condemned by the Restrictive Practices Court, on the basis of interference by unlawful means.[20] These decisions can be criticised on the ground that the 1956 Act does not make agreements illegal, merely presuming them void as contrary to the public interest.[21] In contrast, Article 85 states that practices within its ambit are prohibited and Council Regulation 17, Article 15, provides that the Commission may fine enterprises which have wilfully or through negligence infringed Article 85: surely this must constitute unlawful means?

In a case involving an international element the English courts would have to apply the private international law rules on torts.[22] Would such a tort be committed in the place where the loss is incurred or in the place where the agreement is made? It is submitted that any place where the damage is suffered is a place of commission when damage is an essential ingredient of the tort, as with breach of statutory duty or interference by unlawful means.[23]

Prior to the entry of the U.K. into the Common Market a breach of Article 85 was not actionable as a tort in England unless the act complained of was also contrary to our legislation or constituted a conspiracy to injure the plaintiff without the defence of protection of the defendant's own interests. After entry, it seems possible that actions in tort may lie as long as the prohibited agreement gives rise to a civil action in the country where the tort is committed.

19. See Rew, 'Actions for damages by third parties under English law for breach of Article 85 of the E.E.C. Treaty', 8 *C.M.L.Rev.* (1971) 462.

20. *Daily Mirror Newspapers* v. *Gardner*, [1968] 2 Q.B. 762, C.A.; *Brekkes* v. *Cattel*, [1971] 2 W.L.R. 647. See also *Acrow Ltd* v. *Rex Chainbelt*, [1971] 3 All E.R. 1175.

21. See Guest and Hoffman, 81 *L.Q.R.* (1968) 310. See also more general criticism in Winfield and Jolowicz, *Tort*, 1971, p. 471.

22. After *Boys* v. *Chaplin*, [1971] A.C. 356, H.L., these appear to be that if an alleged tort is committed abroad an action on it in England will succeed only if it is (a) actionable as a tort by English domestic law, and (b) gives rise to civil liability under the law of the place where it is committed. English internal law alone is applied to torts committed in England.

23. See *contra*, *George Monro* v. *American Cyanamid Corp.*, [1944] K.B. 432, C.A.; *Cordova Land Co.* v. *Victor Bros.*, [1966] 1 W.L.R. 793. The point was left open by the P.C. in *Distillers Co. Ltd* v. *Thompson*, [1971] 2 W.L.R. 441. See also note 18 above

The courts of all the Common Market countries may need eventually to determine whether the intention of the Treaty is to give a remedy to the individual harmed by a restrictive practice.[24]

II. INTERPRETATION OF TREATY PROVISIONS

Provisions of the Treaty and laws made by its authority may raise issues of private international law by a second route. Community law contains terms like 'domicile', 'nationality', 'contract' and many more which may need to be defined. Where such a question arises, Article 177 may oblige or give a discretion to the national court to bring the case before the European Court for a ruling on the meaning of legislation. The Court has repeatedly held that it has no power in such cases to interpret national law or to decide on the compatibility of national law with Community law.[25]

If a word or phrase is used in Community legislation, its interpretation must be basically a matter of Community law. However, in deciding on the meaning of a particular term the Court may refer to national law concepts, either in the law of an individual member State, or generally accepted by all or the majority of the member States.[26] When it does this it is not interpreting national law but creating Community law by the comparative law method, just as the English court might be persuaded to develop its rules in a particular way, having heard evidence of Australian or Canadian law on the same point.

It is likely that the European Court would decide that the definition of nationality should be referred to the law of each individual State.[27] It would, in effect, create its own rule of private international law: that nationality must be referred to the law of the country of which nationality is claimed.[28] In *Nold* v. *High Authority*[29] a Coal and Steel Community case, it was held that the capacity of a company to appear before the court and the validity

---

24 See Rew, *op. cit.*, at p. 470 for some foreign authorities.

25. See, for example, the *Costa–E.N.E.L.* case, [1964] C.M.L.R. 454.

26. Article 215(2) specifically refers to the general principles common to the laws of the member States to determine the non-contractual liability of the Community.

27. For the view of the English courts on this matter see *Oppenheimer* v. *Cattermole*, [1972] 3 All E.R. 1106, C.A.; *Stoeck* v. *Public Trustee*, [1921] 2 Ch. 67, 82 *per* Russell J.

28. See the definition of U.K. citizenship attached to the Treaty of Accession, 1972, Cmnd. 4862, 1.

29. No. 18/57, 5 *Receuil*. 110.

of the authority given to an agent to act on its behalf would be referred to the law of the company's registration. The marital status of an individual, which might be very relevant in a social security case, would probably be referred to his 'personal law'. (Another possibility would be to refer to the law of the country where a benefit is being claimed.) Here, however, we encounter a difficulty. Most of the original member countries treat the law of a man's nationality as being his personal law, whereas English courts have always preferred the test of domicile. A specific example of a case where this problem arises is in relation to Article 52 of the *Convention on Jurisdiction and Reciprocal Enforcement of Judgments* (1968),[30] which provides, *inter alia*, that in order to determine the domicile of a party his domestic law shall be applied if, in accordance with this, his domicile depends on that of another person. It is submitted that domestic law in this case must be the law of nationality in preference to domicile, as otherwise there would be a submission to the law of the domicile of the question of where a person *has* his domicile —a *circulus inextricabilis*. A U.K. citizen's domestic law would be the system in force in that part of the United Kingdom with which he was most closely connected.[31]

In the *Meinhardt* case[32] the divorced wife of a Community official claimed part of his widow's pension on his death. Her entitlement depended on the E.C. staff regulations, which gave her the right to an amount assessed according to the maintenance awarded by the German divorce court and the length of her marriage. The European Court referred to the national law to determine the legal effects of the divorce, but stressed that the right to the pension was ultimately a matter for Community law. (In this case the Court took judicial notice of German law without hearing evidence of it.)

Though these questions of individual capacity and status may necessitate a reference to the law of one country only, more general concepts should probably be developed in the light of the laws of all the member States. 'Public policy', for example, which appears frequently in Community legislation,[33] could not be left to the interpretation of each national court without inequality creeping in.

---

30. See below, p. 190. In June 1971 the ministers of Justice of the Community agreed to give to the Court of Justice the power of interpreting this convention and the Convention on Mutual Recognition of Companies (1968). Neither convention is yet in force in the U.K.

31. See s. 6(2), Wills Act, 1963; *Re O'Keefe*, [1940] Ch. 124.

32. [1973] C.M.L.R. 136.

33. E.g. Arts. 36, 48 and 56 of the E.E.C. Treaty.

Indeed, a directive on the general limits of public policy has already been issued.[34]

In many cases it is clear that the European Court should avoid reference to national law and should develop Community rules by examining the policy and aims of Community legislation. One example was the *Unger–Hoekstra* case,[35] where it was held that the definition of the word 'worker' in Article 51 of the Treaty is a matter of Community law, because the policy of the Treaty is to ensure uniform treatment for all workers, whatever their nationality. 'Were the meaning of the term to depend on national law, each member State would then be able to modify the concept of "migrant worker" and to arbitrarily exclude [*sic*] certain groups of persons from the protection of the Treaty.'[36] One solution of this problem is to attach detailed interpretation sections to Community legislation; a new Regulation 1408/71 which came into force in 1973 is designed to solve the many difficult questions of interpretation which have arisen from Regulation 3/58 (social security of migrant workers).[37]

One such case was *Zusatzversorgungskasse des Baugewerbes V.V. A.G. v. van Hamond*[38] The defendant owned a building firm in Holland but for many years acted as contractor in the Krefeld area for German firms. His employees were Dutch nationals who lived in Holland and returned there daily or at weekends. It was a term of their contract of employment that they were employed on the same terms as the defendant's other employees who worked in Holland. A collective bargain, legally enforceable by German law, was made between representatives of German building employers and the German building workers' trade union. This obliged the employer to provide for additional insurance cover over and above the State insurance scheme for his workers. Contributions were to be paid to the Zusatzversorgungskasse. The defendant argued that the collective bargain did not apply to his employees because their contracts of employment were governed by Dutch law, even though they were employed to work in Germany.

The German court would ordinarily have applied Dutch law, according to its rules of private international law, and therefore

34. *J.O.* 850/64.
35. [1964] C.M.L.R. 330. See also [1973] C.M.L.R. 35 ('offer').
36. A similar solution (i.e. considering the policy behind Community law as paramount) was eventually applied to the definition of 'own scrap' under the scrap equalisation scheme of the E.C.S.C. See [1966] C.M.L.R. 146.
37. See Mathijsen, *A Guide to European Community Law*, 1972, p. 52.
38. [1971] C.M.L.R. 585.

would have held for the defendant. However, Regulation 3 provided that employees working within a member State were subject to the laws of that State, even if they lived in the territory of another member State, for the purpose of social insurance benefits. The German court referred the matter to the European Court for a ruling as to whether the words 'laws of that State' in Regulation 3 were confined to internal law or also included rules of private international law. The answer must be that since the intention of the regulation was to confer on foreign workers the same benefits as were given to nationals of the host country, the regulation referred to German internal law only.

III. HARMONISATION AND APPROXIMATION OF LAWS

The third way in which the Treaty may affect rules of private international law is by bringing about changes in them. Article 220 provides that member States shall, as far as necessary, enter into negotiations with each other with a view to ensuring for the benefit of their nationals a variety of advantages. Two conventions were concluded by the six after such negotiations: *the Convention on the Mutual Recognition of Companies* (29 February 1968) and the *Convention on Jurisdiction and Recognition of Judgments* (27 September 1968).[39] I shall now deal in detail with the latter.

The implementation by the United Kingdom of the Convention on Jurisdiction and Recognition will bring about fundamental changes in English private international law. It is a convention of the 'double' type, that is, it deals not only with the enforcement of judgments obtained abroad but also with the right of the court to adjudicate on a case involving a foreign element. The convention has a troubled history.[40] In 1964 a committee of experts from the

39. An English translation of the text of the convention can be found in Campbell, *Common Market Law*, supplement No. 1, 1970, p. 157. See Newman, 'Jurisdiction and recognition of judgments in the European Economic Community', in *Legal Problems of an Enlarged European Community*, 1972, p. 58. The convention is now in force in the original six member States (from 1 February 1973). The new member States have undertaken in Art. 3 of the Treaty of Accession to accede to the conventions provided for in Art. 220 of the E.E.C. Treaty. Negotiations have begun, and a working group of governmental experts has commenced discussions. The definition of 'domicile' is one matter of debate. A committee has been appointed under the chairmanship of Lord Kilbrandon to advise in any matters which may arise in the course of the negotiations.

40. See de Winter, 17 *I.C.L.Q.* (1968) 706; Hay, 16 *Am. J. Comp. Law* (1968–69) 149; Nadelmann, 5 *C.M.L.Rev.* (1968) 409 and 82 *Harvard L.R.* (1968) 1282; Graupner, 20 *I.C.L.Q.* (1971) 367.

E.E.C. countries published a draft convention prepared for the six Common Market countries only. It provided that henceforth the chief basis for jurisdiction in any of the courts of the Common Market was to be that the *defendant* was domiciled within the jurisdiction.[41] This ruled out the assumption of jurisdiction on the basis of nationality of plaintiff or defendant, domicile of the plaintiff or presence of assets of the defendant within the jurisdiction, let alone the mere physical presence of the defendant which is the basis of jurisdiction *in personam* in the common law countries. It also proposed a system which would abolish the need for bilateral agreements on the reciprocal enforcement of judgments by providing that all judgments rendered in one State had to be enforced in other member States unless obtained in violation of the jurisdictional provisions of the Convention.

At the same time, the Hague Conference on Private International Law, of which the U.K. and the U.S. are members, was considering a general convention on the recognition and enforcement of foreign judgments. At an extraordinary session in 1966 these countries expressed disquiet that the Common Market convention extended only to cases where the defendant was domiciled in an E.E.C. country and allowed the use of other bases of jurisdiction against foreign domiciliaries. As an example, Article 14 of the French Civil Code provides that a French court has jurisdiction over any action where the plaintiff is a French national. This means that a French national, even though domiciled and resident in California, can sue a Californian defendant on a Californian contract in a French court.[42] (In practice, of course, he would be unlikely to do this unless the defendant had assets in France.) The Common Market draft did nothing to change this situation, though it prevented the French court from assuming jurisdiction if West Germany, for instance, were substituted for California in the example.

In the light of these criticisms the Common Market experts held another meeting in 1966 and added a new article, Article 59, to the draft. This provides that the member States of the E.E.C. can make individual agreements with non-member States not to enforce against the domiciliaries of such States judgments rendered at jurisdictionally improper forums. However, these provisions have to

41. 'Domicile' is used here in the sense of permanent residence and does not carry the special meaning attached to it in English law.

42. Other 'excessive' grounds of jurisdiction specifically mentioned in the convention (Art. 3) are domicile or residence of the *plaintiff* and the presence of property of the defendant within the jurisdiction.

be part of a general convention on the recognition and enforcement of judgments.[43]

What is the position of the U.K. after accession? Article 63 of the Common Market convention obliges new members of the E.E.C. to accept it as the basis of their duty under the Treaty of Rome to facilitate the enforcement of judgments within the Community. The British government has recognised that English law will have to be changed to bring it into line with the convention.[44] In the Treaty of Accession, Article 3(2), the new member States have undertaken to accede to the conventions provided for in Article 220 of the E.E.C. Treaty and to the protocols on the interpretation of those conventions by the Court of Justice signed by the original member States. A working party of government experts has already started discussions. Meanwhile, the Jurisdiction and Judgments Convention has come into force in the original six member States (on 1 February 1973). The Convention covers all civil and commercial judgments, but not the status and capacity of natural persons, marriage regimes, wills or inheritances, bankruptcies, social security and arbitration. Further conventions may be agreed on these matters.[45] Though jurisdiction within the Community is to be based primarily on the domicile of the defendant, other courts (e.g. in matters of contract the court of the place of performance, though not the place of contracting or the proper law of the contract) may also have jurisdiction. In certain exceptional cases, e.g. actions concerning land, there is exclusive jurisdiction regardless of domicile, in this case in the courts of the State where the land is situated. There are detailed rules about insurance, credit sale and hire-purchase agreements.

The second half of the convention deals with the recognition and enforcement of foreign judgments. Judgments rendered in one contracting State shall be recognised and enforced in the other contracting States without a special procedure being required. There are a few exceptions to this principle, the most important being that no State is required to give effect to a judgment contrary to its own rules of public policy.

43. In 1968 the Hague Conference on Private International Law recommended that its members should make every effort within existing treaty obligations to renounce the exercise and recognition of jurisdiction based on excessive and inappropriate grounds.

44. See chapter III by Dr White *ad fin.*

45. A draft bankruptcy convention is now under discussion: see Hunter, 21 *I.C.L.Q.* (1972) 482.

The entry of Britain into the Community will increase the importance of private international law. It will also create difficulty, because the concepts and rules of English law are so different from those of civil law countries. It is therefore essential that the twin processes of the creation of uniform laws and the harmonisation of laws of member States be successfully pursued.[46]

46. The *Bulletin* of the European Communities, vol. 5, No. 8, 1972, p. 55, reported that a Committee of Experts on Private International Law had just finished preparing a preliminary draft convention on the law to be applicable to contractual and extra-contractual obligations. The text of the draft would be submitted to member States' governments for their comments. The committee was going ahead with the preparation of a second preliminary draft convention on the law applicable to tangible and intangible assets.

Chapter XV

THE POSITION OF OVERSEAS ASSOCIATED STATES IN THE E.E.C.

A. Oye Cukwurah

I. THE IDEA OF ASSOCIATION WITH THE EUROPEAN COMMUNITY

Association between the European Economic Community and a third State, a union of States or an international organisation, is one aspect of the external relations of the European Communities.[1] In a memorandum of 26 February 1959, which was prepared at the request of the Council of Ministers, the Commission of the E.E.C. set out what was generally regarded as the Community's attitude towards association.[2] Briefly, the memorandum emphasised that association status provides an alternative to full membership of the Community reserved exclusively to European States under Article 237 of the Treaty of Rome of 1957 by allowing the associated State (European or non-European) to establish an important structural link with the Community. In other words, association with the Community is not to be confused with full entry. Thus in his speech to the European Assembly in September 1959 Professor Hallstein strongly stressed that:

The creation of the E.E.C. is a political act. Those responsible for the E.E.C. have never hitherto represented any view other than that the final aim and the real justification of their efforts is the intention of furthering the political unification of Europe. Such is declaredly not the aim of association . . . Association pursues economic aims. Consequently, the institutional element in association is of much less importance than institutional matters in our own E.E.C.[3]

1. See Stanley Henig, *External Relations of the European Community—Associations and Trade Agreements*, London, 1971; see also Ralf Dahrendorf's 'foreign policy plan' in *European Community*, No. 9, September 1972, p. 4, and 'The Communiqué issued by the Nine' after their summit conference in Paris on 19–20 October 1972, in *European Community*, November 1972, pp. 6–7, 26.

2. See K. R. Simmonds, 'The Community and the neutral States', 2 *C.M.L.Rev.* (1964–65) 5–20, at p. 12.

3. *Ibid.*

Normally all West European States are expected to join the E.E.C. But for one reason or another some of them have first resorted to associate relationship, which, as the memorandum states, 'is essentially flexible in form and in the connection it may establish between the Community and the associated States'. Some of them are known to have concluded association agreements purely as an interim measure because they are not economically strong enough to accept full membership in the E.E.C. immediately.[4] Unlike these European associates, however, overseas associated States are permanent outsiders to the Community and are no more than beneficiaries of what one commentator called Europe's 'act of faith in international co-operation as the means of helping the poor countries to free themselves gradually from their poverty'.[5] William Zartman has aptly described their position as one where 'the weak confront the strong'.[6] Granted that association agreements tend to minimise the adverse consequences created for developing countries by the Community's policies, the fact remains that in most of the existing agreements the balance of advantage invariably favours the E.E.C. more than the poorer partner. In any case, the memorandum of 1959 to which we referred above had made it quite clear that association must, whatever its form, be directed toward the guiding objectives laid down in Article 2 of the Rome Treaty of 1957, in which article the interests of outsiders such as overseas associated States are not immediately contemplated.[7] It can, therefore, be said that developing countries are by reason of their peculiar circumstances thrown into an uneasy choice of deciding either to leave Europe alone at great economic cost to themselves or to accept the Community's offer of associate status but not without the possibility of some kind of strings attaching to the relationship.

4. See, for example, the associations agreements with Greece (1961), Turkey (1963), Malta (1971) and Cyprus (1972).

5. See Pierrre Drouin (of *Le Monde*), 'Need to redefine responsibilities towards Third World' at p. xiii of 'Europe in 1975', *The Times*, London, 23 February 1972, special supplement.

6. See 1 William Zartman, *The Politics of Trade Negotiations between Africa and the European Economic Community*, Princeton, N.J., 1971.

7. Article 2 provides: 'The Community shall have as its task . . . to promote throughout the Community an harmonious development of economic activities, a continuous and balanced expansion, an increase in stability, an accelerated raising of the standard of living and closer relations between member States belonging to it.' The preamble to this treaty, however, expresses the intention of member States 'to confirm the solidarity which binds Europe and overseas countries' and the desire 'to ensure the development of their prosperity, in accordance with the principles of the United Nations'.

II. ASSOCIATION UNDER PART IV OF THE ROME TREATY

At the time of the negotiations preparatory to signing the Treaty of Rome, four of the foundation members of the E.E.C., namely France, Belgium, the Netherlands and Italy, were still administering sizeable dependent territories overseas. France, in particular, was giving preferential treatment to imports from a number of her former colonies. So, too, did Italy to imports from Libya, a former colonial territory.

Initially, Community member States did not envisage any structural link with these overseas territories. At best, special provision would have been made to ensure that each member State could continue to carry out its responsibilities for its own dependent territories and, within limits, give preferential treatment to imports from those places.[8] France, however, felt differently. For towards the end of the negotiations she insisted on a new and special relationship between the Community as a whole and her own dependent territories. In this connection it has been pointed out by William Zartman that for France, and to a lesser extent Belgium, the economies of their colonies were inseparably tied to the metropolitan country by a system of preferential trade, budgetary and commercial subsidies, and/or expatriate personnel and investment, and the economic needs of their colonies had grown beyond the metropolitan countries' ability to handle them alone.[9] Apart from these economic realities in 1957, France was also inevitably operating under the influence of the preceding year's Suez crisis. All these developments fairly explain France's intransigence on the question of the Community's relationship with former colonies.

In order to ensure French participation in the emerging Community, the other five foundation members were constrained to give in to France's demands, which in effect introduced a new dimension to their original idea of European co-operation. But instead of confining the benefits and commitments of association to French overseas dependencies alone, it was decided to throw the new arrangement open to virtually all their existing dependent territories overseas.

8. See William Gorell Barnes, *Europe and the Developing World—Association under Part IV of the Treaty of Rome*, Chatham House–P.E.P., European Series, No. 2, 1967, p. 5.
9. See William Zartman, *op. cit.*, pp. 6, 9 (f. 4); see also Werner Feld, *The European Common Market and the World*, Englewood Cliffs, N.J., 1967, p. 114.

At first the identification of eligible overseas territories presented some difficulties. There were, for instance, the Maghreb States of Tunisia and Morocco, which had newly become independent and were competing favourably in European trade with some Community members. Algeria, another Mediterranean State, which was then being treated as an integral part of France, was deeply engulfed in a revolutionary struggle. It also constituted a problem for the Community. As if to complicate matters, Italy raised the inclusion of Somalia, its trust territory, and Libya, its former colony. And the Netherlands pressed forward with her interests in the West Indies.[10] Following varying proposals, it was eventually agreed to install progressively a free trade area between members and associates, and, while Algeria would have to be included, it would be so only under circumscribed conditions. Tunisia and Morocco would be assured of the possibility of eventual association through the declarations of intent appended to the Treaty of Rome.[11]

It was, therefore, against the background of such precipitate last-minute compromise that agreement was finally reached in Paris in February 1957, thereby clearing the way for the Treaty of Rome[12] to be signed on 25 March 1957. The 'non-European countries and territories which have *special relations* with Belgium, France, Italy and the Netherlands' were by the decision of these European powers associated with the Community in accordance with the general provisions contained in Part IV (Articles 131–6) of the Treaty and, in greater detail, in an implementing convention attached to the Treaty whose duration was limited to five years. Article 227(3), repeating part of Article 131 of the Rome Treaty, specifically identifies the countries and territories in question as 'those listed in Annex IV to this Treaty'.

There is no textual explanation of the phrase 'special relations' as it applied to associates in the Treaty of Rome. But in the context of its use and in view of the common colonial background and identity of the 'non-European countries and territories' in question it is suggested that the expression pertains to the colonial bond existing between the four foundation member States of the Community and their respective overseas dependencies.

10. See 1. William Zartman, *op. cit.*, pp. 9–10.
11. *Ibid.*, p. 11. See also the Final Act and Declarations annexed to the Treaty of Rome, Tunisia and Morocco, in fact, became partially associated with the Community in 1969.
12. See *Treaty setting up The European Economic Community*, H.M.S.O., London, 1967.

As we show below, the absence of any textual interpretation of this phrase provoked a fresh controversy over the subject of association when the colonial associates became independent, as it were, prematurely, in response to the 'wind of change' in Africa.

It was stressed in Part IV of the Rome Treaty that the purpose of association is 'to promote the economic and social development of the countries and territories and to establish close economic relations between them and the Community as a whole'.[13] As was later revealed in the memorandum of 1959 to which we referred above, the modalities of their association were of necessity directed towards the guiding objectives laid down in Article 2 of the Rome Treaty concerning the Community itself.

For instance, in trade with the countries and territories in question, member States were to apply the same treatment as they applied to themselves. Similarly, in trade with member States and with the other countries and territories, each colonial associate was to apply the same treatment as was applied to the European State with which it had special relations.

Member States were to contribute towards the capital investment or financial assistance required for the progressive development of the colonial associates. And participation in tenders and supplies for such investments were to be open on equal terms to all nationals (natural and legal) of member States or of the colonial associates.[14]

Nationals, firms and companies of member States were to enjoy the rights of establishment (i.e. rights to establish businesses and supply services) within these countries and territories on a non-discriminatory basis. The same rights were to be accorded to the associated dependencies.[15]

The special arrangements for association also included the mutual abolition, according to the same timetable as that laid down for the abolition of customs duties between member States, of customs duties both between all member States on the one hand and all colonial associates on the other and between the associated dependencies themselves. But the colonial associates were permitted to

13. Article 131 of the Rome Treaty.   14. Article 132.
15. Article 132, Rome Treaty. This provision, under Art. 16 of the implementing convention, also applied to Algeria and the French overseas departments of Guiana, Martinique, Guadeloupe and Réunion.

levy 'customs duties which meet the needs of their development and industrialisation or produce revenue for their budgets'.[16] However, whenever such duties were retained by the colonial associates they were not to discriminate between imports from different member States.

There was also provision for freedom of movement in member States of workers from colonial associates and in the associated countries and territories of workers from member States.[17]

Among other important details contained in the implementing convention were provisions for a development fund[18] to provide financial assistance for the associated dependencies and stipulations for import and tariff quotas.

The development fund was established in response to France's claims that she could not extend trade concessions to her European partners without receiving their assistance in financing economic development in her overseas territories.[19] It was administered by the Commission, whose duty it was to allocate the fund between the overseas countries and territories in proportions laid down in an annex to the implementing convention. Procedures were also laid down for the subdivision of these allocations between social and economic projects,[20] and between the various projects submitted under each of these heads.

On import quotas,[21] that convention provided that member States should apply to the colonial associates the provisions of the Rome

16. Article 133, Rome Treaty.

17. Subject to the provisions relating to public health, public security, and public policy (*ordre public*), this was to be governed by agreements to be concluded subsequently with the unanimous approval of all member States. See Art. 135, Rome Treaty.

18. Implementing convention, Arts. 1–7. The fund was of the total of 581,250,000 E.P.U. units ($581,250,000). Of this sum, France and Western Germany would each contribute $200,000,000; Belgium and the Netherlands each $70,000,000; Italy $40,000,000 and Luxembourg $1,250,000. The fund was to be allocated to the overseas territories of the four member countries concerned as follows: France $511,200,000; the Netherlands $35,000,000; Belgium $30,000,000 and Italy $5,000,000.

19. See Werner Feld, *The European Common Market and the World*, 1967, at p. 116.

20. The general programmes were to contain projects for financing (*a*) particular social institutions especially hospitals, teaching or technical research establishments and institutions for vocational guidance, and advancement among the peoples of the countries concerned; (*b*) economic capital investment of general benefit and directly connected with the implementation of a programme which includes productive and concrete plans for development.

21. See Art. 11 of the convention.

Treaty relating to the elimination of quantitative restrictions; and that in any associated country and territory where import quotas existed there should be certain minimum global quotas for all member States other than the member State with which the country or territory had special relations; that any existing quotas for these member States should be converted into global quotas;[22] and that these quotas should be increased annually by the application of the relevant provisions of the Treaty.

Under a protocol annexed to this convention, imports from third countries of unroasted coffee into Italy and the Benelux countries and of bananas into the Federal Republic of Germany amounting to 90 per cent of the consumption[23] in 1956 were also allotted tariff quotas.

The purpose of these quotas was to guarantee traditional trade links with unassociated African and Latin American States for the duration of the association agreement. For, as part of the last-minute compromise at the Paris meeting of February 1957 to which we have referred, Germany was to be allowed quotas for non-associated exports of tropical products, and the common European tariffs on tropical products were to be applied progressively so as not to harm non-associated exports suddenly.

THE ASSOCIATED COUNTRIES AND TERRITORIES

The overseas countries and territories[24] which became colonial associates of the E.E.C. were Senegal, the Sudan, Guinea, the Ivory Coast, Dahomey, Mauritania, the Niger and the Upper Volta (in former French West Africa); the Middle Congo (now Congo–Brazzaville), Ubangi-Shari (now the Central African Republic), Chad and Gabon (in former French Equatorial Africa); Saint Pierre and Miquelon, the Comoro archipelago, Madagascar and dependencies (now the Malagasy Republic), the French Somali Coast, New Caledonia and dependencies, the French settlements in Oceania, the Southern and Antarctic territories; the autonomous republic of Togoland; the French trusteeship territories in the

22. Thus in a French overseas territory there would be a global import quota for imports from, for example, Belgium, Germany, Italy and the Netherlands, in place of previously existing individual import quotas from each of these countries.

23. See Curzon, 'Neo-colonialism and the European Economic Community', *Y.B.W.A.* (1971), p. 120.

24. These overseas countries and territories are specifically listed in Annex IV of the Treaty of Rome.

Cameroons; the Belgian Congo (formerly Congo–Leopoldville, now Zaire) and Ruanda–Urundi (now the separate States of Rwanda and Burundi); the trusteeship territory of Somalia under Italian administration, and Netherlands New Guinea.

As is evident from the above list, most of the colonial associates dropped their former names in the Rome Treaty soon after independence.[25] It may be pointed out, too, that Algeria and the French overseas departments of Guiana, Martinique, Guadeloupe and Réunion were not associated to the Community under Part IV of the Treaty of Rome. Instead, certain general and special provisions of the Rome Treaty applied to them under Article 227(2). Again, Surinam and the Netherlands Antilles were not on the original list of associates. Surinam became associated with the E.E.C. on 1 September 1962, following a Council decision of 23–5 October 1961. The first Chamber of the Netherlands States General approved the association of Surinam with the E.E.C. on 18 July 1962, after previous approval by the second Chamber. The Netherlands government accordingly extended its ratification of the Treaty of Rome to Surinam (or Dutch Guiana) in August 1962. Thereafter it became associated with the Community.[26]

The association of the Netherlands Antilles raised certain problems for the E.E.C. in view of the important position held by petroleum products among Antilles exports and the extent of petroleum refining operations carried on in its territory.[27] However, after protracted negotiations the member States, on 13 November 1962, signed a convention revising the Rome Treaty for the purpose of making the special association system defined in Part IV applicable to the Netherlands Antilles. The negotiations began on 14 June 1960. The E.E.C. Council of Ministers agreed on the terms of association on

25. Other name changes include that of the Sudan, which after its independence became known as Mali and should not be confused with former Anglo-Egyptian condominium, the present Republic of Sudan. The Netherlands New Guinea was later returned to Indonesia and renamed West Irian. And since 1966 the French Somali Coast has been changed to the French territory of the Afars and Issas.

26. See *Keesing's Contemporary Archives*, 1962, p. 18980. It was provided under the declarations of Intent attached to the Treaty of Rome that member countries might offer participation in the Community to certain independent countries such as Morocco, Tunisia and Libya, and to the autonomous territories of the Netherlands Antilles and Surinam.

27. A protocol on mineral oils and certain of their derivatives is attached to the Treaty of Rome. In the case of the Netherlands Antilles it was necessary to prevent any competition unfair to the oil industry of certain member States (especially Germany and Belgium) by excessive exports of Venezuelan oil from the refineries in Curaçao.

14 November 1961, and a convention implementing these terms[28] was approved by the Council on 6 February 1962.

THE FIRST FIVE YEARS OF ASSOCIATION BETWEEN THE COMMUNITY AND OVERSEAS DEPENDENT TERRITORIES AND COUNTRIES

The duration of the association agreement of 1958 was for five years, which put the expiry date at 31 December 1962. It had been believed that within that period the full benefits of association would be felt by both sides to the agreement. But the accomplishment of such expectations depended very much on Community members' early success in consolidating their relations *inter se*. There was, for instance, the functional problem of each member State immediately adjusting its national economy and policies to absorb additional commitments under the Rome Treaty. At the same time the economic attachment of colonial associates directly to the Community instead of indirectly through the metropolitan country without changing the colonial nature of their political relationship with the metropolitan country created a novel situation in which the balance of advantage inevitably favoured the nationals of the European States with which the respective overseas countries and territories had special relations. In practice, too, full benefit from association with the E.E.C. was paradoxical in the absence of political independence of the associates. Some of the associates were, in fact, precluded from taking full benefit of the Treaty provisions or the association agreement by reason of their peculiar international status. This is particularly true of the Treaty proviso, or safeguard clause, permitting the colonial associates to maintain customs and fiscal duties for development, industrialisation or budgetary purposes.[29]

Generally, duties on imports provided much of the budgetary income of the former colonies concerned. To that extent the safeguard clause was important. But their revenue practices were not uniform. For instance, all the French African colonies relied on non-discriminatory fiscal duties to raise revenue. On the other hand, the territories of former French West Africa (Senegal, Sudan, Guinea, the Ivory Coast, Dahomey, Mauritania, Niger and Upper Volta)

28. See *Treaty setting up the European Economic Community*, H.M.S.O., at p. 113; see also *Keesing's Contemporary Archives*, 1962, p. 18979; *ibid.*, 1965, p. 20833; *Official Journal*, No. 150, pp. 2413–19.

29. For a detailed comment on the implementation of the 1958 association agreement in the first five years, see 1 William Zartman, *op. cit.*, at pp. 13–18.

also applied tariffs to goods from third parties. But the trust territories of France (the Cameroons and Togo), of Italy (Somalia) and of Belgium (Ruanda–Urundi) as well as the Belgian Congo (now Zaire) and French Equatorial Africa (Congo–Brazzaville, Ubangi-Shari or the present Central African Republic), Chad and Gabon) were limited to using non-discriminatory fiscal duties because of the 'open door' conventions attached to their trusteeship or colonial agreements. Under these instruments the dependencies in question were precluded from discriminating on the basis of the country of origin of the imports and, therefore, even if they had wanted to invoke the safeguard clause, they were constitutionally incompetent to avail themselves fully of its benefit.

Again, under the Treaty of Rome the elimination of tariffs and quotas was to take place gradually over a period of twelve to fifteen years. Since the Treaty provisions for the colonial associates covered only the first five years of this transition period, it is doubtful whether the full effects of the measures were felt by them by 1962, when in the normal process the association agreement would have been re-negotiated. Granted that there was an increase in the purchases of the associates' tropical products by the E.E.C. over the first five years, however, as Zartman rightly pointed out, 'much of the increase was due simply to increased consumption and not to the fact that European trade was diverted from third parties by increasingly preferential conditions for the associates' exports'.[30]

Again, either because of bureaucratic delays or on account of the failure of member States to contribute promptly to the European Overseas Development Fund (F.E.D.O.M.), the allocation of aids to the associates was slower than scheduled.[31]

It needs to be added that the 1958 association agreement had not run its full cycle before some of the colonial associates became independent. This change in their political status necessitated a new form of arrangement if they were to continue their link with the European Community. The Yaoundé Convention, as we shall show below, established the new association arrangement.

As is pointed out above, under Part IV of the Rome Treaty the implementation convention had a five-year duration in the first

30. 1. William Zartman, *op. cit.*, p. 15; see also Werner Feld, *op. cit.*, p. 115, where it is stated that 'some of the exports of tropical goods originating from non-associated States actually increased, whereas exports from the associated countries up to 1962 rose only minimally'.

31. See 1. William Zartman, *op. cit.*, pp. 16–18.

instance. For subsequent periods Article 136 of the Treaty states that:

Before the Convention . . . expires, the Council shall, by unanimous decision, determine what provision to make for a further period, on the basis of the experience acquired and of the principles set forth in this Treaty.

It was, however, laid down that in any case customs tariffs would continue to be reduced in accordance with the general principles, and that the introduction of a common tariff applying both to the member countries and to their overseas territories would be proceeded with. Accordingly, Article 14 of the implementing convention provides:

After the date of expiry of this Convention and until provisions covering association for a further period have been adopted, quotas for imports into the countries and territories on the one hand, and into the member States, on the other hand, in respect of products originating in the countries and territories, shall remain at the level set for the fifth year. The arrangements in respect of the right of establishment in force at the end of the fifth year shall also be maintained.

In the normal course of things, this was the planned process of gradual change. But there is some doubt as to whether the Community members reckoned with the possible independence of the colonial associates within the five-year duration of the implementing convention.

III. ASSOCIATE STATUS UNDER THE YAOUNDÉ CONVENTIONS

When the colonial associates within Africa became independent in 1960, the year of the United Nations Declaration on the Granting of Independence to Colonial Countries and Peoples,[32] the continuation under Part IV of the Rome Treaty of their associate status was opposed mainly by the Federal Republic of Germany and the Netherlands on the ground that independence implied the end of their special relations with member States of the Community. The opposing States, rather, called for a new agreement on the basis of Article 238 of the Rome Treaty, which empowers the Council of the E.E.C. to conclude 'agreements creating an association involving reciprocal rights and obligations, joint action and special proced-

32. See Ian Brownlie, *Basic Documents in International Law*, second edition, 1972, p. 187.

ures' with a third country, with a union of States or with an inter-national organisation.

A majority of the new African States concerned had been French colonies, all of which, except Guinea, had voted 'YES!' during the referendum on President De Gaulle's 1958 constitution for France and the colonies, thereby remaining in the French community.[33] In reply to members of the Community opposing the continuation of association for the African States under Part IV, France had explained that through the French community and bilateral co-operation agreements[34] which she had signed with the newly inde-pendent francophone African and Malagasy countries the 'special relations' of Part IV were maintained. The whole point in dispute had arisen principally from the fact that Germany and the Nether-lands were reluctant to continue subscribing to the Community's common fund through which aid would flow to the associated States having special relations with the E.E.C. if the independent members among them were not excluded.[35]

The controversy was eventually resolved and thereafter the member States and the Council of the E.E.C. on one side, and the eighteen independent African and Malagasy States on the other, concluded a new agreement, the *First Yaoundé Convention*,[36] which took its name from the capital of the Cameroun Republic, where it was signed on 20 July 1963. The independent African States in question are Burundi, Cameroun, the Central African Republic, Chad, Congo–Brazzaville, Zaire, the Ivory Coast, Dahomey,

33. Prior to the formation of the Organisation of African Unity (O A.U.), these francophonic States—Cameroon, Central African Republic, Chad, Congo–Brazzaville, Congo–Kinshasa (now Zaire), Dahomey, Gabon, Ivory Coast, Mala-gasy Republic, Mauritania, Niger, Ruanda, Senegal, Togo, and Upper Volta—established the sub-regional economic grouping, the Afro-Malagasy Common Organisation (O.C.A.M.). See Ian Brownlie, *Basic Documents on African Affairs*, Oxford, 1971, p. 25; Mauritania, an original member, withdrew on 24 June 1965.

34. On the current agitation by some of the French-speaking African States, especially Mauritania, the Malagasy Republic, Cameroon and Niger, for a revision of their co-operation agreement with France, see *West Africa*, No. 2905, 12 Feb-ruary 1973, p. 213; No. 2907, 26 February 1973, pp. 258–9; No. 2910, 'Pom-pidou's dominoes', 19 March 1973, pp. 361–2; No. 2911, 'The many faces of co-operation', 26 March 1973, p. 395.

35. As stated above, overseas countries and territories associated with the E.E.C. under Part IV of the Rome Treaty or in the spirit of Part IV enjoyed not only trade relations with the Community but also received investment and development aids through the medium of the European Development Fund and the European Investment Bank.

36. For the text of the 1963 Yaoundé Convention see *Convention of Association between the E.E.C. and the African and Malagasy States associated with that Community, and Related Documents*, H.M.S.O. London, 1965.

Gabon, Upper Volta, the Malagasy Republic, Mali, Mauritania, Niger, Rwanda, Senegal, Somalia and Togo.

There was, however, no indication in the preamble to the new convention whether it was a continuation, albeit in modified form, of the original association under Part IV or whether it was an entirely new agreement,[37] such as one that can arise under Article 238 of the Treaty of Rome. The convention came into force on 1 June 1964 and, after five years' duration, expired on 31 May 1969. Thereafter, following a protracted negotiation between the E.E.C. and the eighteen African and Malagasy associates, a *Second Yaoundé Convention*[38] renewing the first, with modifications, was initialled in Luxembourg on 29 June 1969, and similarly signed in Yaoundé on 29 July 1969. It came into force on 1 January 1971. It is still in force and is due to expire on 31 January 1975, when, as we shall show later, a new association with the enlarged European Communities is expected to take its place. The main provisions of the two conventions are discussed below.

E.E.C. COUNCIL DECISION OF 25 FEBRUARY 1964 ON ASSOCIATION ARRANGEMENTS FOR OVERSEAS DEPENDENT TERRITORIES AND FRENCH OVERSEAS DEPARTMENTS

When the First Yaoundé Convention was signed on 20 July 1963 it became necessary also to make fresh arrangements for association under Part IV of the Rome Treaty for the remaining overseas dependent territories and French overseas departments which, like Algeria, were formerly covered under Article 227(2) of the Rome Treaty.[39] This was done by a parallel decision of the E.E.C. Council of 25 February 1964, which, like the First Youndé Convention, came into force on 1 June 1964 and thereafter superseded the pro-

37 See Okigbo, *Africa and the Common Market*, 1967, p. 46.

38. For the text of the Second Yaoundé Convention see *International Legal Materials*, 1970, pp. 485–506.

39. Article 227(2) provides: 'With regard to Algeria and the French overseas Departments, the general and particular provisions of the Treaty relating to:

—free movement of goods,
—agriculture, save for Article 40 (4)
—the liberalisation of services,
—the rules of competition,
—the protective measures provided for in Articles 108, 109 and 226,
—the institutions,

shall apply as soon as this Treaty comes into force.'

visions of the implementing convention (provided for in Article 136 of the Rome Treaty) concerning the association with the Community of overseas countries and territories.

The overseas possessions in question are the territories of French Polynesia, New Caledonia, Wallis and Futuna Islands, the Comoro Islands, French Somaliland (now the territory of the Afars and Issas), Saint Pierre and Miquelon, the southern and Antarctic territories, the Netherland Antilles and Surinam. Also on the list are the French overseas departments of Guiana, Martinique, Guadeloupe and Réunion.[40] As under the 1958 association agreement, the basis of association with these overseas dependent countries and territories remains their 'special relations' with France and the Netherlands respectively. It follows, therefore, that Part IV of the Rome Treaty may well remain relevant only for as long as member States or other European countries acceding to the Treaty of Rome have overseas dependencies qualified to be associated with the Community under it. Otherwise this section of the Treaty, unless it is somehow amended, will eventually lapse for lack of subject-matter.

THE PRINCIPAL PROVISIONS OF THE YAOUNDÉ CONVENTIONS

The main provisions of the Yaoundé Conventions,[41] which are broadly identical, cover trade, financial and technical co-operation, right of establishment, services, payments and capital, and institutions which form the structural link with the Community. According to Article 1 of both conventions, these provisions are directed towards 'the promotion of co-operation between the contracting parties with a view to furthering the economic and social development of the associated States by increasing their trade and putting into effect measures of financial intervention and technical co-operation'. Improving on Yaoundé I, however, Article 1 of Yaoundé II also adds that by means of these provisions, which are discussed below, the contracting parties intend to develop their economic relations, to strengthen the economic structure and economic independence of the associated States and promote their industrialisation, to

40. On the parallel decision of the E.E.C. on the association arrangements between the Community and overseas dependent territories and French overseas departments, see *Keesing's Contemporary Archives*, 1965, pp. 20832, 20833.

41. We shall henceforth refer to these instruments wherever applicable as Yaoundé I and Yaoundé II respectively.

encourage African regional co-operation and to contribute to the advancement of international trade.

1. *Reciprocal trade concessions.* The commercial provisions in Yaoundé II essentially represent a continuation of the previous association regime between the six founder member States of the E.E.C. and each of the eighteen associated African and Malagasy States. These provisions represent the underlying principle of the association as the establishment of a free trade area, which presupposes that trade between the parties should be free of tariff and quota restrictions. But in fact the commercial provisions do not comply fully with this traditional pattern of free trade.

For instance, products originating in the associated States enter the Community free of customs duties and charges having equivalent effect under conditions similar to those governing trade between member States.[42] The E.E.C., however, excludes from the free trade concessions most of the agricultural products coming within its Common Agricultural Policy.[43]

Again, the eighteen associates similarly grant non-discriminatory preferences to products of E.E.C. member States.[44] But at the same time they are permitted to maintain or reintroduce tariffs and quotas against E.E.C. products so as to further their economic development, or protect infant industries or for revenue purposes.[45]

These circumscribed preferences which the eighteen associates extend in return to the E.E.C. member States are, indeed, the 'reverse preferences' about which there has been so much discussion and controversy dating back to the colonial association agreement under Part IV of the Rome Treaty. For developed market economy countries like the United States of America, as non-members of the E.E.C., charge that the reverse preferences prevent the association arrangements from complying with Article XXIV of the General Agreement on Tariffs and Trade (G.A.T.T.), which, by way of exception to Article 1 of G.A.T.T,[46] permits the formation of customs unions and free trade areas with other countries.[47] In a recent

42. See Yaoundé I, Art. 2; Yaoundé II, Art. 2.
43. See Yaounde I, Art. 2(4); Yaoundé II, Art. 2(2).
44. See Yaoundé I, Art. 3; Yaoundé II, Art. 3.
45. See Yaoundé I, Art. 3(2); Yaoundé II, Art. 3(2); see also Treaty of Rome, Art. 133(3).
46. On G.A.T.T. see Alexandrowicz, *World Economic Agencies*, London, 1962, pp. 215–51.
47. Article 1 of G.A.T.T. provides that: 'with respect to customs duties and charges of any kind imposed on or in connection with importation or exportation

pronouncement on the subject, for example, Representative Wilbur Mills, chairman of the House's Ways and Means Committee in the United States, was reported to have stressed that it would be a travesty of the principle of extending tariff preferences to developing countries if the United States were to extend these preferences 'to countries that give discriminatory reverse preferences to the European Community or any other industrialized country'. He also added that the United States does not 'seek this petty concession from the developing countries and . . . expects that other wealthy and powerful trading countries will not insist on these demands'.[48]

Now, to the United States' charge that reverse preferences discriminate against other suppliers, and that their proliferation erodes the G.A.T.T. 'most favoured nation' principle, the Community's attitude appears to be that 'G.A.T.T. rules authorise the network of association and trading agreements which the Community maintains or is negotiating with many countries in Europe and elsewhere'.[49] Examining 'U.S.–E.E.C. relations after Nixon's victory', one commentator, therefore, remarked on the issue of trading agreements that 'For a combination of political, historical and economic reasons, the Community says that the policy of preferential agreements is part of its drive to provide development aid to the Third World and to avoid the re-erection of trade barriers in Europe.'[50]

---

or imposed on the international transfer of payments for imports and exports . . . any advantage, favour, privilege or immunity granted by any contracting party to any product originating in or destined for any other country shall be accorded immediately and unconditionally to the like product originating in or destined for the territories of all other contracting parties'. Developing countries, to which group associates of the E.E.C. belong, are critical of G.A.T.T., although its chief purpose is to encourage nations to reduce tariffs and other trade barriers on a multilateral, reciprocal, non-discriminatory basis. They label G.A.T.T. the 'rich countries' club' and argue that tariff bargaining is extremely unequal when it takes place between rich, powerful nations and poor, weak ones, and that *reciprocal* free trade between advanced and developing countries will simply force developing countries to remain in primary production, subject to all the disadvantages of such specialisation. See Eric Stein and Peter Hay, *Law and Institutions in the Atlantic Area*, New York, 1967, pp. 266–7. On the relation of the E.E.C. Association Treaty to G.A.T.T., see *ibid.*, pp. 411–18; William Gorell Barnes, *Europe and the Developing World, cit.*, pp. 9–13.

48. See *West Africa*, No. 2912, 2 April 1973, p. 444; *ibid.*, No. 2911, 26 March 1973, p. 399, for David Newson's (U.S. Assistant Secretary of State for African Affairs) review of U.S. policy towards Africa for the Royal Commonwealth Society, London, where the subject of 'reverse preferences' is also raised; see also Gerard and Victoria Curzon, 'Neo-colonialism and the European Economic Community', *Y.B.W.A.*, 1971, pp. 118–141, at pp. 125–6.

49. See *European Community*, No. 12, December 1972, pp. 6–7, at p. 7.

50. *Ibid.*, p. 7.

2. *Financial and technical co-operations.* The Yaoundé Conventions, it is generally believed, have been most beneficial to the associates in matters of financial and technical co-operation.[51] Indeed, out of the world's twenty-five least developed countries, eight—namely, Burundi, Chad, Dahomey, Mali, Niger, Rwanda, Somalia and Upper Volta—are among the eighteen associated African and Malagasy States. Thus, for most of them the aid policy under the Yaoundé Convention type of association, which is lacking in other forms of association to be discussed later, has a special appeal.

The European Development Fund (E.D.F.) is the principal instrument for carrying out the Community's financial and technical aid policy in the associated States and in certain other countries and territories overseas. It is administered by the Commission and financed by the member States. The Yaoundé Conventions, however, permit the European Investment Bank (E.I.B.), principally designed to promote European regional development, to finance development in the associated countries.

Now, in 1958, when the Community first set up the E.D.F., the sum of $581 million was made available for making non-repayable grants during 1958–63 so as to further social and economic development in the eighteen associates. This was in addition to direct bilateral aid from individual Community countries.[52]

For the 1964–69 period, total aid provided through the fund under Yaoundé I was increased to $800 million (including $70 million for other territories still linked to the E.E.C. member States).[53] Of the amount given to the eighteen associates, $620 million were in the form of outright grants and the remaining $110 million in the form of loans (including $46 million as 'soft' loans, that is, at specially low interest rates).

Yaoundé II increased the fund to $1,000 million, including $82 million for the Community's overseas dependent territories. Of the $918 million given to the eighteen associates, $748 million are in the form of outright grants, $80 million as soft loans and $90 million as loans from the European Investment Bank.[54]

Initially the fund's activities[55] concentrated mainly on infra-

51. On financial and technical aid provisions, see Yaoundé I, Arts. 15–28; Yaoundé II, Arts. 17–30.
52. See *European Community: the Facts*, European Communities Press and Information, May 1971, p. 25.
53. *Ibid.*
54. *Ibid.*
55. See *European Development Aid*, Commission of the European Communities,

structure projects such as roads, ports, railways, buildings, water supplies and telecommunications, which are considered the basis of general economic development. The social aspects of development (schools, hospitals and medical services) also received considerable attention. Lately its activities cover other important fields such as agriculture and agricultural diversification. Progressively, too, the Community is also encouraging the industrialisation of the associated States, although such encouragement is still smaller than the associates have been pressing for.

3. *Rights of establishment and the free movement of capital.* Under the Yaoundé Conventions the provisions on the right of establishment or the provision of services are, as in preferential trade arrangements, based on the principle of non-discrimination in the associated States against nationals and companies from the E.E.C. member States, subject to reciprocity with respect to nationals and companies from the associated States in the member States.[56] The rights grounded in these provisions are substantial and include 'the right to engage in and to exercise self-employed activities; to set up and manage undertakings and, in particular, companies; and to set up agencies, branches or subsidiaries'.[57] In effect, this wide scope given to rights of establishment precludes the associated States from adopting any measure the effect of which would be to reserve participation in certain enterprises exclusively to their own nationals.[58] It is also doubtful whether in real terms the associates can take, or indeed are taking, full advantage of the reciprocity of these provisions. For, as Professor Onitiri, the Director of the Nigerian Institute of Social and Economic Research, Ibadan, has rightly pointed out, 'the prospects that the nationals of the Associated States will be in a position to establish enterprises in the member countries of the E.E.C., on any significant scale, would appear, at best, to be both remote and unlikely'.[59]

General Directorate, Press and Information, pp. 29–30. See also *West Africa*, No. 2888, 16 October 1972, pp. 1381–2.

56. See Yaoundé I, Art. 29; Yaoundé II, Art. 31.

57. See Yaoundé I, Art. 31; Yaoundé II, Art. 33.

58. As is aimed at, for instance, under the Nigerian Enterprises Promotion Decree, 1972 (Federal Republic of Nigeria *Official Gazette*, No. 10, vol. 59, Lagos, 28 February 1972.)

59. Onitiri, 'Britain, the Commonwealth and Europe', a paper (as yet unpublished) presented at the annual general meeting of the Nigerian Society of International Law held at the Parliament Buildings, Agodi, Ibadan, on 16–17 March 1973.

The signatories also undertake to free payments and capital movements connected with the facilities for establishment:

Each Signatory State undertakes . . . to authorize payments relating to trade in goods, to services and capital and to wages, as also the transfer of such payments to the member State or Associated State in which the creditor or the beneficiary is resident, in so far as the movement of such goods, services, capital or persons has been liberalized in implementation of this Convention.[60]

4. *The institutions of the Association.* Yaoundé II retains the institutional provision of Yaoundé I, and accordingly, establishes the following organs for the structural link between the E.E.C. and the eighteen associated African and Malagasy States.

The Association Council[61] consists of members of the E.E.C. Council of Ministers, members of the E.E.C. Commission and one member of the government of each associated State. It meets at least once a year, and the chairmanship is held in turn by a member of the E.E.C. Council and a member of the government of an associated State.

The Association Council is empowered to take decisions binding on the contracting parties, to formulate such resolutions, recommendations or opinions as it may deem necessary to achieve the common objectives and to ensure the smooth functioning of the association arrangement. It can also review periodically the results of the association arrangements, taking into account the objectives of the association.

The Association Committee. The Association Council is assisted in the performance of its functions by an Association Committee,[62] composed of one representative from each member State, one representative of the E.E.C. Commission and one representative of each associated State. Its chairman is provided by the State which is presiding over the Association Council. In other words, the chairmanship procedure here is the same as for the Association Council.

This Committee, whose duties and powers are defined by the Association Council, ensures the continuity of co-operation necessary for the smooth functioning of the association. That is to say, the Committee conducts the day-to-day business of the association.

The Parliamentary Conference[63] of the association consists of members of the European Parliament and members of the parliaments of

60. See Yaoundé I, Art. 35, and Yaounde II, Art. 37.
61. See Yaoundé II, Arts. 42–46.   62. See Yaoundé II, Arts. 47–51.
63. See Yaoundé II, Art. 52.

the associated States. It meets once a year and annually receives from the Association Council a report on its activities. The ninth session of the Parliamentary Conference took place last April in Kinshasa, Zaire,[64] where the parliamentarians discussed, *inter alia*, the harmful effects of dollar devaluation on the associated States.

The Court of Arbitration[65] of the association deals with disputes in association matters which the Association Council fails to settle. It is composed of five members, namely a president who is appointed by the Association Council and four judges chosen among persons whose independence and competence can be fully guaranteed. Two of the judges are nominated by the Council of the European Communities and the other two by the associated States.

A recent dispute which is illustrative of matters that can be referred to the Arbitration Court is the unfortunate incident over 'melons and green beans'.[66] The dispute arose from a regulation (to which the eighteen associates vigorously objected) limiting duty-free entry of imports of certain fruits and vegetables from the associated States to a limited period of the year. This regulation was drawn up early in 1972 by customs officials entrusted with protecting Italian fruit and vegetable growers from North African competition. The eighteen associates argued that the items in question (1,800 tons of fruit and vegetables as against 20 million tons a year traded within the E.E.C.) had been allowed in duty-free at all times and that the new regulation violated the Yaoundé Convention, making a mockery of the Community's repeated promises to help the associated States market their produce in the Community.

The associated African States, therefore, raised the matter at the Luxembourg session of the Council of Association on 10 October 1972. They also threatened to take the offending regulation to the Arbitration Court. At this point the Luxembourg Foreign Minister, Gaston Thorn, called away from his mother's funeral to participate in the debate, suggested that a former president of the Commission,

64. See *West Africa*, No. 2914, 16 April 1973, p. 517. Prior to the Kinshasa meeting of the Parliamentary Conference of the Association, the European Parliament, meeting in Strasbourg, changed the name of its committee for relations with Afro-Malagasy States to the Committee for Development and Co-operation.

65. See Yaoundé II, Art. 53.

66. Gemini News Service, GE 227, 16 October 1972. See also *West Africa*, No. 2888, 16 October 1972, p. 1381, and Robert Taylor, 'Towards a common policy on development aid', *European Community*, No. 11, November 1972, p. 10; *African Development*, December 1972, p. 14.

Jean Rey, be asked to mediate. Only the Italians objected to this suggestion, and to prevent the situation from deteriorating even further the other E.E.C. partners put the issue to a vote, at the end of which the Italians were outvoted.[67]

SOME CRITICISMS OF THE YAOUNDÉ CONVENTIONS

The existing eighteen associates, as we shall show later, are suspicious of the enlargement of the Yaoundé association to include anglophone Commonwealth African States. Apart from such anticipatory fears, the associates seem to entertain certain grievances against the Community. There is disappointment, for example, at the lack of appreciable increase in the level of exports from associates to the E.E.C. and over deterioration in the terms of trade, which seem to cancel out other benefits.[68] Thus at the recent ninth session of the Association Parliamentary Conference in Kinshasa, Zaire, M. Yace, President of the Ivory Coast National Assembly, who was chairman of the conference, according to reports[69] said that Africa wanted the E.E.C. to give priority to imports of African manufactured goods. Europe should help Africa organise itself to the maximum, and not just increase development grants from the European Development Fund.

For some time, too, the eighteen associates have felt that a guarantee of some kind for the prices of basic commodities would be more rewarding than any preferences, particularly so when the real value of such preferences is being offset or affected by the introduction of generalised preferences.[70] This subject, indeed, came up during

67. On subsequent reports on the fruit and vegetable episode, see *West Africa* No. 2905, 12 February 1973, p. 207; No. 2913, 9 April 1973, p. 474; No. 2912 2 April 1973, p. 444.

68. See *West Africa*, No. 2888, 16 October 1972, p. 1381.

69. See *West Africa*, No. 2914, 16 April 1973, p. 517.

70. See *West Africa*, No. 2888, p. 1381. In response to demands by the United Nations Conference on Trade and Development (U.N.C.T.A.D.), the E.E.C. introduced, in July 1971, a generalised tariff preference system for manufactured goods from some ninety-six developing countries commonly known as the 'Group of 77'. See *European Community*, 1 January 1972, pp. 21–3; U.N.C.T.A.D. aims (but without much success yet) at advancing a generalised preference scheme whereby industrialised countries (like the E.E.C. countries) would give preferential rates of a non-reciprocal and non-discriminatory nature to most manufactured goods from developing countries in order to increase the latter's export earnings, promote their industrialisation and accelerate their economic growth.

The Council of Ministers of the E.E.C. decided in June 1972 to extend the Community's generalised tariff preference scheme to Cuba, Bhutan, Fiji, Bangladesh, Bahrein, Qatar, the Gulf States, Oman, Sikkim, Nauru, Western Samoa

President Pompidou's visit to Niger and Chad, two of the associates, in February 1972. In words which underlined the French government's full awareness of the injustice in the rise in price of industrial products while primary products stay the same or even fall, President Pompidou reportedly stated in Niamey, Niger, that '. . . we shall not cease to intervene with all the people with whom we are dealing, and particularly our European partners, to make sure that African products have their fair place in world trade'.[71]

IV. ASSOCIATION UNDER THE DECLARATION OF INTENT OF APRIL 1963

At the signing of the First Yaoundé Convention on 20 July 1963 the representatives of the E.E.C., pursuant to the declaration of intent adopted by the E.E.C. Council at its meeting of 1–2 April 1963, declared their readiness to negotiate agreements with any non-member countries who so requested whose economic structure and output were comparable with those of the associated States.[72] The proposed agreements were to take one of the following patterns:

1. Accession to the (First) Yaoundé Convention according to the procedure laid down in Article 58 of that convention, in which case such State 'shall . . . enjoy the same rights and be bound by the same obligations as the associated States'.
2. Association agreement with mutual rights and obligations, particularly in matters of trade; or
3. Commercial agreements to facilitate and expand trade between the E.E.C. and these countries.

---

and Tonga (all new members of the 'Group of 77'). Requests from Mediterranean countries (Turkey, Greece, Malta, Israel, Spain) and Roumania to join the scheme faced strong opposition by France and the Netherlands, which argued that the scheme is supposed to be limited to Third World States and that an overall agreement with the Community's Mediterranean neighbours could meet their needs. However, other members support the Commission's proposal that they be included, with restrictions for Spain and Israel because they are more developed. Yugoslavia already benefits from the preferences as a member of the 'Group of 77'. See *European Community*, No. 7–8, July–August 1972, p. 4.

In practice the E.E.C. generalised preference scheme is largely beneficial to the more advanced Asian and Latin American countries and not to Africa, where manufacturing for export is in its infancy; see *African Development*, December 1972, p. 3.

71. *West Africa*, No. 2852, 11 February 1972, p. 142.
72. See *Keesing's Contemporary Archives*, 1965, p. 20833.

Undoubtedly, the non-member States which the representatives of the E.E.C. had in mind were mainly the overseas Commonwealth countries, many of which had anxiously awaited the result of Britain's negotiations for entry into the Community. Some nine days after the signing of the First Yaoundé Convention these negotiations broke down completely and, not long after that, some of these Commonwealth developing countries, hitherto critical and unenthusiastic about association with the E.E.C.,[73] changed their minds and began exploring the possibilities of negotiating association arrangements with the Community.

In the light of the declaration of intent stipulations, suggestions of association agreements with India, Pakistan and Ceylon were refused because the structure of their economies and the importance of their manufacturing industries raised problems not envisaged under Part IV of the Treaty of Rome.[74] On the other hand, Nigeria and the States of the East African community (Tanzania, Uganda and Kenya) succeeded in signing association agreements with the Community under Article 238 of the Treaty in preference to accession to the First Yaoundé Convention. In both cases, a 'mixed procedure' was adopted whereby both the member States of the Community and the Council of the E.E.C. on the one hand and the respective African States on the other signed the association agreement. The adverse effect of such a procedure, as we show below, is that the failure of any member State of the E.E.C. to ratify the agreement prevented the particular association coming into force.

ASSOCIATION WITH NIGERIA—THE LAGOS AGREEMENT

On 16 July 1966 Nigeria and the E.E.C. signed an association agreement in Lagos, capital of the Nigerian federation.[75] The Lagos agreement would have expired on the same date, 31 May 1969, as the First Yaoundé Convention. It was, however, overtaken by the events of the Nigerian crisis and subsequent civil war (1966–70).

---

73. See *Keesing's Contemporary Archives*, 1962, pp. 19009–13.

74. See Okigbo; *Africa and the Common Market*, 1967, p. 46.

75. See *Agreement Establishing an Association between the European Economic Community and the Republic of Nigeria*, July 1966, published by the Nigerian Federal Ministry of Information. See also *International Legal Materials*, vol. 5, 1966, pp. 828–58. On the crucial closing stages of Nigeria's negotiations with the E.E.C., see *West Africa*, No. 2501, 8 May 1965.

For the Lagos agreement expired without coming into force, for lack of ratification. A Nigerian proposal to implement that agreement before ratification by the Community and its member States was rejected by the E.E.C.[76]

Although the Lagos agreement did not take effect, it is nevertheless necessary to examine, at least briefly, its main provisions in view of the fact that they seem to have influenced the pattern of the association agreement which the E.E.C. later signed with the East African community. It has three main sections, namely trade; right of establishment and services, payments and capital transfers; and institutions.

Under the terms of the 1966 Lagos agreement, all Nigerian exports, except cocoa beans, groundnut oil, palm oil, and plywood and similar products,[77] would have entered the Community's market free of customs duties and charges having equivalent effect.[78] Nigeria in turn would have removed all customs duties and charges under the terms of Protocol No. 2 from some twenty-six commodities imported from E.E.C. countries,[79] except when such duties were necessary to meet its development needs or industrialisation requirements or in the event of balance-of-payment difficulties.[80] The four export commodities excluded from duty-free entry into the E.E.C. were subjected to a tariff quota based on the average of Nigeria's exports of these products to the E.E.C. in the years 1962, 1963 and 1964, after which they were to be subject to normal Community duties. The Nigerian association agreement has, therefore, been rightly described as 'essentially a modified tariff agreement covering a limited volume of trade between the E.E.C. and Nigeria', as the trade provisions were not 'aiming at either a full-fledged customs union or a free trade area'.[81]

Nigeria also agreed not to discriminate between the nationals of one Community country and another in matters of right to establish businesses and supply services as defined in articles 16 and 17 of the agreement. This meant in effect that Community member States

76. See *Keesing's Contemporary Archives*, 1967, p. 21887.
77. Article 2(1).   78. Article 2(1).
79. Article 3(1).   80. Articles 3(2), 6(2).
81. See Costonis, 'The treaty-making power of the E.E.C.: the perspectives of a decade', 5 *C.M.L.Rev* (1967–68) 421–57, at p. 427. Following the publication of the draft agreement in 1965, both the United States of America and Britain officially objected to its terms, on the ground that the agreement, which introduced preferences for the E.E.C. and Nigeria in each other's markets, would not establish a free trade area and would not, therefore, conform to G.A.T.T. rules. See *Keesing's Contemporary Archives*, 1967, p. 21887.

would have been better placed in Nigeria than Britain,[82] for example, notwithstanding the benefits enjoyed in the British market by Nigerian exports under the Commonwealth preference scheme.

Conspicuously absent from the Lagos agreement were provisions according Nigeria economic aid and provisions establishing strong institutional ties between the parties.

The agreement provided for only one organ, the Association Council,[83] to be composed of members of the E.E.C. Council and Commission as well as members of the government of Nigeria. It was empowered to take decisions binding on the parties, to examine all matters concerning the implementation of the association agreement and to review periodically the results of the association arrangements.

There was, however, also provision for an *Ad hoc Arbitration Tribunal* to handle any dispute concerning the interpretation or the application of the association agreement unresolved by the Association Council.[84]

The explanation for this rather tenuous structural link between Nigeria and the E.E.C. lies, perhaps, in the fact that Nigeria, unlike the Afro-Malagasy associates, was less prepared or disposed to be tied too closely to Europe in return for trade and development aid. It must be pointed out that the failure of the Lagos agreement to take effect, for the reasons stated above, did not in any way stop the existing trade relations between Nigeria and individual member States of the E.E.C., even throughout the civil war years, although these were subjected to the Community's common external tariff whenever applicable.[85] Since the civil war Nigeria has been having a fresh look at the enlarged European Communities,[86] which we shall discuss later, especially in connection with the offer of association to some Commonwealth countries under the Accession Treaty of January 1972.

82. That is, before Britain's entry into the Community.
83. Article 21. A similar organ exists under the Yaoundé Convention, see p. 212 above.
84. See Art. 25 of the Lagos agreement.
85. This fact is confirmed by the *Annual Abstract of Statistics* of Nigeria's import and export trade published by the Federal Office of Statistics, Nigeria, 1966, 1967, 1968, 1969 and 1970.
86. Following the ratification of the Accession Treaty of 22 January 1973, membership of the Communities has now increased to nine from the original six.

ASSOCIATION WITH THE EAST AFRICAN COMMUNITY—
THE ARUSHA CONVENTION

Two years after the Lagos agreement, the partner States of the East African community[87] (Kenya, Tanzania and Uganda) signed a similar association agreement with the E.E.C. at Arusha, Tanzania, on 26 July 1968. This agreement, commonly known as the 'Arusha Convention',[88] was, like the Nigerian association agreement, based on the E.E.C. declaration of intent of 1963. Exploratory talks leading to its being signed had commenced as far back as February 1964.

The Arusha Convention, which was signed by member States of the E.E.C., the E.E.C. Council and the partner States of the East African Community, also suffered from the disadvantages of 'mixed procedure' to which we referred in connection with the Lagos agreement. It had expired automatically with the First Yaoundé Convention on 31 May 1969 without entering into force. For only Belgium, Kenya, the Netherlands, Tanzania and Uganda had ratified it. But, unlike Nigeria's association agreement, the Arusha Convention was saved by the decision of the E.E.C. Council, which, on 28 May 1969, authorised the Commission to enter into negotiations with the East African countries with a view to concluding a *provisional agreement* which would incorporate some of the provisions of the previous convention of 26 July 1968. It was against this background that the Arusha Convention was renewed on 24 September 1969, and, as was intended, it took over the main provisions of the first agreement.[89] It has been in force since 1 January 1971 and, like the Second Yaoundé Convention, will expire on 31 January 1975.

Following the same pattern as the one signed in July 1968, the new Arusha Convention likewise covers matters of trade; right of establishment and services, payments and capital transfer; and institutions. Indeed, its framework is reminiscent of the Lagos Agreement discussed above.

87. For more details about the East African Community, see Ingrid Doimi di Delupis, *The East African Community and Common Market*, 1969; see also Akwunmi, in *Journal of World Trade Law*, vol. 6, No. 2, 1972.

88. See *International Legal Materials*, 1970, pp. 741–68; see also *Keesing's Contemporary Archives*, 1968, p. 22978.

89. Negotiations for the renewal of the agreement with certain modifications, took place in Brussels from 30 June to 10 July 1969. See *Keesing's Contemporary Archives*, 1969, p. 23632.

On trade, the new Arusha Convention provides that the E.E.C. will suspend customs duties and quantitative restrictions on imports of all East African products except cloves, coffee and canned pine-apples, which compete with exports of the eighteen associated Afro-Malagasy States and for which tariff quotas were fixed of 56,000 tons per annum for coffee, 860 tons for tinned pineapple, and 100 tons for cloves. These three commodities so restricted happen to be of major importance to the three East African countries.

Again, for products competing with agricultural production within the Community the Community also grants some conces-sions on a few products such as beef and veal, and some fruits and vegetables but, as Professor Onitiri has rightly pointed out, 'these have been fairly marginal, usually involving removal of import duties but maintaining the more substantial internal levies'.[90]

The Arusha Convention States in turn grant the E.E.C. States tariff preferences. They undertake to remove some tariffs and quotas on imports of some fifty-eight products from the Community, except where industrialisation, government revenue or balance-of-payment requirements dictate otherwise. Comparatively, the 'free' trade provisions of the Arusha Convention are as circumscribed as those of the Lagos agreement.

The provisions of the Arusha Convention on right of estab-lishment and services, payments and capital transfer, and institu-tions (Association Council and Ad hoc Tribunal) are exactly the same as for corresponding areas in the Lagos agreement discussed above, and therefore need not be repeated here.

In passing, it may be pointed out that the present political dispute between Tanzania and Uganda, following the overthrow of Obote's regime by President Idi Amin, is seriously threatening the continued existence of the East African community.[91] It is not unlikely, too, that this period of uncertainty has considerably undermined the interests of the Arusha Convention States within the European Community. In particular, the internal stress, unless smoothed out in time, may well constitute a clog in their preparations for the forthcoming negotiations with the enlarged Communities.

90. Onitiri, *Britain, the Commonwealth and Europe, op. cit.*
91. See 'East African Community—the beginning of the end?', *The Renaissance*, Enugu, Nigeria, 28 February 1973, p. 13.

V. ASSOCIATION UNDER THE ENLARGED COMMUNITY: OPTIONS OPEN TO COMMONWEALTH AFRICAN STATES

As stated above, the Yaoundé and Arusha conventions will expire on 1 January 1975, but talks with the Communities for their renewal and for new associations under the enlarged Communities will begin on 1 August 1973.

Under the Accession Treaty[92] of 22 January 1972, which was signed in Brussels by the Communities on one side and Denmark, Ireland, Norway[93] and the United Kingdom on the other, Common-wealth countries in Africa, the Caribbean, the Indian Ocean and the Pacific have been offered three options on future relations with the enlarged Communities.[94] The countries concerned, commonly referred to as the 'associables', are to decide whether:

(a) to accede to a renewed Yaoundé Convention; or

(b) to conclude some other form of association under Article 238 of the Treaty of Rome, 1957, as the kind exemplified by the Arusha Convention; or

(c) merely to negotiate a special trade agreement with a view to facilitating the developing trade with the Communities.

The Commonwealth 'associables' concerned are Barbados, Bots-wana, Fiji, Gambia, Ghana, Guyana, Jamaica, Kenya, Lesotho, Malawi, Mauritius, Nigeria, Sierra Leone, Swaziland, Tanzania, Tonga, Trinidad and Tobago, Uganda, Western Samoa and Zambia.[95] They are required to make their choice known as soon as possible after accession by Britain and the other new member States of the Communities, though their present trading arrangements with the United Kingdom will be maintained until 31 January 1975, when the present Yaoundé Convention and the Arusha Convention will expire. In other words, these independent Commonwealth countries must be ready to begin negotiations on the basis of their respective decisions as from 1 August 1973.

92. See European Communities Treaty, Brussels, 22 January 1972, Parts I and II, Cmnd. 4862–I and Cmnd. 4862–II, London, H.M.S.O., 1972.

93. During various referenda on the Accession Treaty Norwegians subsequently voted to stay out of the Communities.

94. See Protocol No. 22 to the Accession Treaty of 22 January 1972.

95. See Annex VI to the Act of Accession.

The offer in section I of Protocol No. 22 of the Accession Treaty is supplemented by the provision in section III of the protocol concerning the 'firm purpose' of the Community to safeguard 'the interests of all the countries referred to in this Protocol whose economies depend to a considerable extent on the export of primary products, and particularly sugar'.[96]

On the other hand, to safeguard the existing special relations between the E.E.C. and the African and Malagasy Yaoundé group of States, section II(2) of Protocol No. 22 further stipulates that:

The accession of the new Member States to the Community and the possible extension of the policy of association should not be the source of any weakening in the Community's relations with the Associated African and Malagasy States which are parties to the Convention of Association signed on 29 July 1969

and that

The Community's relations with the Associated African and Malagasy States ensure for those States a range of advantages and are based on structures which give the Association its distinctive character in the fields of trade relations, financial and technical co-operation and joint institutions.

In a tone of finality section II(3) adds:

The Community's objective in its policy of association shall remain the safeguarding of what has been achieved and of the fundamental principles referred to above.

There is an element of contradiction in these two separate provisions, which must inevitably set the 'associables' thinking about the reality of the offer of association extended to them under the Accession Treaty in the light of this most-favoured-group qualification attached to this offer. In fact, these guarantees given to the Yaoundé associates recall to mind the solemn assurance which President Pompidou of France gave to them during his tour of Mauritania, Senegal, the Ivory Coast, Cameroun and Gabon in February 1971. In a speech in Yaoundé, Cameroun, he said, *inter alia*:

96. The second paragraph of section III of Protocol No. 22 states that the 'question of sugar will be settled within this framework, bearing in mind with regard to exports of sugar the importance of this product for the economies of several of these countries and of the Commonwealth countries in particular'. See also Protocol No. 17 on the import of sugar by the U.K. from the exporting countries and territories referred to in the Commonwealth Sugar Agreement. See also *The United Kingdom and the European Communities*, Cmnd. 4715, H.M.S.O., London, 1971, pp. 28–9.

Nobody can be unaware that there is every chance that the E.E.C. will in the near future undergo a fundamental development in that its enlargement will finally be accepted to include Great Britain and other European countries which have asked to become members. This profound change is evidently likely to have repercussions on the links with associated African States that arise from the Yaoundé Convention. That is a problem with major and multiple implications that rightly preoccupy all our African friends. This is why I wish to solemnly state in this city of Yaoundé that France in so far as she is concerned will intervene at the appropriate moment.[97]

In spite of these solemn assurances and guarantees, the fears and suspicion of the associates against the enlargement of the Yaoundé-type association to cover anglophone African States linger on. Thus, at Fort Lamy, Chad, during the visit of President Pompidou in February 1971, there was undisguised reference to preoccupation by the associates with 'the economic potential of the African Commonwealth countries, whose future association with the E.E.C. could affect the existing balance of co-operation between the E.E.C. and the existing eighteen associated Yaoundé States'.[98] Some of the associates, especially the major traders in primary produce, such as the Ivory Coast, see the enlargement as a continuation of a process in which all the privileges enjoyed as French colonies have been slowly whittled away.[99]

The Commonwealth independent States, on their part, are individually affected by greatly varying circumstances. Nigeria's case, for instance, is quite different from those of Botswana, Lesotho and Swaziland, which are faced with the extremely tricky problem of compromising their customs union with *apartheid* South Africa.[100] However, over and above their particular interests these African States must remain constantly aware of the dominant interest of Africa as a whole. In this connection Professor Onitiri suggests that

The ideal procedure would . . . be for all African countries to whom the offer of association has been made to agree before the negotiations begin on how the various options should be defined so as to take into account some of the global political and economic considerations . . . as well as the specific long term interest of Africa as a whole.[101]

97. See *Daily Times*, Lagos, Nigeria, 14 July 1971, pp. 11–18, at p. 17—a special article published on French national day.

98. See *West Africa*, No. 2852, 11 February 1972, p. 143. During this second tour of Africa, President Pompidou also visited Niger.

99. See *West Africa*, No. 2888, 16 October 1972, p. 1381.

100. As to special provisions in the Accession Treaty concerning Botswana, Lesotho or Swaziland, see Protocol No. 22, section II(3).

101. Onitiri, *op. cit.*

Working towards such a common approach does not necessarily mean that all African countries would choose the same option, although the European States, or at least their spokesmen, seem to suggest that the Yaoundé-type association is best for African States.[102]

BRITISH DEPENDENCIES AND PART IV OF THE
TREATY OF ROME, 1957

Under the Accession Treaty of 22 January 1972 all British dependent territories (and the Anglo-French condominium of the New Hebrides) are offered association under Part IV of the Treaty of Rome of 1957 discussed above.

Gibraltar and Hong Kong are excluded from the list of these dependent overseas territories, which include the Bahamas, Bermuda, British Antarctic territory, British Honduras, British Indian Ocean territory, the British Solomon Islands protectorate, the British Virgin Islands, Brunei, the Cayman Islands, the Central and Southern Line Islands, the Falkland Islands and dependencies, Gilbert and Ellice Islands colony, Montserrat, the New Hebrides (with France), Pitcairn Island, St Helena and dependencies (Ascension and Tristan da Cunha), the Seychelles, the Turks and Caicos Islands, West Indian associated States (Antigua, Dominica, Grenada, St Lucia, St Vincent, St Kitts–Nevis–Anguilla).[103]

Gibraltar will participate in the E.E.C. under Article 227(4) of the Treaty of Rome, which applies to 'the European territories for whose external relations a member State is responsible'. But since Gibraltar is not part of the United Kingdom's customs territory, it has been agreed, at Gibraltar's request, that she should not be included in the customs territory of the enlarged Community.[104]

102. The E.E.C. Commission, for instance, has let it be known privately that it would prefer all the Africans to opt for the Yaoundé Convention. Again, Lady Tweedsmuir, the British Minister of State, speaking at a diplomatic and Commonwealth writers' lunch in London in October 1972, was quoted as saying that it was her personal opinion that the Yaoundé Convention was the best choice, and if asked, the British government would suggest this. See *West Africa*, No. 2888, 16 October 1972, p. 1381. Thus Robert Taylor, in his article entitled 'Towards a common policy on development aid' in *European Community*, No. 11, November 1972, at p. 10, states that '. . . Britain and the Community see the Yaoundé model as the best suited to the Commonwealth countries . . .'

103. See *The United Kingdom and the European Communities*, Cmnd. 4715, *op. cit.*, p. 30.

104. See *The United Kingdom and the European Communities*, Cmnd. 4715, *op. cit.*, p. 30.

Hong Kong, on the other hand, will be included within the scope of the E.E.C. scheme of generalised preferences.[105]

For some time now the Commonwealth 'associables' have been exploring the possibilities of maintaining a united front in the forthcoming talks with the Communities. In this way they hope to have 'much greater strength and leverage in negotiations'.[106] However, the overall results of the various conferences, meetings and consultations held in furtherance of this objective indicate that agreement on a common approach by the associates and 'associables' is not going to be easy.

In April 1972 officials from all Commonwealth countries met at Marlborough House, London,[107] and decided, *inter alia*, that the twenty Commonwealth 'associables' should ask the Commonwealth Secretary General, Arnold Smith, to sound out the francophone African countries for a meeting. Coincidentally, at a conference of the eighteen associates at Nouakchott, Mauritania, at exactly the same time, M. Djim Sylla (of Mali) who is the Secretary General of the Co-ordinating Committee of the Associated African States and Malagasy (A.A.S.M.), was briefed to sound out the Commonwealth countries about a meeting. The chance for both sides came at U.N.C.T.A.D. III, which was held in Santiago, Chile, in April 1972, where M. Sylla met Mr Hunter of New Zealand, who is the Deputy Secretary General of the Commonwealth, and the two men discussed the proposed conference.[108]

The francophone group wanted a meeting of Ministers to be held in Europe and some real negotiation. On the other hand, the Commonwealth 'associables' wanted a lower-level meeting held in Africa as a starting point. In the end the compromise was to hold a

105. See p. 214 (note 70), on generalised tariff preferences; see also Protocol No. 22 of the Accession Treaty, section II(4).

106. See *African Development*, September 1972, p. 14.

107. See *The Times*, London, 6 April, 1972, pp. 13, 15. A second conference was held there in July 1972. See B.B.C. newsreel, 25 July 1972.

108. See *African Development*, September 1972, p. 13. At the invitation of the Commonwealth Secretariat, M. Seydou Djim Sylla visited London in December 1972 and held a meeting with Commonwealth representatives. According to the same report, the francophone associates, through M. Sylla, invited the Commonwealth 'associables' to a meeting in Brussels in January 1973; see *West Africa*, No. 2896, 11 December 1972, p. 1642.

meeting of senior officials in Geneva in September 1972. Thereafter there would follow a meeting of Ministers of all thirty-eight countries (i.e. associates and associables together) before the end of the year. However, the Santiago *rapport* by the representatives of the two groups did not last long. It was torpedoed by suspicions among the francophone group, possibly inspired by France, concerning the role of the Commonwealth Secretariat and the alleged efforts of Britain to reduce French influence in the French-speaking African countries.[109] This unhappy development led to a drawing back on the francophone side. In France itself there followed a change of government, with M. Messmer succeeding M. Chaban-Delmas as Premier, which was interpreted as heralding a harder line.[110]

The idea of a September joint meeting of the associates and Commonwealth 'associables' in Geneva was consequently abandoned. The francophone countries thereafter wanted the thirty-eight to meet in Africa for talks at Ministerial level, which meeting would not, however, take place until after the twenty 'associables' had declared their position on the three choices.[111]

The picture changed dramatically during the September 1972 conference in London of the Commonwealth Finance Ministers,[112] when Nigeria's Federal Commissioner for Finance, Alhaji Shehu Shagari, in his address to that assembly, announced Nigeria's rejection of an association agreement with the European Communities. He stated, *inter alia*, that:

The Nigerian Government has been studying the implications of the British move as well as options offered by the E.E.C. to developing countries whose interests are likely to be affected. We in Nigeria are not convinced that the Yaoundé Convention, with its reverse preferences, or the Lagos-type agreement, with quota limitations, is capable of meeting our needs. It is, therefore, all the more necessary for us to intensify the search for an arrangement that will best serve Nigeria's national interests. It is in such a context

109. See *African Development*, September 1972, p. 13.
110. See report of his general policy statement in *West Africa*, No. 2888, 16 October 1972, p. 1403.
111. See *African Development*, September 1972, p. 13. According to other reports, when the Commonwealth representatives met at the Commonwealth Secretariat late in 1972 they were unable to agree either on a Ministerial meeting of their own group or on one with the eighteen associates. The date of 22 January 1973 was proposed for a Commonwealth Ministerial meeting, which would have been prior to any joint meeting, with the associates, but even that date was reportedly not adopted. The Commonwealth States were said to be divided over contact with the associates and to be critical of the Commonwealth Secretariat. See *West Africa*, No. 2896, 11 December 1972, p. 1642; No. 2912, 2 April 1973, p. 427.
112. See *New Nigeria*, Kaduna, Nigeria, 25 September 1972, p. 15.

that we will look into the third option of a special trade agreement when the time comes.[113]

Again, prior to a recent visit to Nigeria of André Bettencourt,[114] Minister Delegate in the Foreign Ministry in Paris, Dr Okoi Arikpo, Nigeria's External Affairs Commissioner, gave an interview to *Agence France-Presse* in which he was quoted as saying that Nigeria intended to make it very clear to France that she did not want her own relations with the E.E.C. within the framework of the Yaoundé Convention, since this put limitations on the manufacturing and semi-processing of goods, while 'we have plans to process most of our primary products and sell them either as semi-processed or completely processed goods'.[115]

All along, Nigeria had adopted a 'wait and see' attitude and made no attempt to turn Commonwealth countries away from the idea of association. Now that she has taken a firm stand on the question of future relations with the Communities, it is not inconceivable that she may well lead an African campaign against the association offer.[116] In that case the enlarged Community must either modify the existing pattern of its relation with developing countries or take measures to minimise the adverse effect of Nigeria's stand on associates and 'associables' alike.[117] It is generally believed that the

113. Prior to this declaration, Nigeria's Head of State, General Yakubu Gowon, had told the visiting British Defence Secretary, Lord Carrington, that Nigeria would give careful thought to the proposed British entry into Europe and decide what was best for her. Writing on 'Options facing Commonwealth associables', Carol Cosgrove Twitchet, observed as follows: 'In the aftermath of the Civil War the political situation has undergone profound changes and the present leadership appears highly suspicious of association with the E.E.C.' See *European Community*, No. 10, October 1972, p. 19.

114. See *West Africa*, No. 2905, 12 February 1973, pp. 193–4.

115. *Ibid.*, p. 194.

116. In fact Nigeria is currently advocating the creation of a West African Economic Community, which will be discussed later.

117. Following Nigeria's rejection of association, members of the E.E.C. have made various diplomatic contacts with Nigeria to discuss the E.E.C. question. For example, Nigeria's External Affairs Commissioner, Dr Arikpo was invited to Britain and Ireland, which he visited from 28 November to 3 December 1972. See *West Africa*, No. 2896, 11 December 1972, p. 1669. In January 1973 Lady Tweedsmuir, Minister of State, Foreign and Commonwealth Office, passed through Lagos, Nigeria, on her way to Gambia and Sierra Leone. See *Daily Times*, Lagos, Thursday 25 January 1973, p. 18; One month later, in February 1973, Sir Alec Douglas-Home, British Foreign Secretary, made a four-day official visit to Nigeria. See *Daily Times*, Lagos, Saturday 17 February 1973, p. 32; *West Africa*, No. 2907, 26 February 1973, p. 293. Nigeria's Head of State undertook an official visit to Britain in June 1973.

So far only Mauritius, which is linked with the eighteen associates in the Afro-Malagasy Common Organisation (O.C.A.M.) has acceded to the Yaoundé

recently published 'Deniau memorandum' to be discussed below, is intended to remove the objections raised by Nigeria and other 'associables'. Whether this would persuade Nigeria to change her declared stand remains to be seen.

Outside Africa the impression has been created, and it is generally believed, that Britain's accession to the European Communities 'can act as the catalyst that will lead to a blurring of the francophone–anglophone division of the continent'.[118] But in practice events, especially within Africa, are not hopefully justifying such high expectations. On the contrary, there seems to exist on both sides continuing mistrust and, therefore, because of the far-reaching effect which any ultimate decision taken by the associates and 'associables' may well have on Africa as a whole, the issue of future links with Europe has featured prominently in conferences of various other bodies with an African base or connection. For example, a conference which took place in Dakar,[119] Senegal, from 29 January to 1 February 1973, considered the implications of the enlargement of the E.E.C. for trade and development in Africa. It was sponsored by the Conference of Directors of Economic and Social Research Institutions in Africa (CODESRIA), and the U.N. African Institute. It was organised under the auspices of the Economic Development Institute of the World Bank, the Development Centre of Organisation for Economic Co-operation and Development (O.E.C.D.) and the German Foundation for Developing Countries (G.S.E.).

Similarly, one of the important subjects discussed at the Ministerial meeting of the United Nations Economic Commission for Africa (E.C.A.)[120] in Accra, Ghana, in February 1973 was Africa's attitude to the enlarged E.E.C. and the framework in which

---

Convention, and Gambia is also reportedly interested in Yaoundé-type association. See *European Community*, January 1972, p. 9; *The Times*, London, 17 February 1972, p. 6; *ibid.*, 9 March 1972, p. 5; see also *West Africa*, No. 2822, 16 July 1971, p. 810; No. 2887, 9 October 1972, p. 1349; No. 2888, 16 October 1972, pp. 1381, 1404; No. 2896, 11 December 1972, p. 1674. Representatives of the East African Community began talks with the E.E.C. in Nairobi, Kenya, on the existing Arusha agreement on 21 February 1972. See *The Times*, London, 22 February 1972, p. 5.

118. See *African Development*, September 1972, p. 13. During his visit to Niger in February 1972 President Pompidou, said, *inter alia*, 'I think it is only logical that there should be close co-operation between African countries that speak English and French, and that British entry to the E.E.C. would help that co-operation.' See *West Africa*, No. 2852, 11 February 1972, p. 143.

119. See *West Africa*, No. 2901, 15 January 1973, p. 80.

120. See *West Africa*, No. 2907, 26 February 1973, p. 289.

African States can negotiate with the European Communities. The matter did not come up directly on the agenda, but the various statements made by some of the leading participants do reflect the mood of many African States.

For example, Mr Robert Gardner, the Ghanaian Executive Secretary of E.C.A., said before the meeting that the E.E.C.'s invitation to African States to take up associate status in the Community constitutes a great opportunity for Africa 'to speak to Europe'. It is now open to African governments, in concert, to define in clear terms the type of relations they wish to have with the E.E.C. On his part, the Secretary General of the Organisation of African Unity (O.A.U.), Mr Nzo Ekangaki, said that if a collective association with the E.E.C. was found desirable, then all the forty-one member States of the O.A.U. must negotiate as a body because an instrument negotiated under the auspices of the O.A.U. would be able to cater adequately for the interests of each member without compromising major continental objectives. Furthermore, he reminded the meeting that Africa needed to be aware of, and to ward off, the danger of allowing inter-African economic co-operation to become an instrument at the service of the interests of foreign industrialists and investors instead of using such co-operation as a means to accelerate Africa's development.

At the recent meeting in Abidjan, Ivory Coast, of the trade and planning Ministers of the forty-one member States of the O.A.U.,[121] bringing together the associates and the 'associables', the representatives considered major economic questions, including Africa's future relationship with the enlarged E.E.C., especially the vexed question of a common approach by French- and English-speaking States towards such links. The meeting adopted two major documents, namely a declaration which will be submitted to African heads of State at their forthcoming summit meeting in Addis Ababa in May and a report setting out the conference's position on specific African and world economic and monetary issues.

The representatives failed to agree on a common approach in the negotiations with the E.E.C. But the conference rejected the E.E.C. 'reciprocity policy' by denouncing the Community's practice of demanding African trade concessions to the Community in return

121. See *Daily Times*, Lagos, Nigeria, 10 May 1973, p. 9; *ibid.*, 14 May 1973, p. 40; *ibid.*, 15 May 1973, p. 13. The Abidjan meeting opened on 9 May 1973. Among other things, it set up a Council of African Finance Ministers to determine Africa's financial relationship with the outside world.

for preferential treatment for their exports to the Community. This, however, was not acceptable to several members of the French-speaking group of countries already associated with the E.E.C., which States grant such reverse preferences[122] to Europe because of what President Senghor of Senegal once described as 'the symbolic equality of the free trade area and the dignity involved'.[123]

One significant thing about the Abidjan decisions was that the African States represented there acted with full knowledge of the recent memorandum published by the Community which contains, as we show below, modifications meeting some of the African criticisms, including their objection to reverse preferences. Their stand at Abidjan, therefore, reaffirms how strongly they feel about some aspects of the association arrangements at present in operation.

In fact the publication of this innovative memorandum was timed to coincide with the important meetings in Nairobi, Kenya, and Kigali, Rwanda, of representatives of what has become known as the Lagos group of twelve Commonwealth African countries.

The Trade Ministers from these countries (i.e. Botswana, Gambia, Ghana, Kenya, Lesotho, Malawi, Nigeria, Sierra Leone, Swaziland, Tanzania, Uganda and Zambia) met in Lagos, Nigeria, on 16 February 1973 to decide their countries' relationship with the E.E.C. following Britain's entry.[124] The meeting resolved, among other things, to set up a secretariat under the auspices of the East African community,[125] to be supplied with additional personnel from Nigeria, Ghana and Botswana as it becomes necessary. The group agreed to hold its next meeting in Nairobi for a further study of the matter. This took place[126] in April 1973, that is, following another meeting of the group during the Accra meeting of the U.N. Econo-

122. On criticisms of reverse preferences by non-member developed market countries (e.g. the United States of America), see above, pp. 208–9, and note 81.

123. President Senghor recently toured France, Belgium, Italy and Tunisia as chairman and spokesman of O.C.A.M. (see note 33 above). He held interviews (e.g. with the French newspapers *Combat* and *Le Figaro*) and made speeches in support of continued links between Europe and Africa. Addressing the European Commission in Brussels, he said, 'We will continue to give to Europe the preferences she has enjoyed in our markets as much for considerations of human dignity as for commercial and juridical reasons.' See *West Africa*, No. 2912, 2 April 1973, p. 425; *ibid.*, No. 2913, 9 April 1973, p. 463.

124. See *Daily Times*, Lagos, 17 February 1973, pp. 1, 30; *New Nigeria*, Kaduna, 19 February 1973, p. 20; *West Africa*, No. 2906, 19 February 1973, p. 252; *ibid.*, No. 2912, 2 April 1973, p. 426.

125. Before the Lagos meeting the delegation from the East African Community had visited Sierra Leone and Ghana.

126. Nigerian Broadcasting Corporation (N.B.C.) news, 6 April 1973.

mic Commission for Africa, and contact was made there with Rwanda's Minister of Commerce, who is the current chairman of the Council of Association which brings together in Brussels Ministers of the nine E.E.C. countries and the Yaoundé Convention associates.[127] Later on, a Ministerial delegation representing Nigeria, Kenya, Tanzania, Uganda and Sierra Leone went to Kigali, capital of Rwanda,[128] for further discussions, and thereafter to Georgetown, Guyana, to act as observers at the meeting there of the Caribbean Free Trade Area (CARIFTA)[129] and to discuss the E.E.C. offer of association.

VI. THE DENIAU MEMORANDUM

An important new document to which we referred earlier on is the European Commission's memorandum[130] on future relations between the E.E.C. and the associated States in Africa, as well as potential associates in Africa, the Caribbean, the Indian Ocean and the Pacific, which was published in April 1973. The new document was presented to the European Parliament, meeting in Luxembourg, by M. Jean-François Deniau,[131] the Commissioner

127. See *West Africa*, No. 2912, 2 April 1973, p. 426.
128. *Ibid.* See also *West Africa*, No. 2910, 19 March 1973, p. 380; No. 2911, 26 March 1973, p. 411.
129. See *West Africa*, No. 2912, 2 April 1973, pp. 427, 444; see also 'Caribbean integration' (editorial), *Daily Times*, Lagos, 16 April 1973, p. 3. See also *West Africa*, No. 2903, 29 January, p. 145, and Fuat Andic, 'The development impact of the E.E.C. on the French and Dutch Caribbean' reviewed in 8 *Journ. Comm. Market Studies* (1969) 19–49. The Caribbean States are concerned about the E.E.C. reverse preferences because of the United States' unwillingness to extend its generalised preference scheme to countries which it felt discriminated against U.S. goods in favour of E.E.C. products.
130. See *West Africa*, No. 2912, 2 April 1973, pp. 426, 427; No. 2914, 16 April 1973, p. 490–1; No. 2915, 23 April 1973, p. 557, No. 2917, 7 May 1973, pp. 599–600; No. 2918, 14 May 1973, pp. 634–5, see also *Daily Times*, Lagos, 12 May 1973, p. 8.
131. M. Deniau, the commissioner responsible for external relations with developing countries, especially those associated to the E.E.C., has since left the E.E.C. Commission to take up a Ministerial job in France as the new Secretary for Co-operation. See *West Africa*, No. 2915, *cit.*, at p. 579. During his visit to London in July 1972 Jean-François Deniau had proposed the use of pacts like the Commonwealth Sugar Agreement to increase the export earnings of less developed countries, whose position was steadily deteriorating while the more industrialised countries were benefiting. In 1950 the less developed countries had handled 30 per cent of world trade; by 1960 it was down to 25 per cent; and in 1972 the total was less than 20 per cent. In 1960 their combined trade deficit had been $1 billion; in 1972 it was $3 billion a year. A system of compensation was, there-

responsible for its preparation.[132] In this position paper a number of aspects of the Yaoundé Convention have been substantially modified so as to maintain 'the difficult balance between the need for the existing associates to feel they are not losing anything by accepting more States into association, and the suspicions of the existing arrangements which have been expressed by those known as 'associables'.[133]

The document, according to reports, deals essentially with three subjects, namely trade, support for commodity prices, and development aid. But it also throws some light on how negotiations with the 'associables' are to take place.

On trade, the document proposes the maintenance of the free trade system, which, it states, is 'the only guarantee to the associated States in accordance with G.A.T.T. rules of free access to the Community market and which by itself represents the contractual element of the Association'.[134] But the E.E.C.'s new document no longer insists on the controversial 'reverse preferences'. Thus it stresses that the free trade system does not entail any obligation to grant preferences to the Community. For associated States will 'retain complete tariff autonomy in their relations with third countries, and complete freedom to negotiate on such matters'.[135]

Considering that the tariff advantages of association have been progressively reduced by the application of generalised preferences and that development aid cannot provide equitable compensation, the memorandum contains proposals for the stabilisation of export revenues from certain commodities of the associated countries. This 'new dimension' of association arrangement involves setting up a system of compensatory payments which would give the countries concerned an assurance of stable and adequate income for certain primary products without interfering with market mechanisms.[136] Some of the products suggested for the scheme, according to each

fore, needed to provide guaranteed minimum prices and minimum quantities for their exports, particularly those from countries dependent mainly on one product. See *European Community*, No. 7/8, July–August 1972, p. 3.

132. The contents of the memorandum were also explained to the Eurafrican parliamentary meeting in Kinshasa in April 1973. See *West Africa*, No. 2914, 16 April 1973, p. 517.

133. See *West Africa*, No. 2914, *cit.*, p. 491.

134. See *West Africa*, No. 2914, 16 April 1973, p. 490.

135. See *West Africa*, No. 2914, *cit.*, at pp. 490–1. This innovation is introduced without reference to President Senghor's attachment to 'reverse preferences', as we explained above, see p. 230.

136. See *West Africa*, No. 2914, *cit.*, at p. 491.

country's dependence on the income expected from them and their price instability, include sugar, groundnuts and groundnut oil, cotton, cocoa, bananas and copper.

This scheme, it has been pointed out, will in no way affect international agreements, which the E.E.C. will continue to work for; nor, since it is linked to export revenues rather than price stabilisation as such, will it affect market prices. The memorandum makes it clear that the system shall be essentially financed by the E.E.C. (a feature that may well provoke adverse reactions in some E.E.C. countries), in addition to the financial resources envisaged within the framework of the new European Development Fund.[137]

On aid, the document also makes a number of innovations. In addition to increasing aid to regional projects and to 'least developed countries', the memorandum proposes transferring the European Development Fund to the budget of the Community, whereas previously it had a separate budget.[138] Apparently the aim here is to 'give the European Parliament a measure of increased control, and also have the advantage of ensuring continuity of aid in the bridging period between funds, which have to be completely renewed periodically'.[139] In such a case there will be none of the usual delays which in the past had led to the commencement of each new fund on a later date than intended.

Another ameliorating proposal in this connection is that the participation of associated States in the fashioning of financial and technical co-operation shall be strengthened, and their participation in the running of the European Development Fund shall continue. There is also an acknowledgment that the institutions of the association are imperfect, and 'the conditions for a real dialogue should be improved'.[140]

Additional proposals in the memorandum relate to the pattern of the anticipated negotiations with the 'associables'. Here the E.E.C. seems prepared to show greater flexibility. There is not going to be any insistence on the three rigid options (Yaoundé, Arusha or trade agreement) originally offered to the 'associables'. It is also stated that there can be no question of limiting the scope of the

137. See *West Africa*, No. 2914, *cit.*, p. 491. On financing the scheme, M. Deniau, at a news conference in the Berlaymont building (the Commission's headquarters in Brussels), raised the possibility that countries might use the proceeds of very good years to pay back part of the assistance they received in very poor ones.
138. See *West Africa*, No. 2914, *cit.*, at p. 491.
139. *Ibid.*
140. *Ibid.*

negotiations by setting up any prior conditions. At the same time, however, it is made clear that the negotiations with the 'associables' (now due to begin on 1 October) will be concerned with some form of 'association', and that the other formulae of Protocol 22 of the Accession Treaty of 1972 will be 'negotiable at the appropriate time by the Community with those States which so desire'.[141]

There is also a hint of a possible enlargement of the E.E.C.'s offer of association to all African States south of the Sahara and not just former European colonies.[142]

These proposed changes are in effect the first step towards the adoption of 'an overall policy of development co-operation on a world-wide scale' as defined in paragraph 11 of the communiqué issued by the nine member States of the Community after their summit conference in Paris[143] on 19–20 October 1972. This projected new policy contains, in particular, the following elements:[144]

the promotion in appropriate cases of agreements concerning the primary products of the developing countries with a view to arriving at market stabilization and an increase in their exports; the improvement of generalized preferences with the aim of achieving a steady increase in imports of manufacture from the developing countries; an increase in the volume of official financial aid; an improvement in the financial conditions of this aid, particularly in favour of the least developed countries . . .

VII. CONCLUSION

The decision to accept or to reject the Communities' offer of association or trade agreement is a crucial one for the overseas developing countries concerned. Without exception, both the present associates among them and the 'associables' are mainly producers of primary products anxious to obtain high and stable prices for their products. In addition, most of them have a long-term

141. See *West Africa*, No. 2914, *cit.*, at p. 491.

142. *Ibid.* For example, the inclusion of Sudan, Liberia and Ethiopia. During President Pompidou's visit to Ethiopia in January 1973, Emperor Haile Selassie was quoted as saying that Ethiopia was considering an association with the enlarged Community. See *West Africa*, No. 2903, 29 January 1973, p. 155. Similarly, during a recent visit to Liberia Sir Alec Douglas-Home, the British Foreign Secretary, 'welcomed Liberian interest in a relationship with the E.E.C.'. See *West Africa*, No. 2906, 19 February 1973, p. 250.

143. See the 'Summit' issue of *European Community*, No. 11, November 1972, pp. 6–7, 26.

144. *Ibid.*, at p. 26; see also Francois-Xavier Ortoli (President of the Commission), 'The new Europe's next tasks', *European Community*, March 1973, p. 3.

programme for industrialisation which, however, cannot take off without a stable economic base or external assistance. These developing countries cannot compete favourably as individual States against the developed market countries without first attaining a reasonable degree of industrialisation. The question, then, is whether attachment to the E.E.C. is the only way out for these overseas countries and, if not, what other alternatives are open to them.

None of the developing countries can conveniently ignore the dominant position of the Communities in world trade but, as it appears, the considerations which will determine what type of relationship each one of them establishes with the Communities go beyond the general questions of trade and aid.

It is not unlikely that some of the 'associables' among them who have expressed strong misgivings about associate status do so as a result of the criticisms which the associates level against the Yaoundé Convention.[145] Over the years, for instance, the Yaoundé associates' trade with the Communities, contrary to expectations, has not increased more than that of the other developing countries, some of whom are benefiting from the Communities' generalised tariff preference scheme without taking on any reciprocal obligations similar to the ones that obtain under the association agreements. To that extent, therefore, the preferential treatment accorded to associates seems to have been cancelled out, in which case it has not brought the disadvantages that were feared by the non-associates. Many non-associates like Nigeria have profitably carried on existing trade relations with individual member States of the Community, taking care, of course, to diversify their trade relations so as to minimise the adverse effect of the Community's common external tariff (C.E.T.) on their exports, especially when they finally lose the Commonwealth trade preference now that Britain has to apply the C.E.T. to goods of non-associates entering her traditional market.

It is, indeed, significant that barely four months before the opening of talks on the basis of Protocol No. 22 of the Accession Treaty,[146] the Communities have come out with a memorandum[147] which, if finally approved, will completely alter the fundamental character of previous association arrangements with overseas developing countries. Impliedly, this substantial innovation in a way amounts to an admission by the Communities of basic faults in the

145. See pp. 223–6 above.
146. See p. 221 above. 147. See p. 231 above.

formulae under which both the Yaoundé and Arusha conventions had originally operated. In that case the present misgivings of the 'associables' cannot be said to have been misplaced in the first place. It remains to be seen whether most of them, especially the leading ones like Nigeria, will respond favourably to the changes and opt for some form of association. However, in view of the declaration which the O.A.U. States adopted at Abidjan[148] recently, it appears, at least on paper, that the African States which can afford to do so would reject association and opt for commodity or trade agreements, even if they have to do so at some economic cost to themselves.

Many of the 'associables' in Africa are preoccupied with the movement towards continental co-operation and unity, and consequently any suggestion of structural links with Europe is viewed by such 'associables' with some reservation. For instance, at the London Conference of Commonwealth Finance Ministers in September 1972, Alhaji Shehu Shagari, Nigeria's Federal Commissioner for Finance, stated, *inter alia*, that: '. . . . African countries should come together and unite in spite of the well-known obstacles. We do not have to do this under the umbrella of the enlarged European Economic Community but on our own system'.[149]

It was, indeed, in furtherance of this system that Nigeria entered into agreement with the Republic of Togo late in 1972 to establish the nucleus of a West African Economic Community,[150] transcending colonial boundaries and linguistic divisions. Under this arrangement it is agreed that appropriate officials of the two countries should meet to work out areas in which Nigeria and Togo can co-operate, for example, transport and telecommunications, trade,

148. See p. 229 above.
149. See *West Africa*, No. 2887, 9 October 1972, p. 1349.
150. See *West Africa*, No. 2898, 25 December 1972, p. 1733. Contrast this Community with the *Economic Community of West Africa*, grounded on the articles of association signed at Accra, Ghana, on 4 May 1967 by Dahomey, Ghana, Ivory Coast, Liberia, Mali, Mauritania, Niger, Nigeria, Senegal, Sierra Leone, Togo and Upper Volta. See Ian Brownlie, *Basic Documents on African Affairs*, pp. 58–62. Contrast it also with *Communauté Economique de l'Afrique de l'Ouest* or C.E.A.O., bringing together the French-speaking West African States of the Ivory Coast, Mali, Mauritania, Senegal and Upper Volta (with Togo and Dahomey accorded observer status), established under the final treaty signed at Abidjan in April 1973; and succeeding the *Customs Union of West African States* (U.D.E.A.O.) which they set up previously. See *West Africa*, No. 2765, 6 June 1970, p. 622; No. 2915, 23 April 1973, p. 579; No. 2917, 7 May 1973, p. 594; No. 2918, 14 May 1973, pp. 629–30; see also *Daily Times*, Lagos, 18 April 1973, p. 32, and *European Community*, No. 7–8, July–August 1972, p. 5.

industry, money payments and movement of factors of production. The abolition of transit tax on goods moving from one of the two countries to the other was recommended, as such barriers are not conducive to trade development.[151]

The long-term objective of such regional arrangements is to work gradually towards an eventual union between the West African Economic Community sponsored by Nigeria and Togo and other sub-regional functional economic groupings in Africa such as the East African Economic Community[152] and the Central African Economic and Customs[153] Union in the hope of producing in Africa a political structure and economic force necessary to stand out to the rest of the world as equal partners.

In the months before negotiations finally begin there is bound to be an intensification of meetings and manoeuvres by the associates and the 'associables' on both sides of the Atlantic. For the overseas developing countries, dialogue with the European Communities is unavoidable. No doubt, better results will be achieved if many of the countries concerned approach the talks in concert; but in the absence of a common approach each country has to go it alone. However, whether the overseas States pursue the negotiations jointly or severally, they will for the foreseeable future find themselves in a position in which the weak confront the strong.

151. See *African Development*, October 1972, p. 12.
152. See Ian Brownlie, *Basic Documents on African Affairs, cit.*, p. 63.
153. See *ibid.*, p. 46.

LIST OF CASES CITED

ARTICLES OF THE E.E.C. TREATY
REFERRED TO IN THE TEXT

243

INDEX